LANGUAGE OF
THE MENTALLY RETARDED

The edited proceedings of a conference sponsored by the National Institute of Child Health and Human Development and hosted by the University of Kansas Bureau of Child Research, Lawrence, Kansas, February 16–18, 1970. Technical editor, Robert K. Hoyt, Jr.

Richard L. Schiefelbusch, Director of the Kansas Center for Mental Retardation and Human Development, Lawrence, Kansas City, and Parsons, Kansas.

NICHD–Mental Retardation Research Centers Series

LANGUAGE OF THE MENTALLY RETARDED

Edited by
Richard L. Schiefelbusch, Ph.D.

616.85
L287

UNIVERSITY PARK PRESS
BALTIMORE • LONDON • TOKYO

Copyright © 1972 by University Park Press

All Rights Reserved

Printed in the United States of America

By Edwards Brothers, Inc.

No part of this publication may be reproduced or transmitted in any form or by any means, electronic or mechanical, including photocopy, recording, or any information storage and retrieval system, without permission in writing from the publisher

Library of Congress Cataloging in Publication Data
Main entry under title:

Language of the mentally retarded.
   "The edited proceedings of a conference sponsored by the National Institute of Child Health and Human Development and hosted by the University of Kansas Bureau of Child Research, Lawrence, Kansas, February 16-18, 1970."
   Includes bibliographies.
   1. Mentally handicapped—Language—Congresses.
I. Schiefelbusch, Richard L., ed. II. U.S. National Institute of Child Health and Human Development. III. Kansas. University. Bureau of Child Research.
RC570.L36   616.85'5   70-169194
ISBN 0-8391-0629-7

UNIVERSITY PARK PRESS
Chamber of Commerce Building
Baltimore, Maryland 21202

CONTENTS

ABOUT THE HOST CENTER vii

LIST OF PARTICIPANTS xi

FOREWORD: *Gerald D. LaVeck* xiii

PREFACE: *Michael J. Begab* xv

INTRODUCTION: *Richard L. Schiefelbusch* xvii

Psycholinguistic Approaches to Language and Language Development

A PSYCHOLINGUISTIC VIEWPOINT OF THE LANGUAGE ACQUISITION PROCESS:
Kenneth F. Ruder 3

SEMANTIC FEATURES IN LANGUAGE DEVELOPMENT: *Lois Bloom* 19

SYNTACTIC STRUCTURE AND LANGUAGE DEVELOPMENT IN RETARDATES:
Wilbur A. Hass and Sarah K. Hass 35

THE DEVELOPMENT OF REFERENTIAL SKILLS IN CHILDREN:
Seymour Rosenberg 53

Language Training

A SYSTEMATIC APPROACH TO LANGUAGE TRAINING: *William A. Bricker* 75

ADVENTURES IN SIMPLISTIC GRAMMAR: *Donald M. Baer, Douglas Guess
and James A. Sherman* 93

OPERANT LANGUAGE DEVELOPMENT: THE OUTLINE OF A THERAPEUTIC
TECHNOLOGY: *Todd R. Risley, Betty M. Hart and Larry Doke* 107

Approaches to the Description and Delineation of Defective Speech

THREE APPROACHES TO SPEECH RETARDATION: *Gerald M. Siegel* 127

A BEHAVIORAL SYSTEM FOR ASSESSING LANGUAGE DEVELOPMENT:
Dona L. Hedrick and Elizabeth M. Prather 143

A PROGRAM OF DEVELOPMENTAL RESEARCH IN AUDIOLOGIC PROCEDURES:
  Robert T. Fulton 169

THE LANGUAGE-RELATED BEHAVIOR OF DYSPHASIC CHILDREN:
  Paul S. Weiner 189

Experimental Procedures

SAMPLE-MATCHING TECHNIQUES IN THE STUDY OF CHILDREN'S LANGUAGE:
  Peter S. Rosenberger, Lawrence T. Stoddard and Murray Sidman 211

THE ROLE OF VERBAL PROCESSES IN SHORT-TERM MEMORY:
  Earl C. Butterfield and John M. Belmont 231

INDEX 249

ABOUT THE HOST CENTER

The Kansas Center for Mental Retardation and Human Development consists of three separate physical facilities located at the university campus at Lawrence, the Parsons State Hospital and Training Center, and the University of Kansas Medical Center in Kansas City. Each of the sites emphasizes different research areas, but there is considerable overlapping of interest and a concerted effort to mount an internally cohesive program of independent and collaborative research.

The rationale for the program of research and research training at the center is based on several fundamental issues: (1) Mental retardation is seen as a dynamic, developmental disorder subject to preventive, ameliorative, or educational procedures starting in infancy and extending through the life cycle. (2) The problem is both biological and behavioral and requires interdisciplinary collaboration from several relevant fields. (3) The complexity and breadth of the problem calls for a sustained coordinated effort by investigators who study the retardate in both controlled and naturalistic environments. (4) Many scientists and service personnel need the products of the research centers in a form which they can understand and use. (5) Because the number of investigators and settings concentrating on research in mental retardation are relatively few in number, the center should undertake the training of additional research specialists to extend the scientific manpower pool to other settings.

In keeping with these premises, the Kansas Center has undertaken a broadly based, multidisciplinary program of research in mental retardation. Prominent among the biological areas to be studied are reproductive physiology, metabolism, and neurophysiology. Of equal importance are areas generally regarded as behavioral—educational, interpersonal, and environmental. In a real sense, however, many, if not most, of the problems in these various areas—learning disabilities, sensory impairments and perceptual disorganization, language impairments and communication disorders, seizures, neonatal disorders, etc.—lend themselves to a combined biobehavioral approach.

The extent of the research investment in the Kansas settings permits systematic, procedural attacks upon a number of such problems pertaining to the retarded. The researchers have longstanding experience in developing research that calls for a combination of disciplines and experimental approaches. These sustained investments should result in a significant number of valuable products for those who work with the retarded. Examples of such productivity already exist. Kansas now has several exemplary programs which are making daily contributions to the understanding and training of mentally retarded children and adults. One such program involves both scientific and technological investigations of mentally retarded children and the production of educational methods and materials for optimizing their behavior. This center should significantly increase the range and value of the products which this research and training amalgam can produce.

A dual role of scientist and technologist has been accepted by many of the investigators in the Kansas setting. These programs and their structures draw on improved scientific knowledge to provide data and specific assistance in areas where this has been nonexistent, incomplete, or inadequate. The Kansas program has been developed to fully utilize the skills and knowledge of speech clinicians, audiologists, special educators, linguists, psychologists, and related service and technical personnel in a systematized, cooperative, and functional manner. There are few places in the United States where there is such a diverse concentration of disciplines attempting to integrate methodologies in the education and training of retarded children. With a continuing and expanding emphasis on biological and psychobiological research, this center promises to be increasingly progressive and comprehensive.

In order to establish a research center capable of producing significant research products in accordance with these issues, we have sought to develop approaches to problems common to the various units which make up the Kansas Center while also encouraging each setting to strengthen those features unique to it. This includes constructing novel laboratory equipment and instrumentation for the control of experimental variables, since such equipment is often a requirement of a number of investigators at all settings. We have also sought to develop procedures that will generalize to the natural environments of the settings.

We have sought also to provide common support facilities, including standardized format for data analysis, and to develop media products for the dissemination and distribution of the results of the research efforts. A pilot project is to establish common parameters for data acquisition and processing within the research unit at the Lawrence setting. In this way we hope to create a data processing model there which will prove applicable to the other settings.

In the area of publications, the director's staff now includes the technical and creative personnel required to produce nearly any desired media product, from broadcast quality motion pictures to simple in-house research reports. In a little over three years, eighteen 16-millimeter films have been produced to disseminate the results of research and to demonstrate exemplary or model environments which apply behavior analysis techniques to the problems of mental retardation and related aspects of human development. In addition to numerous articles in scientific journals and mass circulation publications, a book on audiology recently has been published and two books relating to the language of the mentally retarded are now in preparation.

The above areas are designed, of course, only to augment and support the main thrust of the research. They contribute to the design and implementation of research and to the demonstration and dissemination of the results. During the past few years there has been a steady tendency, not only to follow the original stated goals and subgoals, but also to continue to refine those statements into finite thematic areas of investigation. This has resulted in a progression which examines the problem of mental retardation from conception to the optimum development of life skills in persons handicapped by retardation. The rationale is thus to touch on the whole continuum—to design, develop, demonstrate, and disseminate data stemming from research in several thematic areas including:

    Physiological Processes of Reproduction
    Fetal and Neonatal Development
    Biochemical and Metabolic Factors
    Neurophysiology
    Sensory and Perceptual Development
    Language and Verbal Behavior
    Depriving Environments
    Learning Disorders and Special Education

LIST OF PARTICIPANTS

DONALD BAER, *University of Kansas*
BETTY BARTON, *NICHD*
MICHAEL BEGAB, *NICHD*
LOIS BLOOM, *Columbia University*
WILLIAM BORTHICK, *University of Colorado*
DORIS BRADLEY, *University of North Carolina*
WILLIAM BRICKER, *George Peabody College for Teachers*
EARL BUTTERFIELD, *University of Kansas Medical Center*
JOHN CHAVES, *Children's Hospital Medical Center, Boston*
ROSS COPELAND, *University of Kansas*
ROBERT FULTON, *University of Kansas*
CHARLES GALLOWAY, *George Peabody College for Teachers*
SARAH HASS, *Shimer College*
WILBUR HASS, *Shimer College*
DONA HEDRICK, *University of Washington*
GERALD KISSIN, *Albert Einstein College of Medicine, New York*
D. D. KLUPPEL, *University of Wisconsin*
CALVIN KNOBELOCH, *University of North Carolina*
LYLE LLOYD, *NICHD*
ELOISA DE LORENZO, *Instituto Interamericano del Niño*
RUSSELL LOVE, *Vanderbilt University*
MARILYN LOWELL, *University of California at Los Angeles*
NANCY MARSHALL, *University of Oregon*
ROBERT MATTOS, *George Peabody College for Teachers*
JAMES MCLEAN, *University of Kansas*
JON MILLER, *University of Wisconsin*
JOHN MEIER, *University of Colorado Medical Center*
KAZUO NIHIRA, *University of California at Los Angeles*
DONALD O'GRADY, *University of Cincinnati*
ELIZABETH PRATHER, *University of Washington*

TODD RISLEY, *University of Kansas*
SEYMOUR ROSENBERG, *Rutgers University*
PETER ROSENBERGER, *Walter E. Fernald State School*
KENNETH RUDER, *University of Kansas*
RICHARD SCHIEFELBUSCH, *University of Kansas*
JAMES SHERMAN, *University of Kansas*
MURRAY SIDMAN, *Harvard Medical School*
GERALD SIEGEL, *University of Minnesota*
JOSEPH SPRADLIN, *University of Kansas*
PAUL WEINER, *University of Chicago*

FOREWORD

Approximately six million persons in our society evidence impaired behavior during some part of their life span because of subnormal intelligence. To the nation, they represent a potential loss of human resources, to their states and communities a financial and humanitarian burden of care and concern, and to their families the ultimate in personal misery and tragedy. By whatever measurements are applied, mental retardation is a major social problem. Its solution warrants the full commitment of our scientific talents and resources.

The first giant step forward toward this objective was the enactment of Public Law 88-164 to construct centers for research in mental retardation and related aspects of human development. The twelve centers which have been created under this program constitute the primary research thrust of this country to understand the causes of this complex phenomenon and to seek methods for its prevention and amelioration. Scientists representing many disciplines are already intensively engaged in independent and collaborative research to unravel the critical issues involved.

The scope of the research programs at the centers covers a broad spectrum of investigations ranging from cell biology at the molecular level to remediation of language and reading skills. Between these extremes lie numerous studies in the neurosciences, biochemistry, genetics, reproductive physiology, and the behavioral and social sciences. Only through a multifaceted and multidisciplinary approach can we hope to plumb the mysteries of human development.

New discoveries, however dramatic they may prove to be, are not the end product of any complex research enterprise such as mental retardation. Knowledge is interrelated, interdependent, and cumulative. Periodically it must be synthesized, analyzed, disseminated, applied, tested, and refined.

The Mental Retardation Research Centers, because of their shared objectives and uniquely comprehensive approach to this field of research, are especially well equipped to construct the mosaic of understanding so essential to the solution of this problem. The systematic exchange of scientific information on topics of import to the field is an essential step. The staff of the Institute is planning to hold a series of seminars and to publish proceedings on selected aspects of mental retardation.

We embark on this venture in the hope that the promotion of scientific exchange under the leadership of the National Institute of Child Health and Human Development and the Mental Retardation Research Centers will contribute to our objectives of reducing the numbers of retarded persons and enhancing the quality of life for the individuals already handicapped and for their families as well.

GERALD D. LaVECK, M.D.
Director
The National Institute of Child Health
and Human Development

PREFACE

MICHAEL J. BEGAB

MICHAEL J. BEGAB is head of the mental retardation research centers program for the National Institute of Child Health and Human Development. He has seventeen years of experience in the mental retardation field, including work in institutions and in diagnostic centers, as well as consultation at the national level. He has an M.A. degree in Social Work from the University of Chicago and a Ph.D. degree in sociology from the Catholic University of America.

During 1963–64 he was special assistant to the President for Mental Retardation. His service includes offices in numerous professional organizations in mental retardation, and he has approximately 35 publications in a wide range of professional journals and conference proceedings. His writings are concerned largely with social work practice and education and the sociological aspects of mental retardation. Dr. Begab is presently an Associate Editor of the American Journal of Mental Deficiency.

The Mental Retardation Research Centers Program was initiated in 1963 under legislation providing construction grants for research centers in mental retardation and related aspects of human development. A total of $26 million in Federal funds and approximately $14 million from university and state funds have been expended for this purpose. Of the twelve centers awarded grants, nine are now fully constructed and operational. Two more will be completed by the end of 1972, the third by 1973.

The centers differ considerably from each other in the breadth and depth of their research in specific areas. Some are broadly multidisciplinary, including representation from the medical schools and many of the graduate departments within their university, and embracing the behavioral, social, and psychological science. Others are multidisciplinary in a narrower sense; within the biomedical profession and biological sciences they embrace a wide range of subspecialties in biochemistry, neurology, genetics, pediatrics, embryology, etc. Still others are primarily behavioral in orientation as represented by psychology, education, sociology, and anthropology.

The intent of the legislation was to mount a major national attack on mental retardation and its related aspects, utilizing research as one of the major tools to be applied. Retardation had been a problem of chronic national neglect by the scientific community. It was recognized by the planners of this program that no single discipline could solve the complex mysteries surrounding the causes, prevention, and treatment of this condition. They were convinced that only as disciplines were brought together in a setting conducive to interdisciplinary and collaborative effort could we begin to get needed answers.

Clearly, each center can approach the problem of mental retardation in its own way. It has been the Institute's philosophy from the very beginning, however, that an independent, internally cohesive approach to the problem is not sufficient to a national effort—similar cohesion between centers must also be achieved.

The National Institute of Child Health and Human Development has, in effect, entered into a partnership with the centers, not as a silent partner providing only fiscal support, but as an active partner bringing the centers together through various structures and mechanisms to weld them into a single operational effort to solve the problems of mental retardation.

As one step in this direction, the center directors, under Institute urging, have organized into an informal unit whereby their collective planning and activity may yield more beneficial results to themselves and to national goals than could be anticipated through independent action. We have also attempted to promote the exchange of scientific information and the development of a communication network so that resources are channeled into the most promising directions. In this way, we hope that priorities will be established without influencing the direction any particular center may take in its exploration of the problem. At the same time we strive to avoid unnecessary duplication, to identify knowledge gaps, and to move the entire field of research in mental retardation forward in the most constructive manner possible.

The legislation requires that each center be legally committed to carrying out research in mental retardation and related aspects of human development for a 20-year period. We recognize that Congress and other interested organizations and individuals will be checking the progress of the centers to see whether mission-oriented research is effective in problem solving. We have confidence that it is, and we believe our partnership philosophy will help increase center effectiveness. This seminar reflects this philosophy.

In our efforts to develop a communication network, it is fitting that the subject of this first seminar is related to communications. Research issues in language acquisition and development demand the attention of our best scientific minds, for deficits in language and communication represent the most common traits the retarded share with each other.

This seminar is the first in a series on different critical aspects of the state of knowledge and research needs in mental retardation being sponsored by NICHD. These seminars will be cosponsored by each of the centers in turn, but will not be limited exclusively to participation by center personnel and will draw appropriately on experts from other settings. The second conference will focus on the problems of antenatal diagnosis.

We hope that each conference will develop a publication on the most up-to-date knowledge on different aspects of the problem and result in a series of scientific reports on basic and applied research in mental retardation. Through this approach we hope to advance center programs and perhaps contribute to the field in general. In implementing this center-Institute leadership role we may move forward the frontiers of our knowledge in mental retardation and ultimately facilitate its prevention and treatment.

INTRODUCTION

RICHARD L. SCHIEFELBUSCH

RICHARD L. SCHIEFELBUSCH was granted a Ph.D. at Northwestern University in 1951. From 1949 to 1956 he was director of the Speech and Hearing Clinic at the University of Kansas and in 1956 became director of the Bureau of Child Research. In that position he has been instrumental in developing research and training efforts in the field of mental retardation and related handicaps. In 1959 he became a full professor on both the University and the Medical Center campuses and in 1969 was named to the rank of Professor of the University.

Since 1966 Dr. Schiefelbusch has directed the Kansas Center for Mental Retardation and Human Development with facilities at Lawrence, Kansas City, Kansas and Parsons. As director of several research projects on language of the mentally retarded, his publications include a number of works in the fields of speech, language and communication.

The participants in this conference were drawn from several professional fields. They represent a variety of working assumptions about language and are studying various aspects of language and language problems. Linguistic theory and linguistic data occupied much of the attention of participants. Developmental issues were also carefully examined in reference to language acquisition, as were interpersonal variables as they affect the relationships between speakers and listeners. Reciprocal factors (contingencies) are shown to influence communication events. Finally, physiological features were discussed in studies of defective language. Taken together, these areas represent a complex combination of information about language functions.

This was not the first group to undertake a dialogue relative to these fields. An overview of the language of the mentally retarded was undertaken at the University of Kansas in 1963. The proceedings were subsequently published in *Language and Mental Retardation,* available through Holt, Rinehart, and Winston (1967). Other authors have also presented work in this area, in particular, Spreen (1964), Jordan (1967), and Schiefelbusch (1969).

One characteristic of recent reviews and studies referenced by these works has been an increasing attention to the delineation of issues. The authors have specified the frames of reference they have used, and they referred to the applied and basic literature from which the methods described were drawn. Although they were somewhat less successful in describing the parameters of the language content that they index, the previous studies gave much useful information from which to plan this publication. Therefore, it was with a great deal of optimism that we approached the conference and anticipated the product of the interchange. A total of thirteen papers were presented. They are grouped here under categorical headings to make the content more meangful and to make the sequence more useful.

The first section is *Psycholinguistic Approaches to Language and Language Development.* The section includes four papers. The first, "A Psycholinguistic Viewpoint of the Language Acquisition Process," by Ruder, provides a general unified framework, commencing with current linguistic theory and encompassing available developmental psycholinguistic data. His model focuses upon phonological, syntactic, and semantic components. It is based primarily upon a generative transformational theory.

The following chapter on "Semantic Features of Language Development," by Bloom, includes findings from a longitudinal study of the emerging grammars of toddlers and a discussion of the possible relevance of her findings to the treatment of language disorders. The purpose of the research was to investigate the development of linguistic behavior in relation to aspects of the child's experience. Her study is based upon the assumption that it is possible for an observing adult to interpret the semantic intent of children's utterances. With this assumption as a starting point, she has been able to study single-word and two-word responses to determine grammatical relations. " . . . It was possible to propose rules of grammar to account for the inherent sematic relations that underlie the juxtaposition of words in early sentences."

Her data suggest several treatments for language disorders associated with mental retardation, including the arrangement of words in sentences before attempts are made to teach morphological inflection, noun, verb, and adjective forms. She concludes that research in the language of the retarded must devote attention to the situational and behavioral context of speech events as well as to the linguistic form of utterances. It would follow that treatment situations should be manipulable in order to provide environmental assistance for learning specific linguistic structures.

The chapter entitled "Syntactic Structure and Language Development in Retardates," by Hass and Hass, starts with the assumption that grammar should show how closely syntactic structure is bound to the basic features of communication. The authors are especially interested in three faces of syntax: namely, surface structure, semantic representation, and transformations. The interests of these authors are compared to Osgood's model, which has been used for developing the ITPA and the Semantic Differential. The primary focus of the paper is on transformational features, and for this work they use the seminal concepts provided by Chomsky. Four practices for intervention in language training are also considered. These practices are verbal bombardment, labeling (tacting), grammar drills, and structured communication. The authors conclude by suggesting that one must select the plan for language training out of an observation of the roles the individual plays in communicating with others. These roles may be clarified by examining the function marked or left ambiguous in the sentences we use.

The fourth chapter in the psycholinguistic series is by Rosenberg. In "The Development of Referential Skills in Children," Rosenberg is concerned with the referential processes which underlie human communication and the development of referential processes in children. In brief, he is concerned with how a speaker selects his verbal repertoire in communicating with his listener. He is concerned also with the ways in which a listener correctly or incorrectly identifies his speaker's reference from his speaker's utterances. He uses an interpersonal model in dealing with this process. The research design is set up to account for the participation of both the speaker and the listener in the referential system. He is also interested in the referential processes in children, particularly in the stages which he has referred to as *vocabulary development* and *comparison-stage development*. He points out that it is not clear whether a retardate has difficulty with language primarily because of his small vocabulary or because he is simply unable to make appropriate comparisons to select the proper response. He points out a current need in research methodology for a precise means for investigating these questions. His paper provides a methodology with some preliminary data showing results which can be attained with his approach.

As a group, these papers present interesting approaches and raise intriguing questions regarding further application of linguistic and psycholinguistic procedures to language description and intervention with children. The retarded do not come in for a strong illustrative review in these studies, because for the most part the authors have not worked extensively with the retarded. However, the approaches do have a prominent place in language research with the retarded.

The next section includes three papers which pertain to *Language Training*. The first of these is by Bricker. "A Systematic Approach to Language Training" combines psycholinguistic theory with a range of past research using the operant model. He puts these two procedural systems together by using psycholinguistics to provide the structure of language, and by using behavior modification to represent the functions which sustain language activities included in training. Systems analysis was used to lattice both systems into a sequential training plan.

The chapter by Baer, Guess, and Sherman, "Adventures in Simplistic Grammar," describes behavioral functions. This research focuses upon specific features of linguistic acquisiton. They analyze the actual process of instruction and attempt to formulate an effective intervention strategy for language training. A single subject is described and data are examined to determine if language instruction can include generative possibilities.

The next chapter, "Operant Language Development: The Outline of a Therapeutic Technology," by Risley, Hart, and Doke, also represents a combination of behavioral procedures and linguistic issues. The immediate goal is the instruction of language with preschool ghetto children. The important feature of their remedial program is the imitation training which they assume to be crucial to a normal development of language. Therefore, when vocal imitation is absent, they begin a language training program designed to establish this imitation function. The imitations are then elaborated into words and phrases of increasing length and complexity. The next step is to transform such imitative vocalizations into rudimentary language. This is accomplished by using imitation to establish appropriate labeling of objects, events, and relationships in the child's environment. They take advantage of the naturally occurring events and reinforcers in the environment. The environment is arranged so the child can obtain reinforcers only with the help of the attending adult. In order to advance this system they found it necessary to devise a procedure to reliably record the linguistic events occurring in spontaneous speech.

The next section may be labeled *Approaches to the Description and Delineation of Defective Speech*. The four papers in this section all utilize procedures developed in the field of speech pathology and audiology. The first paper, "Three Approaches to Speech Retardation," by Siegel, also utilizes the procedures developed in behavior modification and linguistic areas. He uses the behavioral frame of reference to suggest how speech is learned and how speech may break down during the developmental process. He presents the remedial process within a general framework of interpersonal events showing how it is possible for the clinician and the child to relate effectively in the learning process. He points out that linguistics provides a way of talking and planning for the instruction of language which is highly essential to any effective program. Language instruction after all is a process of implementing linguistic systems which improve the complexity and effectiveness of a child's language.

Hedrick and Prather describe a "Behavioral System for Assessing Language Development." They assume that speech and language clinicians must evaluate language to find a starting point for training. The model they present is based primarily upon receptive and expressive functions. They report on a preliminary study they have undertaken to develop and define their system. They suggest that both cross-sectional and longitudinal follow-up studies will be necessary to fully develop their approach to assessment.

Fulton describes "A Program of Developmental Research in Audiologic Procedures." His report is based upon work at Parsons State Hospital and Training Center by Spradlin, Lloyd, and Fulton. Their procedures are sometimes referred to as operant audiometry. Their research deals with the response features of the severely retarded child in a way which adds to the reliability of efforts to sample their hearing characteristics. Their work has led to an elaborate form of audiological assessment through which a variety of features and characteristics of the hearing sensitivity of the retarded subject can be determined. The work completed and the work planned is designed to provide a means to obtain complete and elaborate hearing evaluations of the severely retarded.

Weiner reports on "The Language-Related Behavior of Dysphasic Children." He suggests that methods employed in studies of language and language-related behavior of dysphasic subjects and the knowledge gained from these studies may be used in considering the problems of the mentally retarded. He carefully analyzes the literature that describes both adult and child dysphasics and their problems in receptive and expressive speech. He points out that the vagueness of the descriptions of children's language makes it difficult to establish the degree to which correspondence is found among the various studies. He then describes ongoing research with mild aphasic children at the University of Chicago Medical School. He found that these children were deficient in auditory vocal functioning and in the learning of linguistic rules. Several features of the clinical approaches used in his study are applicable to the mentally retarded. One is a form of diagnostic testing. This approach includes attempts to help the child overcome specific deficits found in the diagnostic examination. It represents an effort to minimize the effects of the child's deficits by using a visual approach as much as possible when auditory functioning is poor.

INTRODUCTION xxi

The final section includes two papers combined under the heading of *Experimental Procedures*. The first chapter in this section, by Rosenberger, Stoddard, and Sidman, is entitled "Sample-Matching Techniques in the Study of Children's Language." The technique includes both verbal and non-verbal sample and choice materials and incorporates the use of a reinforcing consequence which immediately follows each correct response by the subject. Their procedure is completely automated. They initially applied the technique to study the effects of acquired brain disease upon normally developed language and children of normal intelligence. Three cases are included in their presentation. They find that auditory-visual equivalences are important to language skills and that these equivalences may be studied by essentially non-verbal techniques in the proper laboratory setting. They have also used auditory-visual word-matching to teach reading to mentally retarded subjects. They found that matching spoken words to pictures and printed words can be taught without explicitly teaching oral reading and therefore completely without the intervention of a teacher.

Butterfield's chapter relates to "The Role of Verbal Processes in Short-Term Memory." Specifically, he uses the technique of verbal rehearsal to enhance short-term memory in various subjects, including mentally retarded children. In studying both the acquisition and the retrieval functions, he speculates that normal persons supplement the retarded by giving them both an acquisition and a retrieval strategy, and that poor memory performance on the part of the retarded may be caused by inappropriate or ineffective acquisition and retrieval strategies. If this assumption is true, he may be able to have all the retarded subjects under study performing like normal adults, as far as the tasks under consideration are concerned.

The thirteen studies included here represent samples of research currently underway in the Mental Retardation Centers or in work settings that are highly relevant to the programs currently going on in the Centers. Subsequent language conferences should be held to examine other selected areas of language research. This publication should thus be considered as the beginning of a series of efforts to analyze progress in the Centers for Metal Retardation and Related Aspects of Human Development.

In anticipation of future language conferences it is essential that an active communication between Centers be established and maintained. It is hoped that this publication will contribute to that end. Our eventual objective should be to increase the number and the scope of language research projects in the Centers, and to promote a communication network among investigators within the Centers. This network should include a traffic of published manuscripts and working papers, e.g., prepublication or preliminary report versions of research projects. In that manner we should be able to make more rapid progress in this critical and complex field of research.

In introducing the content of this conference it is appropriate to acknowledge the special contributions of Miss Betty Barton of NICHD and Mr. Ross Copeland of the Bureau of Child Research for their skill in planning and arranging the Conference. Also the participants wish to commend the expertise of Mr. Robert Hoyt in editing the conference discussions which appear in the book, and the good judgment and understanding of Dr. Michael Begab in guiding the format of the entire undertaking.

REFERENCES

Chomsky, N. *Aspects of the theory of syntax.* Cambridge: MIT Press, 1965.
Jordan, Thomas E. Language and mental retardation: A review of the literature. In R. L. Schiefelbusch, R. H. Copeland, and J. O. Smith (Eds.), *Language and mental retardation.* New York: Holt, Rinehart and Winston, 1967.
Osgood, C. E.; Suci, G. J.; and Taunenbaum, P. *Measurement of meaning.* Urbana: University of Illinois Press, 1957.
Spreen, Otfried. Language functions in mental retardation: A review. I. Language development, types of retardation and intelligence level. *American Journal of Mental Deficiency,* 1965, *69,* 482–494.
Spreen, Otfried. Language functions in mental retardation: A review. II. Language in higher level performance. *American Journal of Mental Deficiency,* 1965, *70,* 351–362.
Schiefelbusch, R. L. Language functions of retarded children. *Folia Phoniat.* 1969, *21,* 129–144.
Schiefelbusch, R. L.; Copeland, R. H.; and Smith, J. O. (Eds.). *Language and mental retardation.* New York: Holt, Rinehart and Winston, 1967.

**Psycholinguistic Approaches to
Language and Language Development**

A PSYCHOLINGUISTIC VIEWPOINT OF THE LANGUAGE ACQUISITION PROCESS

KENNETH F. RUDER
University of Kansas
Bureau of Child Research

KENNETH F. RUDER was born November 27, 1939, at Hays, Kansas. In June, 1962, he received the degree of Bachelor of Arts with a major in Speech Pathology from Fort Hays Kansas State Teachers College. In September, 1962, he enrolled in the University of Wisconsin Graduate School. He held a Traineeship from the Vocational Rehabilitation Administration until August, 1963, when he received the degree of Master of Science with a major in Speech Pathology and Audiology. From 1964 until 1966 he served as Director of Speech Pathology Services at Harmarville Rehabilitation Center, Pittsburgh, Pennsylvania. In 1966, he enrolled in the Graduate School of the University of Florida, and in 1969 he received the degree of Doctor of Philosophy. He is a member of Sigma Xi and the Acoustical Society of America, and is currently a research associate at the University of Kansas Bureau of Child Research.

The aim of any language acquisition model is to describe and predict the processes whereby language is acquired. This is an ideal goal, but not the goal of this chapter. We propose instead to provide a general unified framework which encompasses available developmental psycholinguistic data and which at the same time is commensurate with current linguistic theory. A discussion of such theory with all its ramifications is beyond the scope of this chapter, but some basic theoretical background upon which this proposed model is based, and a general overview of some basic principles of a theory of grammar, is in order.

It should first be made clear that in the context of this paper an adequate grammar should account not only for all the sentences of a language, but for all aspects of those sentences. Under those conditions, a grammatical theory confined to syntax alone would be incomplete and inadequate. To account for all aspects of a sentence a theory of grammar should include phonological, syntactic, and semantic components.

Figure 1 illustrates the components of an adequate theory of grammar and the interrelationship among these components. There are essentially three components: the phonological component, the syntactic component, and the semantic component.

The phonological component defines or accounts for sentences of a language in terms of phonological theory, i.e., phonological rules, distinctive features, etc. The syntactic component accounts for the structure of the language; that is, it yields syntactically well-formed structures. The semantic component; in turn, relates to meaning and yields semantically well-formed structures.

To illustrate why an adequate theory of grammar must include at least these three components, let us examine the conditions of an adequate theory of grammar. The first such condition is *acceptabilility*. This says nothing more than that the theory

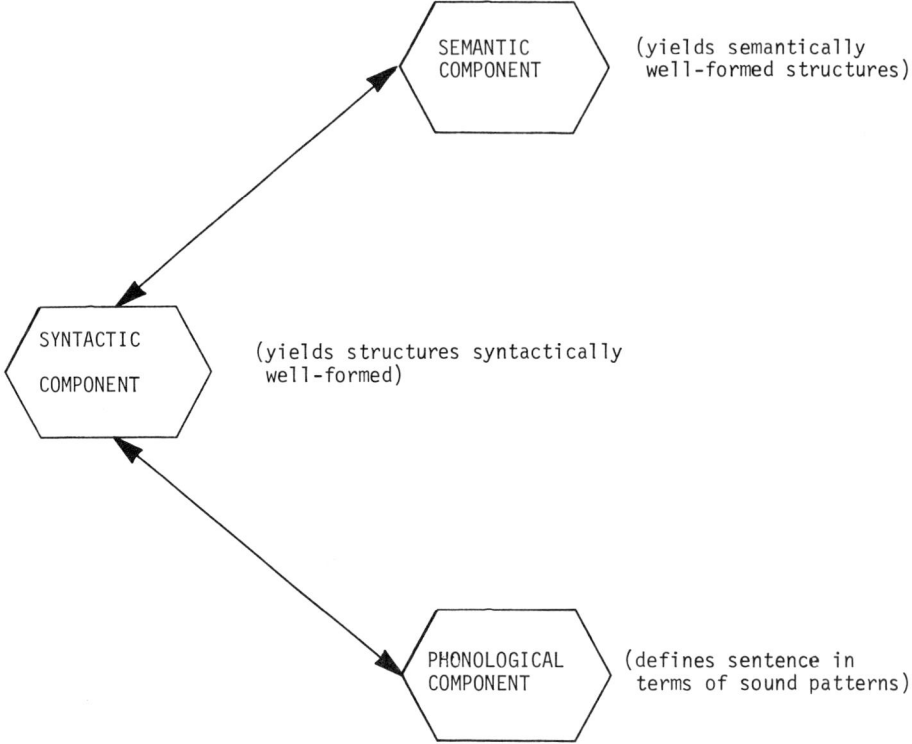

Fig. 1. Components of a theory of grammar. At least these three components are necessary for any theory of grammar to be considered adequate.

should conform to reality. That is the sentences such a theory of grammar would generate would be acceptable as sentences by the native speakers of that language. It is apparent that to be acceptable to native speakers of the language, a sentence must be well-formed on all three components of the grammar previously discussed.

For example, take Chomsky's famous sentence, "colorless green ideas sleep furiously." Syntactically and phonologically that sentence is well-formed. Semantically it is ill-formed because it is essentially devoid of meaning.

The second and third conditions of an adequate theory of grammar are *simplicity* and *generality*. The former condition implies nothing more than the notion that a theory attains its simplest form by building on no other premises than those absolutely required by its object. The generality condition requires that the theory be applicable across all languages. The necessity of these two conditions to any theory of grammar is obvious.

The fourth condition of an adequate theory of grammar is *constructional homonymity*. That is to say, a theory must have a way of dealing with ambiguous utterances. For example, if a sentence were defined only on the phonological level—that is, in terms of the sound patterns—then the phonemic sequence /ə nem/ can be interpreted as either "a name" or "an aim." Such a theory is incomplete since it fails the constructional homonymity requirement. As native speakers of English we know that the two strings mean something different even though the phonological analysis would tend to indicate they are identical. This homonymity, or ambiguity, must be resolved on a higher level; i.e., in the syntactic component. In the same way, we can give examples of syntactic and semantic ambiguity which also have to be resolved with reference to other components of the theory of grammar.

It is apparent that a theory of grammar must include phonology, syntax, and semantics. This is taking a rather broad view of grammar or of language, but it is upon such a general viewpoint of grammar that this psycholinguistic model of language acquisition is based.

A PSYCHOLINGUISTIC ACQUISITION MODEL

To get to the psycholinguistic acquisition model, the conditions for an adequate theory of grammar might also be applied to an adequate model of language acquisition. Several considerations have already been mentioned, namely that the model should be commensurate with current linguistic theory and that it provide a unified framework within which language development data may be discussed. This is necessary if we are to obtain some description of the process involved in acquiring one's native language. To these ends, the model proposed is based primarily on a generative-transformational theory of language (Chomsky, 1965). We could show that this model does meet the requirements for an adequate theory of grammar, but that is beyond the scope of this chapter.

Such a theory places specific constraints on the acquisition model. It requires, for instance, that a distinction be made between linguistic competence and performance; competence referring to the speaker-hearer's knowledge of his language and performance referring to actual use of language in concrete situations.

In the generative-transformational grammar theory, the goal of linguistic description is to describe the linguistic competence of the language user. In this sense, the theory is concerned primarily with an ideal speaker-listener who knows his language perfectly and is unaffected by such grammatically irrelevant conditions as memory limitations, distractions, shifts of attention, etc., which might interfere with the application of his knowledge of the language in actual performance.

While we are dealing with something less than an ideal speaker-listener situation in the study of the language acquisition process, linguistic competence can be a useful concept in describing the linguistic mechanism by which the child generates his utterances at various stages of development. In this sense, a child's linguistic competence may be thought of as a set of rules which govern and regulate his linguistic performance. However, linguistic competence itself cannot be measured directly. Competence can only be inferred from performance data, whether those data are based on imitation, comprehension, or production.

From a body of such performance data, more commonly referred to as a language corpus, the linguist will infer, and attempt to describe, all the generalizations about the language that the child has knowledge of and uses in his language performance. This competence or knowledge is expressed as a set of rules which are models of possible sentences for the child.

It should be emphasized that these rules (a grammar if you will) are models, not descriptions, of sentences in a language corpus. Idiolectal and dialectal variations in performance would be reflected in a strucutral description of a language corpus, whereas such variation would not be reflected in the significant generalizations specified by the grammar of that language.

It is clear, then, that a psycholinguisctic model of language acquisition must incorporate both performance and competence features. Performance is what is observed. Competence in this sense is the inferred rule governing that performance. The developmental stages of performance characteristics of the language acquisition process can be catalogued in terms of conventional descriptions of phonological and morphological development, vocabulary acquisition, use of adult-like sentences, etc. The Templin (1957) and McCarthy (1954) accounts of language development are recent examples of descriptions of some performance characteristics of first language learners.

Describing the stages of development of linguistic competence presents more problems than does a description of performance stages. With performance data, it is relatively easy to point to a specific starting point in the developmental process, be it crying behavior or first-word acquisition (Carroll, 1961). It is not so easy in the case of competence. In linguistic competence, there are two general assumptions regarding its acquisition. You can assume that the child is born without any linguistic competence and it develops gradually from his exposure to a linguistic environment, or you can assume that the child is born with some rudimentary linguistic competence which is then shaped by the environment.

The first assumption would seem to be the more untenable of the two. Such an assumption has a difficult time explaining why the deaf acquire "language" (sign language) despite the fact that they are not exposed to the linguistic environment that normal hearing individuals are. Also, the assumption of no linguistic competence at birth does not account for the universality of some linguistic structures despite varied cultural and linguistic environments. There seems to be no logical reason why we should expect such linguistic similarities across diverse cultures unless there were some innate basis.

The latter assumption, namely, that the child is born with a rudimentary linguistic competence, has been referred to more commonly in terms of an innate capacity for language acquisition. A basic part of this innate capacity is the child's tacit knowledge of language universals (Chomsky, 1965). Linguistic universals refer to universal properties of a generative grammar of natural languages. Linguistic universals may pertain to either the syntactic, semantic, or phonological components of a grammar and are of two types—substantive and formal. Substantive universals are those elements of a grammar which are independent of any language. They include distinctive features, parts of speech (noun, verb, etc.), syntactic categories (subject, predicate), and basic grammatical relations (actor–action–object). Formal universals are more abstract and pertain to properties of natural languages such as the transformational rules of the syntactic component. Whether or not one wishes to attribute such an innate capacity to the child is of little consequence to the general acquisition model to be proposed. The model itself makes no assumptions about innate or acquired initial competence. It does make assumptions about a developing linguistic competence. Figure 2 presents a schematic psycholinguistic model of language acquisition. The model contains both competence and performance aspects, and the input to the model, at every stage of development (see Figure 1) is primary linguistic data—that is, the data to which the child is exposed in his linguistic environment. In the model, this input is shown being filtered through perceptual mechanisms and short-term memory. The effect of perceptual mechanisms on language acquisition is obvious. For example, a deaf child develops language in a different way than does a normal-hearing child. The end products, adult language performances, are not necessarily the same. These difference we attribute primarily to the differences in perceptual mechanisms.

The role of short-term memory in the development of linguistic competence and performance has not been delineated at this time. Some limited evidence concerning short-term memory and language points out that short-term memory is indeed a significant parameter which might affect language acquisition. The data of Wickelgren (1965) show that vowels and consonants are coded in short-term memory as a set of distinctive features. Savin and Perchonock's (1965) data concerning immediate recall of certain sentence types illustrate the relationship between short-term memory and language. However, the exact role of this relationship to the acquisition process remains to be specified.

Within the constraints imposed by the perceptual mechanisms and short-term memory, the primary linguistic data are then processed through the competence component of the model. What this processing is, or how it operates, is not understood. It has been proposed that the child formulates hypotheses about his language environment. These hypotheses are shaped by the linguistic universals. Experience—that is, further linguistic data—provides the criteria against which predictions and hypotheses are judged (McNeill, 1966). Hypotheses are then reformulated and modified, checked against further linguistic data, and again remodified until the hypotheses match the data. At that point, the child's competence should match the adult's. The dynamics of the processing of primary linguistic data is based primarily on introspection and logic and remains to be verified. This is not to say that such a viewpoint serves no useful purpose, since it is at least a point of departure for research into the dynamics of the language acquisiton process.

To continue with the model, we see that the ouput of competence is performance. If there were no environmental factors to consider, such as distractions, shifts of attention, etc., the linguistic competence of an ideal speaker-listener would be mirrored by his performance. However, we are not dealing with an ideal situation. Therefore, the competence aspect can only be inferred from the performance data. Although not specifically indicated in Figure 2, the model does presuppose the afore-

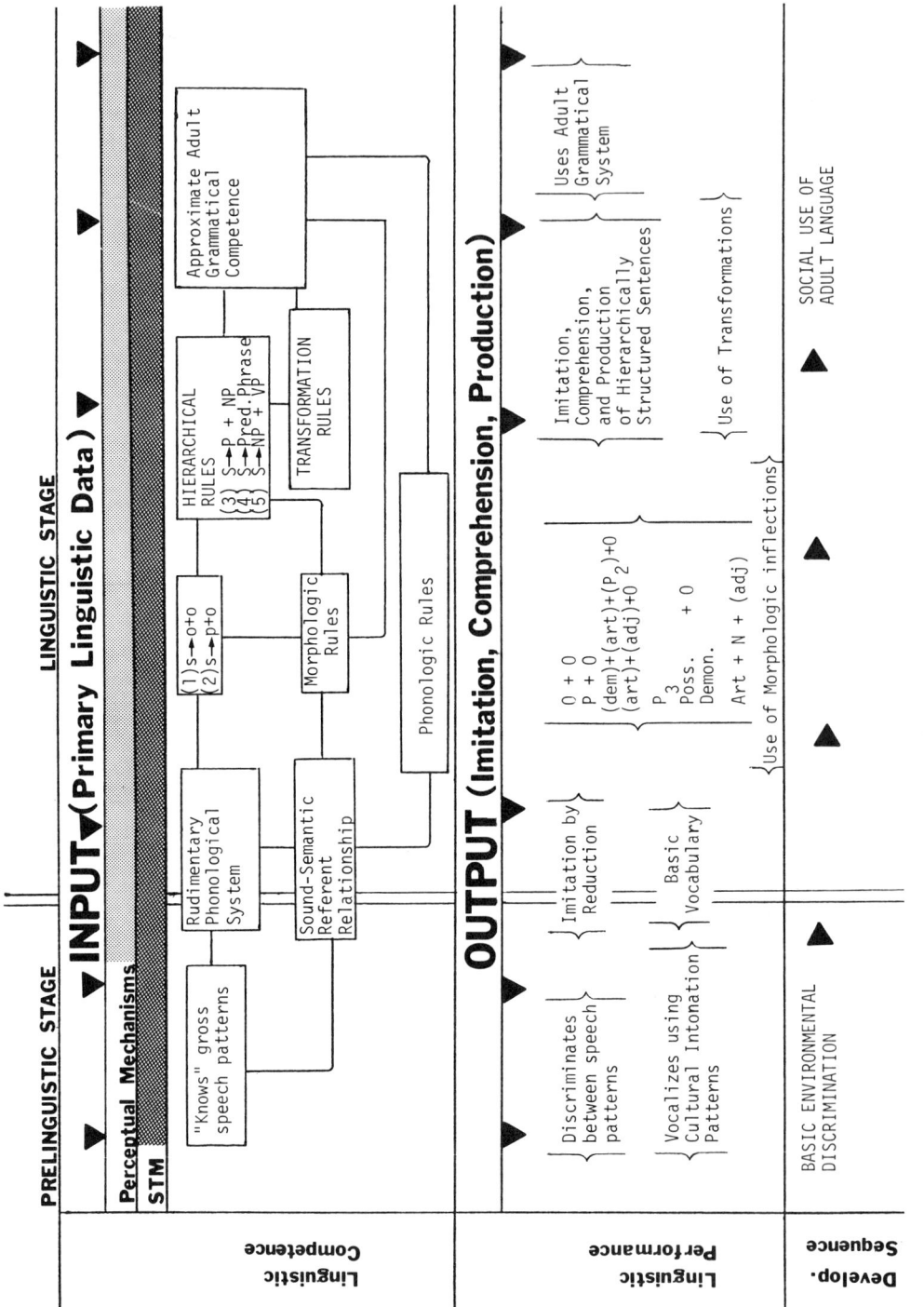

Fig. 2. Psycholinguistic Acquisition Model.

mentioned environmental variables which affect performance and thus make the competence and performance aspects less than a complete match.

Looking at the model from the developmental aspect we see that a distinction has been made between prelinguistic and the linguistic stages of development. This is an arbitrary, rather than a functional, division. Psycholinguistic performance data are limited to stages of development beginning with acquisition of the first word. In other words, this is the first time any conventional linguistic units (i.e., phonemes, morphemes, words, etc.) can be realistically dealt with, hence the division between linguistic and prelinguistic stages of development.

Both the competence and performance aspects in the prelinguistic stage of development are rather sketchily covered. Although there has been considerable literature concerning this stage of development (Carroll, 1961, and Eisenson, Auer, and Irwin, 1963), the relevance of many of their cited parameters to later language acquisition has not been demonstrated. For instance, crying behavior, cooing, babbling, echolalia have traditionally been viewed as practice for later stages of development (Carroll, 1961), but other data indicate that these so-called stages of language development are not prerequisites to later language development. Lenneberg (1966) specifically cites a case of a tracheotimized child who was unable to vocalize through several of these "developmental stages" and yet when he was finally able to vocalize, he produced utterances commensurate with those of his peers, completely skipping the stages of development his peers had gone through during his tracheotimized period. Thus, in at least this case, the "missed" stages of development cannot be viewed as prerequisites for later development.

The early, "prelinguistic," stages of development are thus quite vague, and for the most part undefined. There are several aspects of competence which must be attributed to this stage, albeit in a vague, general form. We do know, for instance, that the child is sensitive to different voices, tones of voices, and in some cases, perhaps even sensitive to intonation and stress patterns, although the data are vague on this point. We must also attribute to the child at this time, a segmenting ability by which he is capable of identifying gross units of language, i.e., words and sentences. Again, the gross dynamics of such a process must yet be specified. In the acquisition model (Figure 2), this particular stage of linguistic competence is covered by the gross term "knows gross speech patterns." The model also shows the skimpy performance data which leads to this inferred competence.

There is a point in the language acquisition process where the prelinguistic and linguistic stages overlap, and that begins somewhere around the age of the first word.

With the age of first word, we have the beginnings of what can be classified as a functional linguistic system for the child. The first word is the initial demonstration that the link between sound and semantic referents has been made. This also signals the first rudimentary phonological system of the child as well as the beginning of vocabulary acquisition as manifested by his linguistic performance.

Again, the dynamic processes involved in this acquisition are not clear, but the model does suggest that the role of verbal imitation is not as much an active part of this process as it is an external indicator of the level of competence. This is depicted in the performance aspect of the model as "imitation by reduction." The literature abounds with examples of children recoding adult utterances into their own phonological system—a type of "imitation by reduction." Ervin (1964) also describes such an imitation by reduction process for the syntactic imitations. In comparing spontaneous imitations of five children to grammars written from her subject's unimitated spontaneous speech, she found no differences in performances which would indicate that imitations were grammatically more progressive than spontaneous non-imitative responses. Scholes (1969) provides further evidence that verbal imitations are futher dependent, at early stages of development, upon words having semantic referents; that is, the word-object semantic relationship has been established. This suggests that while imitation may be used to shape performance, its applicability is limited by the linguistic competence of the language user. In this light, the data can be interpreted as indicating that imitation is not an adequate mechanism to account for the development of linguistic competence in normal children. Note that although imitation by reduction occurs only once in the model, it carried through developmentally in all three components of the grammar (phonology, syntax, and semantics) until such a time as the adult linguistic competence is approximated. In this sense, imitation (as well as comprehension and production in a more functional sense) may be used as an index of the linguistic competence but not a determiner of it.

The remainder of the model is rather straightforward. Performance data (imitation, comprehension, and production) are used to infer linguistic competence and its development. For example, the pivot-open grammatical distinction and the differentiation of the pivot class as described by McNeill (1966), can be reduced to a more simplistic rule. A sentence can be written as an open plus an open word, or the sentence can be written as a pivot plus an open word. These are the two rules the child operates under at this stage of development. Stated a little differently, there are those words which in a multi-word utterance assume a fixed position and there are those words which are free to vary.

To go back to the McNeill data, the pivot words are those which assume a fixed position in an utterance, and the open words can occur either in first or last position; that is, they are free to vary. The differentiation of the pivot class as McNeill describes it is merely an extension of the rules that the child has or was previously credited with. The distinction between words which assume a fixed position and those which are free to vary is a distinction which is also compatible within adult grammatical rules.

For instance, determiners in our language always precede nouns. The differentiation of the pivot class merely demonstrates that this distinction is being refined to the point where it matches the adult distinctions. This process of pilot class differentiation can also be viewed as an example of hypothesis formulation and reformulation on the part of the child, as previously discussed.

In the process of this refinement, it can be postulated that the child is acquiring hierarchical syntactic rules, encompassing noun phrase-predicate phrase performance. A bit of performance evidence which demonstrates that the child has incorporated the hierarchical relationship of phrase structure as a part of his linguistic competence, is the fact that he will use pronouns to represent an entire noun phrase —not just the noun that the pronoun theoretically represents. Development of competence in the use of transformation rules begins during this phase of development, as the model indicates, and development is theoretically complete when the child's linguistic competence matches that of the adult.

Coincident with the development of the competence in the syntactic component (including morphological development) is the development of competence in the phonologic and semantic components of the grammar. Again, it is from the performance data which we infer the competence of the child at these various stages of development. Recent data on the acquisition and use of phonological rules (Menyuk, 1968, and Michel, 1969) have furthered our knowledge in this area. Unfortunately, the study of the semantic component has been largely ignored and specific inferences concerning either competence or performance acquisition are generally lacking.

To sum up our discussion of the model, it might be well to reiterate that the proposed model be viewed as a theoretical framework encompassing relevant psycholinguistic data concerning the nature of language acquisition. Only in a general sense will the model provide any satisfactory explanation of the dynamic processes involved in the acquisition. It does encompass the general theoretical concepts which any specific study of the acquisition process must consider—such concepts as competence and performance, general and specific rule behavior, base structures, transformations, and surface structures. It should also be pointed out at this time that the competence aspect of this model is general enough that it is independent of any specific language—that is, it should theoretically apply to the language acquisition process of any child of any language environment. This, after all, is the ultimate goal of any model of the normal language acquisition process. Through more research and refined theory building, the model, or aspects of it, may be made more specific and more explanatory.

The language intervention model (A Systematic Approach to Language Training) designed by Dr. Bricker can be viewed as a research and training model of more specific parameters of the acquisition process. While the developmental performance sequence of the two models may be similar (the data on which the two models are based are essentially the same), the theoretical conceptions underlying the two models differ considerably. This difference is reflected to some degree by different treatments of the same parameters. Imitation, for instance, is given considerably more weight in Dr. Bricker's training model, whereas the acquisition model based on available data concerning the role of imitation in first language acquisition, plays down the significance of this factor in the normal acquisition process. Other such comparisons between the two models can be made and the differences will probably be more glaring than the similarities. But then it must be remembered that the purposes of the two models are essentially different. The present model attempts to provide a psycholinguistic description of the general processes and relevant data related to the normal acquisition of language. Dr. Bricker's model attempts to intervene and modify aspects of this process with the view toward discovering relevant training parameters and methods for those who do not acquire the language naturally, i.e., the mentally retarded. No doubt there will be mutual influence of the models on each other and the type of research they generate. In the process we can but gain in our knowledge of the normal acquisition process and the degree to which intervention and training can influence this process in both normal and abnormal language acquisition.

SUMMARY OF DISCUSSION

QUESTION: You say that, "While imitation may be used to shape performance, its applicability is limited by the linguistic competence of the language user. In this light the data can be interpreted as indicating that imitation is not an adequate mechanism to account for the development of linguistic competence in normal children." I am not quite sure what you mean by that. If in fact a child can imitate only what he knows about the language, why then is imitation not an indication of competence?

RUDER: I mean that it is not an adequate mechanism to account for development of linguistic competence. The point is that there are no data to show that by working on imitation you are not, in this view, increasing the child's linguistic competence. His imitation is already dependent upon the competence that he has. To my knowledge, there are at present no data to indicate that imitation is a basic process utilized by a child in his progression to adult language competence.

QUESTION: Would you then say that imitation is a reflection of the child's comprehension ability?

RUDER: Yes, in some respects you might make such a generalization. In the view of some of the recent literature you could also say that imitation, as a performance measure, also reflects the level of the child's linguistic competence at a particular stage of development.

QUESTION: Of his competence? Could you measure what the child knows about the language through an imitation?

RUDER: Yes. And when I talk about the imitation by reduction in terms of the model, it's a crude form but it does give you some indication of his phonological system, what type of syntactic rule behavior he has, and in the case of the Scholes' data, some aspect of the child's semantic reference.

QUESTION: Didn't they find that the child could imitate a lot more than he could understand, at least through their picture mode?

RUDER: Yes. However, there are several problems with this, particularly as applied to the mentally retarded. Fraser, Bellugi, and Brown's (1963) finding that imitation is better than comprehension did not hold for *all* subjects. All subjects however, did better in both imitation and comprehension than they did in production. And in comparing normal and mentally retarded imitation-comprehension performance, the data did not match the imitation-comprehension-performance of Fraser, Bellugi, and Brown's subjects.

QUESTION: What differences did you find?

RUDER: With the mentally retarded there was no difference between imitation and comprehension performance. The data were essentially similar for all aspects of this performance.

QUESTION: Is it possible that some of the echolalic children can't handle various kinds of structures because they don't comprehend? And what about the opposite group that finds imitation extremely difficult and are able to comprehend much more than they can imitate?

RUDER: I am not familiar with the data on the performance of retarded children in this regard. However, my exposure to mentally retarded children has included several mongoloids who were very adept at imitation. In fact, they did the opposite of what I point out here. They imitated my utterances up to the limits of their memory span very well. Yet spontaneously they could produce almost nothing. I'm not sure whether they work with the same imitation strategies normal children use. My guess is that they do not.

QUESTION: Assuming we are dealing with a population whose innate capacities differ, either as a result of some biological insult or perhaps on the basis of genetic limitations, how does this model apply? What is the relationship between limited comprehension as reflected in mental retardation and the theory? Are some of the differences that you are alluding to with respect to the intervention approach and this model for acquisition caused by this kind of difference in innate capacities? Does the intervention have to be modified because of differentations in ability to comprehend or imitate?

WEINER: I don't think there is a single language disorder one is going to find among the mentally retarded, but probably a number of different types of language disorders. This makes a difference in the kind of model that will be necessary, the kind of intervention programs that will be necessary.

SCHIEFELBUSCH: I think the intent simply was to present a model of linguistic acquisition. We have a major problem in considering what happens or what exists as a series of events when a person is acquiring the necessary early linguistic structure. If you talk with language therapists or language trainers or language developmentalists, or whatever they may call themselves across the land, they really have vague and confusing concepts of what they are trying to do in relation to what the child can do and what perhaps he should be doing at any point along the line.

QUESTION: What is an acquisition model? You have the adequate features of a theory of grammar, but it is hard for me to know how to recognize an acquisition model walking down the street.

RUDER: In a very restricted sense, an acquisition model should attempt to identify and describe the relevant processes involved in a child's progression toward, and acquisition of, an adult's linguistic competence. In this sense, the model, if you wish to call it that, is based on McNeill's hypothesis formulation—the child being a type of a hypothesis generator who keeps reformulating hypotheses until he comes out with something that matches the input.

QUESTION: That sounds like the power behind the model is terminal behavior by the adult which somehow reaches into childhood and pulls the child along as though there were no impellents along the way except that ultimate terminal behavior. Doesn't that place all the explanatory power in the terminal behavior of the adult rather than the processes whereby the child achieves that behavior?

RUDER: The behavior the child exhibits in terms of his language performance at certain stages is probably adequate for communication with peers, and yet it is not adequate to carry on, say, conversation with an adult after he gets to certain points and wants to communicate with his adult counterparts. We can also talk about this in terms of the child's need to communicate effectively. He's going to keep re-altering. And our grammar, the linguistic rules that adults function by, continually changes to meet the needs of our own effective communication. This is why we can't stand still with a prescriptive type of a grammar. If we do, we end up where Latin is, a nonfunctional language. So I would have to say it is not so much the need to acquire the adult model as it is the need to communicate effectively which impels the child from stage to stage.

QUESTION: There are two variables. One is the set of variables that impels the child to go from stage to stage. The other has to do with the internal logic within the model itself. Why is one stage antecedent to some other? Is this an environmental requirement, or is there something internal to the model or to the child as an organism? Or what moves him along this particular sequence?

RUDER: There is nothing significant in these particular stages other than the child trying to develop and differentiate, to eventually evolve an adult competence.

QUESTION: Do you feel that the model you have discussed is a viable, dynamic, changing model of acquisition that is sensitive to new information, to experience with children acquiring language? Or do you see it as a relatively static, relatively unchanging kind of thing?

RUDER: Any new information that you acquire in terms of a child's performance or of ways you can manipulate that performance are going to add to your knowledge. This may include throwing out parts of what we have attributed to the child's linguistic competence. I tried to set up the model to be general enough so that it would be sensitive to new information and capable of being adapted.

QUESTION: The tremendous overgeneralizations you make about the function of imitation makes me wonder if that statement is really true. Imitation is very functional but only a very small part of some kind of intervention process.

RUDER: There is indeed an argument between two opposing viewpoints on the role of imitation in the process of language acquisition. I am on the fence about it. I am familiar with Ervin's data and McNeill's ideas on the role of imitation and their strict transformational viewpoint. Yet being in an operant conditioning environment for three or four months has given me second thoughts about it. With the limited data available on the role of imitation in the acquisition process, I am not sure that either approach to imitation is correct at this point, but if the model does nothing other than point out or highlight discrepancy between the two ways of thinking, then I think part of the model has served its purpose in that it poses an empirical question which needs further research.

QUESTION: Do you foresee any data that would lead you to discard all or part of your model? In other words, are there any conceivable data that your model can't account for?

RUDER: I am particularly disturbed by some of the data basic to the competence model. This is the pivot-open class distinction. I suspect that the people who have generated these rules must have ignored at least part of the data. I have attempted to replicate this distinction in children's grammars based on mother-child interaction data and failed to come up with such a clear cut classification. Furthermore, not all the utterances by children were strictly nice two-word utterances with nothing else added to them. I believe that this junk or noise, or whatever you want to call it, that accompanies identifiable words in a child's utterance was just disregarded in previous studies. And I am not so sure that we can simply disregard this.

QUESTION: Is the filtration of primary linguistic data, whatever processes are involved in that procedure, where most of the acquisition takes place?

RUDER: Yes. One of the big differences I see between the training model and the model I presented is the primary linguistic data, that is, the data with which the child in the normal acquisition process is presented. He is not presented with a nice, clean, clear-cut, completely grammatical model to follow. He is given performance data, and performance data are in most cases less than completely grammatical. There are parts of utterances, and changes of thought. The child may be answering in one or two words. This is the type of environment he is exposed to. Yet, somehow, with this primary linguistic data, he is able to make relevant generalizations. The training process involves a different input. The input may be something the normal child is never exposed to as primary linguistic data. Input may be a nonsense syllable input, or it may be word input, or it may be a structured, completely grammatical model sentence.

QUESTION: Do you say something is not grammatical because it doesn't conform to your description?

RUDER: There are degrees of grammaticality. There are also degrees of acceptability. We have set up what we called degrees of grammaticality or well-formedness of sentences. Even something every native speaker of English would say is completely well-formed can be manipulated to set up a hierarchy of well-formedness.

QUESTION: Doesn't that confound acceptability with grammaticality?

RUDER: Yes. I was equating the two. The hierarchy of grammaticality is a theoretical issue which is beyond any demonstration. The point is that the child is exposed to utterances which are incomplete, fragmented, and accompanied by many other things in the environment.

QUESTION: In dealing with an interactional process between an organism and certain environmental experiences, does the acquisition model fully account for the differences in the organism? Are we looking at problems of intersensory integration or developmental processes in the child which influence the application or his receptivity to certainly environmental events and his ability to process whatever input information comes to him? Many people say that a child will start talking when he is ready to talk and that it doesn't matter what you do to get him to speak sooner. Does the environment teach the child to have pivot-open class restraints, or does something else impose that restraint on the child? Why doesn't he start out with well-formed, grammatical sentences? What is it that drags him through this chain of performance of development?

RUDER: Something should be added to the constraints of short-term memory or the perceptual mechanisms. We have to consider the development of the biological mechanism. And we have to take into consideration the neurological development of the child, whatever that may be.

QUESTION: This model represents a description of the operations of the nervous system, not necessarily what is happening in terms of synapses. The question is whether it involves formal instruction or manipulation of contingencies in any systematic way. These don't seem to be very powerful in the normal acquisition process. When we talk about something like imitation we have a set number of training events. It might be represented in SR formulation. But at some point in the training sequence the child extrapolates. He gets to generalized imitation. But what is the mechanism operating in generalization? Is there a way of representing the data of language in such a way that we can account for generalization or competencies? Going through a set number of training events you get to generalized competency. Again, is there a formulation contained in Ruder's model that simplifies the language process so we don't have to think about language as just the set of responses that people emit as performance? Back to a previous question of what pushes the child along. Is it the fact that he identifies with adults and therefore wants to talk like adults and therefore begins to strive to construct language? Or is it something within him neurologically that pushes him along? One implication of this language acquisition device is that he is pushed along internally rather than drawn along externally.

RUDER: McNeill does view the neurological component, or whatever you want to call it, the developmental neurological aspects, as propelling the child along. I emphasize the external environment and the need for the child to communicate effectively. I don't know that there are data to support either notion. Both should be looked at more completely in normal acquisition and as motivation in the intervention model.

SCHIEFELBUSCH: We are now getting into the weaknesses or limitations in current linguistics and psycholinguistics. Neither body of literature gives the functions that move the structure from point to point or from stage to stage. This is the main problem in dealing clinically or educationally with someone who is a disordered speaker. You must intervene so as to move the child, and your linguistic data doesn't tell you how to do that. Some say you can't do it except in relation to some surface features or performance characteristics which do not change the basic code or the basic language knowledge functionally. This poses a basic issue to all people who have children confronting them everywhere.

HASS: I could present an alternative interpretation of what McNeill is trying to do. He is not trying to set up an innately programmed timetable which determines everything about child language development. What he is trying to do is account for the regularities in language development in a way that leaves space open for the child to interact with the environment. He has tried in several ways to give an account of the regularities of the child's syntactic structures, saying as little as he can about what the child has to bring to the language task. He says that you can get this mechanism going, that you can get these widely divergent structures that were quite different—pivot and open class, hierarchical structures, transformation—if you assume only one thing, which is base grammatical relations.

That is not too much to assume. At least it's far simpler to assume that kind of mechanism in the child than to say he first starts out with pivot and open, open and open, and then all of a sudden he gets a completely new idea, "I'll do transformation."

If you start out saying that he is working at language from a view which pushes toward basic grammatical relations, then what McNeill is trying to show is that you can get these phenotypically quite divergent structures from the same kind of push the child has in organizing his behavior toward language.

So we should consider McNeill as giving us a recipe for as little innate pre-programming as you need to still get the regularities that you do find in the sequences.

REFERENCES

Carroll, J. Language development in children. In S. Sparta (Ed.), *Psycholinguistics: A book of readings.* New York: Holt, Rinehart and Winston, 1961, Pp. 331–345.

Chomsky, N. *Aspects of the theory of syntax.* Cambridge MIT Press, 1965.

Eisenson, J., Auer, J., and Irwin, J. *The psychology of communication.* New York: Appleton-Century-Crofts, 1963.

Ervin, S. Imitation and structural change in children's language. In E. Lennenberg (Ed.), *New directions in the study of language.* Cambridge: MIT Press, 1964.

Lenneberg, E. H. The natural history of language. In F. Smith and G. Miller (Eds.), *The genesis of language.* Cambridge: MIT Press, 1966. Pp. 219–249.

McCarthy, D. Language development in children. In L. Carmichael (Ed.), *Manual of child psychology.* New York: Wiley, 1954.
McNeill, D. Developmental psycholinguistics. In F. Smith and G. Miller (Eds.); *The genesis of language.* Cambridge: MIT Press, 1966. Pp. 15-84.
Menyuk, P. The role of distinctive features in children's acquisition of phonology. *J. Speech Hearing Res.,* 1968, *11,* 138-146.
Michel, L. The interaction of auditory perception and the phonologics systems in children. Unpublished manuscript, University of Kansas, 1969.
Savin, H. and Perchonock, E. Grammatical structure and immediate recall of English sentences. *J. Verb. Learning Verb. Behavior,* 1965, *4,* 438-453.
Scholes, R. J. On functions and contentives in children's imitations. *University of Florida Communication Sciences Laboratory Quarterly Report,* 1969, *7*(3), 29-33.
Templin, M. C. Certain language skills in children: Their development and interrelationships. University of Minnesota, *Institute of Child Welfare Monograph,* 1957, No. 26.
Wickelgren, W. A. Distinctive features and errors in short-term memory for English vowels. *J. Acoust. Soc. Amer.,* 1965, *38,* 583-588.

SEMANTIC FEATURES IN LANGUAGE DEVELOPMENT

LOIS BLOOM
Teachers College, Columbia University

LOIS BLOOM received her Ph.D. from Columbia University in 1968. From 1958 until 1963 she was the assistant chief of the Department of Speech and Hearing, Institute of Rehabilitation Medicine, New York University Medical Center. She is presently an associate professor in the departments of psychology and speech pathology and audiology at Teachers College, Columbia University.

In the last decade, inquiry into what the child learns when he learns language has focused attention on the formal syntax of children's speech—on descriptions of the arrangements of words in sentences uttered and understood at successive stages. In texts of early child language, some words occur more often and in more varied linguistic environments than do other words. For example, "no" (or "no more") and "Mommy" are just such forms that occur frequently in children's speech, in relatively fixed sentence position, with many different words. In this respect, "no" and "Mommy" could be described superficially as 'pivotal' in their appearance with different substantive words in children's utterances. This 'pivotal' aspect of children's language has been described by several investigators (Braine, 1963; Brown and Fraser, 1963; Miller and Ervin, 1964; McNeill, 1966).

However, such linguistic descriptions of the form of speech provide minimal information about the child's intuitive knowledge of a linguistic code. The development of language necessarily involves more than an increase in numbers of words and their possible combinations. Rather, the linguistic expression is one component of the complex process which also involves cognitive-perceptual growth and development of interaction in a world of objects, events, and relations. Clearly, success in learning to talk depends upon the child's ability to perceive and organize his environment, the language that is a part of that environment, and the relation between the two. The goal of the research discussed below (and reported at length in Bloom, 1970) was to investigate the development of linguistic behavior with specific focus on the relations between children's speech and aspects of their experience related to the speech that they use. This paper will discuss some of the findings from a study of the emerging grammars of three children from the age of 19 months to 28 months (Bloom, 1970), a pilot observation of one child from the age of 9 months to 18 months, and, finally, the possible relevance of this information for the treatment of language disorders in children.

An earlier version of this paper was presented to the Conference on Research in the Language of the Mentally Retarded, at the Bureau of Child Research, The University of Kansas, February, 1970. Part of the research described in this paper was supported by PHS Grant 50F1-MH-30, 001-03 from the National Institute of Mental Health.

EMERGING GRAMMARS

The subjects of the study—Kathryn, Eric, and Gia—were the first-born children of white, college-educated, American-English speaking parents. They were each visited in their homes for approximately eight hours over a period of several days every six weeks. Each sample of spoken language was obtained during (1) play with a selected group of toys, (2) eating, dressing, and toileting, and (3) play with a peer. The syntactic components of generative grammars were proposed for the earliest texts with mean length of utterance less than 1.5 morphemes. The syntactic and semantic development of negation was described until mean length of utterance was approximately 3.0 morphemes (in Bloom, 1970). Kathryn was 21 months old when the study began; Eric and Gia were each 19 months, 1 week old.

In order to propose rules of grammar for early language, judgments were made of the semantic intent of utterances, based upon cues from the context and behavior in the speech events in which utterances occurred. For example, it was clear from nonlinguistic cues in the data that when a child said "Mommy sock" and Mommy was putting the child's sock on the child, there was a different semantic-syntactic relationship between the constituents than when the child said "Mommy sock" and picked up Mommy's sock. Using this kind of information an attempt was made to propose rules of grammar to account for the inherent semantic relations that underlie the juxtaposition of words in early sentences.

The major results of the study could be summarized as follows. The children began to express the basic grammatical relations, that is, subject-verb, subject-object, and verb-object in their early two-word utterances, when subject-verb-object strings did not occur. Although subject-verb-object strings were not produced by the children, these grammatical relationships were postulated in the underlying structure of utterances to account for the inferred semantic interpretation of two-term strings. For example, interpretation of "Mommy pigtail" (Kathryn wanted Mommy to make her a pigtail) implied the existence of an intervening predicate element in the underlying structure of the sentence to specify the hierarchical relationship between "Mommy" as *subject* and "pigtail" as *object*.

Thus, early utterances that have been described in the literature as simply the cooccurrence of two substantive words (x-word plus x-word by Braine (1963), or two open class words by McNeill (1966)) could be explained in terms of the inherent semantic relationship between the constituents. It was apparent that the children in the study were talking about the relations between actors or agents, actions or states, and objects or goals. They did not simply name two referents or two aspects of a referent—simple conjunction—within the bounds of a single utterance. If this were the case, then the order in which the constituents occurred would have been variable, but word order did not vary. The order of constituents reflected the underlying order of basic sentence relations with remarkable consistency—subjects and verbs preceded objects or goals.

It was also not the case that any two words could occur with any possible relation between them. The utterances with two noun forms specified the grammatical relations subject-object ("Mommy pigtail"), subject-locative ("sweater-chair"), the genitive relation ("Kathryn sock"), the attributive relation ("bread book"), and, marginally, conjunction ("umbrella boot"). However, there were no instances of such other possible relations that could hold between two noun forms as identity ("Mommy lady"), disjunction (either-or relation), or direct-indirect object. The fact that expression of certain relationships did not occur was not due to the absence of such relations between objects and events in the environment. The children's utterances were not merely reflections of nonlinguistic states of affairs if it could be assumed that the nonobtained relations existed in the child's experience, for example, giving someting to someone (direct-indirect object). Such selectivity in addition to the impressive consistency of word order provided evidence for assuming that the children's utterances were motivated by an underlying cognitive-linguistic rule system.

The nature of the underlying rules that the child uses to speak and understand utterances cannot be described directly. There is a necessary distinction between a speaker-hearer's knowledge of grammar and the notion of grammar as a linguistic account of that knowledge. The generative grammars that were proposed (Bloom, 1970) represent a formal linguistic account of how such rules specify the inherent grammatical relations that hold between the categories from which lexical items (like "Mommy," "sock," "make") are derived. Such an account specifies the syntax of utterances (the arrangements of forms) that codes the semantic relations among the forms; thus there is a crucial relationship between linguistic structure and underlying cognitive function. This kind of information about the relationship between linguistic structure and certain cognitive notions (such as the relation between agent and object) appears to be inherent in generative rules of grammar—and in this sense, a generative grammar can be seen as a cognitive as well as a linguistic construct (Chomsky, 1968). It was clear that the three children in the study used the linguistic code to signal what they knew of the world of objects, events, and relations.

A similar conclusion was reached by Schlesinger (1971). In his account of early two-word utterances he hypothesized that a model for the production of utterances (a performance model) uses as input certain information about the child's semantic intentions. Moreover, he proposed that these intentions are essentially relational notions which specify the relations that hold between concepts as agent-action, action-object, agent-object. Schlesinger suggested that the relational notions contained in the semantic intentions which are ultimately coded linguistically by the child may represent a universal cognitive organization of experience.

However, the possible grammatical relations (subject-verb, verb-object, subject-object) were not equally represented in the data. Certain relations appeared to be more productive than others—that is, they occurred more often in different situations with different words. Also, the children seemed to differ in their use of each. For example, Eric used the verb-object relation first and utterances expressing this relation were dominant in his speech before he began to use subject nouns in relation to verb forms. The most productive early relationship for Gia and Kathryn was subject-object; Eric never produced such utterances. Schlesinger (1971) reported the productivity of this structural relationship between two nouns in the early speech of two Hebrew speaking Israeli children, and Leopold (1949) described its frequent occurrence in the speech of his daughter Hildegard. In the speech of Kathryn, Eric, and Gia, verb-object strings appeared earlier and were more productive than subject-verb strings.

There are also other kinds of relational notions than those that hold between noun and verb forms or between two noun forms. Certain forms occur frequently in the early two-word utterances of Kathryn, Eric, and Gia (and in the data reported in the literature) that function as syntactic markers or operators with particular semantic intent. The most productive of these function words were "no" (or some other negative element such as "no more" or "all gone") and "more" (or "another"). Other forms such as "here" (and "there"), "this" (and "that") occurred less frequently. These words could be described as 'pivotal'—they were small in number and occurred frequently in fixed position with a variety of different words. However, it was not the case that such words occurred freely with the larger class of substantive words. Rather, their use was motivated by their semantic function; they occurred in speech events that shared features of context and behavior.

The earliest syntactic utterances with "no" (or "no more" or "all gone") occurred in speech events in which the referent named did not exist although there was an expectation of its existence because it had existed previously or the child either anticipated or looked for it. For example, the children said "no pocket" when a pocket couldn't be found, "no fit" when one block did not fit into another, "no more cleaner" when the vacuum cleaner was put away. The earliest use of "no" signaled *nonexistence*. Subsequently, the same form, "no", was used in similar syntactic contexts to signal *rejection*—the referent was imminent or actually manifest in speech events and the child either pushed it away, or turned away, or otherwise negated wanting to have or to do something. For example, Kathryn said "no dirty soap" and pushed away a worn sliver of soap, wanting to be washed with new pink soap. At a still later time, "no" signaled *denial*—the referent was not present in the speech event but it was manifest symbolically in something said. For example, Kathryn said "no truck" when someone offered her a car saying "here's the truck."

"More" occurred in speech events in which the referent named (as in "more read," "more raisin," and "more updown") had occurred previously, and the child either requested or commented on its occurring again. "More" signaled another instance of or the *recurrence* of a referent.

The forms "no" and "more" are inherently relational terms that occurred with constant grammatical function, that is, they did not change grammatical meaning as noun forms did in relation to verb forms or other nouns. Possible variation in meaning—as the use of "no" to signal nonexistence, rejection, or denial and the use of "more" to signal recurrence (and, eventually, the partitive and comparative notions)—did not depend on variable underlying syntactic arrangement.

In summary, the children's earliest sentences could thus be seen as expressing (1) *grammatical relations,* where substantive words such as "Mommy" and "sock" occur with variable grammatical meaning in reciprocal relationship with other substantive words, and grammatical meaning is derived from that interrelation. Substantive words such as "Mommy" and "sock" enter into grammatical relationship with other words in sentences. They are not in themselves relational terms in the sense that they also occur alone in reference to some aspect of experience. Children's earliest sentences also express (2) *functional relations,* where function words such as "more" and "no" operate in linear relationship with other (substantive) words to specify a particular relational aspect of such words (or their referents). Spoken alone as single-word utterances, such words manifestly imply such a semantic relationship to some unspecified aspect of experience.

The studies of children's language in the last decade have focused on the development of grammar, so that after the emergence of grammar (the period most often characterized by the use of two-word utterances) inquiry has been directed toward the subsequent development of increased complexity. There has been little recent attention to the earlier stages. How do children *use* language, that is, single-word utterances, before the appearance of syntax in their speech?

SINGLE-WORD UTTERANCES

The function of pre-syntax single-word utterances as 'holophrastic' has been attributed to observations of the ways in which adults interpret what children say (McCarthy, 1954, p. 525; Lenneberg; 1967, pp. 281–283; McNeill, unpublished). Whether or not such single-word utterances can be structurally represented is an important question for a theory of the origins of grammatical competence. Children appear to understand structural relationships well before they express them in their speech. Furthermore, when they begin to use syntax, they use both relational, function words and substantive words. Do these different classes of words occur singly, and how are they used, before the appearance of syntax?

In a pilot observation of one child (my own daughter Allison) from the age of 9 months to 18 months, it was possible to detect certain developmental trends. Two of the most relevant observations concerned (1) differential use of substantive words and inherently relational terms, and (2) chronological change in the use of substantive words. First, aside from "Mama," "Dada," and a very few other 'names' of familiar experiences (such as "baby" and "car") the development of a vocabulary of substantive words was not cumulative. That is to say, by the age of 14 months, more than 50 different recognizable words were heard, more than once, over a period of a few days, to refer to a recognizable object or person, but did not occur again until several or many months later. Comprehension of these words persisted —they simply were not *said* in similar situations. However, a small group of words were used in this same period of time, frequently and persistently. These words were "no," to express rejection and, subsequently, nonexistence, "more," to express recurrence, "up" and "down," (in contrast); "away" and then "all gone" as a comment on disappearance; deictic "there"; and "stop," as a comment on cessation. It appears that the words which have been described syntactically as functional, inherently relational terms were the predominant forms in Allison's earliest language before the appearance of syntax. Each of these words had identifiable semantic intent in relation to some aspect of the child's experience.

Second, there was a chronological change in the apparent function of substantive words. For example, initially "Mama" was used either as a vocative, or with deixis to point Mama out, as if to say 'that's Mama.' Subsequently, "Mama" was said when Allison pointed to or looked at objects that were associated with Mama, for example, coat, gloves, lunch—objects that she had never named, although her understanding of the names for them was evident. Later, she began to use "Mama" in reference to events in which Mama was the agent, for example, Mama cooking pudding, opening a door, or sweeping the floor. Still later, she used "Mama" in reference to events in which Mama was the object, for example, closing the door to hide Mama in the kitchen.

At 17 months, Allison quite suddenly began to use a great many substantive words—more than 150 such words were counted as used consistently and repeatedly by the time she was 18 months old and noun forms predominated. Moreover, most often these words appeared to occur with no other function than to 'name' or point out the referent in the environment. This sudden increase in so-called naming or labeling behavior has been observed and reported by many students of child language. If pressed to ascribe grammatical function to these utterances, one could say only that they occurred most often as objects of deixis.

However, at the same time, Allison began to produce sequences of two or three words that were not syntactic constructions. Although said in succession, each word occurred with terminal falling contour; there was intervening juncture; and word order was variable. Examples were "door, open" as she passed a door being opened; "door, open, Mommy" wanting Mommy to open the door; "cut, Daddy" pointing to a band-aid on Daddy's finger; "coat, Daddy" pointing to Daddy's coat in the closet; "bed, up" as she tried to climb onto the bed; "powder, Mommy" as Mommy sprinkled powder on her; "powder, Mommy" as Mommy powdered her own face; "up, Daddy" as she pulled Daddy from a chair; "Daddy, door" after Daddy came home; both "Daddy, car" and "car, Daddy" after Daddy left to get the car; "read, more" as she picked up another book to read; "meat, more" as she received another helping of meat; and "more, raisin" as more raisins spilled out of a box. Leopold observed this same linguistic behavior: "two (related) one-word utterances . . . said in succession" just before the emergence of the earliest two-word constructions in his daughter's speech (1949, p. 20). The same behavior was observed in the earliest samples of speech from Eric and Gia, when mean length of utterance was 1.10 morphemes for Eric and 1.12 morphemes for Gia.

A structural description of these utterances in terms of Topic and Comment as the "basic grammatical relation of (the) surface structure" of the constituents (Chomsky, 1965, p. 221) would be appropriate. In this analysis, the Topic is the element stated first—perhaps in order of importance—and the subsequent element is interpretable as Comment. The Topic and Comment designation was offered as an alternative explanation for Gia's early constructions (with closed juncture between the constituents), for example, "balloon throw" as she 'threw' a balloon; "slide go" as she put keys on the slide, and "fly block" as she watched a fly settle on a block. The surface form of adult English sentences can be described similarly, for example, "The ball, I threw *it*" and "The ball, *it* is on the table" where *"it"* represents the topic of the sentence as underlying object and subject respectively.

It is of considerable interest that just before the emergence of syntax in their speech, Gia, Eric, Allison, and Leopold's Hildegard were able to produce related one-word utterances in succession, but without underlying grammatical relationship between the forms. The order in which the elements occurred was variable and the semantic interpretation (and hence the 'structure' of these utterances) was a factor of context and behavior alone. This observation raises important questions about the designation of single-word utterances as 'holophrastic' if such a description implies knowledge of linguistic structure. It appears that children recognize more than one aspect of a referent, or recognize the relationship between aspects of a referent before they express (syntactically) either co-occurrence or relationship. At this stage, when children produce utterances with the surface features of Topic and Comment, they do not use the syntax of the adult model, and there is no evidence from their linguistic performance that they 'know' the syntax in the sense of being able to use it.

However, the fact that such series of single-word utterances occur within the bounds of single speech events provides evidence to support the notion that children are aware of relational aspects of their experience before they are able to code such experience linguistically. This is essentially the conclusion reached by Schlesinger—that children learn notions of agent, action, object as "concepts" which are prelinguistic—although Schlesinger referred only to syntactic data (two word utterances). Children interact in a world of objects, events, and relations and their perceptual-cognitive strategies for apprehending this experience no doubt include the realization of such relational notions as have been discussed. Learning linguistic structure, in this view, would depend on the prior development of certain conceptual structures—as observed by Piaget (1968).

TREATMENT OF LANGUAGE DISORDERS

The data suggest several conclusions that may be applicable to planning treatment for language disorders in children. Limitations which exist for extrapolating conclusions from the results of this study for all children learning language apply as well as application of the results to treatment and evaluation of language pathology. Moreover, one of the most crucial needs in the field of speech pathology is for research directed toward evaluating and comparing treatment procedures for language disorders. For example, whether or not the normative data on language development that are beginning to appear in the literature can or should be directly applied to treating children with delayed language development is an important question (see Bloom, 1967). However, certain observations can be made at this time that should provide hypotheses for such research.

First, the results of the study of emerging grammars confirmed a conclusion that has been reached in every study of language acquisition with children in the earliest stages of the acquisition of grammar. Children learn the syntax of language—the arrangements of words in sentences—before they learn inflections of noun, verb, and adjective forms. Although there may be alternation of certain forms from the beginning—"block," "blocks" and "sit," "sits"—the different shapes of a word occur in free variation. That is, in the early samples, "-s" did not signal a meaningful difference such as making reference to more than one block as opposed to reference to only one block without expression of "-s." Thus, children learn word sequences, for example, "throw block," before morphological contrasts, as between "block" (singular) and "blocks" (plural).

Second, the three children, Kathryn, Eric, and Gia, did not produce constructions that were potentially analyzable as noun phrases as their first (or most productive) syntactic pattern. Rather, the most productive constructions they produced (after utterances with initial /ə/) were those which, in the adult model, cross phrase boundaries: subject-object, subject-verb, and verb-object strings. Although the grammars for Kathryn and Gia specified the derivation of a noun phrase constituent (with an attributive adjective class in Kathryn's lexicon), this structure was far less productive than others which occurred, and Eric did not produce noun phrase constructions at all. Based on these two observations, children appear to learn the expressions "throw block" or "baby (subject) block (object)" before the expressions "big block," "red block," or "blocks."

Finally, the results of this study point to the conclusion that (1) the status of the referent in the context in which an utterance occurs and (2) the child's relation to the referent in terms of behavior are critically important as influences on language performance. There were four discernible contextual variables which coincided with the occurrence of utterances: (1) existence of the referent within the context, (2) recurrence of the referent or addition to the referent after previous existence, (3) action upon the referent, and (4) nonexistence of the referent in the context where its existence was somehow expected.

The importance of the manifestation of the referent in the contexts of speech events was most significant. Single word utterances in the pre-syntax stage and early syntactic utterances most often referred to objects or events which the child was able to see—the majority of utterances which occurred in all of the children's speech functioned as *comments* or *directions,* where the referent was manifest in the context of the speech event, as opposed to reports of past or future events. All of the children used a relational term, "more" or "nother," to signal recurrence of the referent after previous occurrence. The productivity of verb-object and subject-object strings reflected the tendency for the children to talk about objects being acted-upon. And, finally, as might be expected given the foregoing observations, when the children began to express negation as a contrastive notion syntactically, their first negative sentences signalled the nonexistence of the referent. On the simplest level, children appear to learn to perceive and discriminate (and, ultimately, to communicate) (1) such aspects of a referent as its existence, recurrence, or nonexistence and (2) relational aspects of events, before such features of objects as relative size, color, or other identifying attributes.

It might be said that children learn to identify particular syntactic structures with the environmental and behavioral contexts in which they are perceived and then progress to reproducing approximations of heard structures in similar, recurring contexts. In order to use a structure in a new situation, the child needs to be able to perceive critical aspects of the context of the situation. Thus, the sequence in which syntactic structures are learned by the child may be influenced as much by his ability to differentiate aspects of situational context and recognize recurrent contexts, as by such factors as frequency of exposure to structures or their relative complexity.

Children learn to talk because they have something to say, and a model for language acquisition that describes the accumulation of words and word combinations presents only part of the story. Similarly, programs for language therapy that present children with linguistic structure (for example, 'pivot grammar') without attention to content ignore the nature of language. Attention to language pathology must include attention to situational and behavioral contexts of speech events as well as to the linguistic form of utterances.

SUMMARY OF DISCUSSION

QUESTION: What would you suggest we start with then when we try to put words together?

BLOOM: The point I want to make is that the linguistic description of just the form of children's speech says little about what the child "knows" about grammar. Certain conceptual relations (as between actor and object, or the notions of nonexistence and recurrence) can be identified in the earliest syntactic utterances. All investigators of child speech have reported "more" or "no" (or "all gone" or "no more") and constructions with two nouns. Children use some words more frequently than other words simply because of what they mean. It appears that what children learn about linguistic structure depends upon what it is they intend to say, and learning language involves learning the coding of underlying conceptual relations. I would begin language therapy by coding just those conceptual relations that I described in the speech of the normal children that I studied.

QUESTION: Little children speak very much in the here and now. Is this a valid characteristic we can use to distinguish between children and adults?

BLOOM: Yes. If I came in here and said to you, "I sit down," and I sat down, and I said to you, "I stand up," and I stand up, you'd think I was a little bit strange. You can see what I am doing, and I can see what I am doing and there is no reason for me to tell you what I am doing. But a little child who came in here, pressed to say something, would probably say, "sit down," or "I sit down," or "stand up," and we would not be disturbed. Children generally speak about what they can see and hear and what they are doing.

QUESTION: What about very young children who say things like "cookie" or "milk" or "bread" where there are no cookies or milk or bread?

BLOOM: The child will, when he wants something that is not present, name what it is. The cookie isn't there in the environment to be sure, and that's all we can say, but we have some indication about how real it is for the child at the time he is saying it.

QUESTION: Isn't the important thing the relationship between the child and what he is talking about rather than its being there physically in the environment?

BLOOM: That's a good point. What I did was to make the decision that I could have some idea of what the child meant by what he said, not that I could reach the *meaning* of a particular utterance. But I could make a *judgment* about the semantic intent that underlies particular utterances that children make, and that I could do this by relying on clues from the context and behavior in speech events. So that rather than simply looking at and recording only what the child said, I also took into consideration what it is he was talking about and made certain inferences about the semantic intent that underlies what he is talking about.

QUESTION: How can you possibly know what a child means by what he says? Sometimes we don't know what adults mean by what they say.

BLOOM: All you have to do is spend an hour with a young child and you can more often than not know what the child is talking about. Mothers do this all the time. In fact, if mothers didn't understand what children meant much of the time, chances are they wouldn't learn to talk. The child depends on this factor for communication, that somebody has a good idea of what he intends to say, and this no doubt influences how the child learns to talk.

QUESTION: Isn't it really even stronger than that? Shouldn't we know the intent of the speaker in order to do an analysis?

BLOOM: Yes. Since we can't reach the intuition of a young child we have to compensate for it in some way. If a child says "no pocket" in a situation where she is looking for a pocket and a pocket does not exist, there is a different semantic relationship between "no" and the rest of the utterance than when the child says "no sock" and the sock is in fact there but the child does not want to wear the sock. Nonlinguistic cues can make it clear that there is a difference between these two utterances.

QUESTION: Does the mean length of utterance mean anything? Is that measurement all that reliable?

BLOOM: There are problems with using mean length of utterance—it certainly doesn't tell very much about substantive factors of linguistic development. But it does give a superficial index for comparing children and it is the one measure that has survived the old-time count studies as an index for comparing children generally. As such, it is a fairly good one; it does allow us to compare children at particular levels. As long as you recognize the limitations, it is useful.

QUESTION: Would you summarize the major results of your study?

BLOOM: First of all, there were so-called pivot structures in the language of all three children, with "this" and "that," "no," "more," "it," where these small words tended to occur frequently with many different words. However, for two children, utterances containing these words were a small minority of the total number of utterances they used. It was apparent that the grammatical relations subject-verb-object were productive very early. This is not to say that children produced three-term strings, because they did not. As a matter of fact, these children had a very definite constraint on the length of utterance that could be produced, two items in a string. But subject-verb, verb-object, and subject-object were highly productive grammatical relations in early two-word utterances.

QUESTION: Would you explain what "productive" means in that context?

BLOOM: Yes. It is enough for a sentence or a structure to occur once in a sample of adult speech, and be acceptable as "grammatical" to a native speaker, in order to have to account for it in a grammar of the language. To account for all of the unique utterances (occurring only one time) that a child produces is a prodigious task. The use of speech is influenced by outside environmental factors and internal factors as well. So children make "performance" mistakes as adults do, although the children in my study did not make as many "mistakes" as I had expected they would.

Second, children produce structures that do not have an analog in any other utterances they produce. For example, Eric used "no more" plus another word in all expressions of negation—"no more cleaner," "no more milk," "no more noise," "no more toy." He also picked up a doll he was holding, dropped it, and said, "don't want baby." It was clear that "don't want baby" was unique in that particular sample; "no more"—because it occurred in the overwhelming number of instances of negation—was the productive form. I made an arbitary decision for the purpose of analysis: a form or structure that occurred only once was unique; a structure was marginal if it occurred less than five times; and a structure was productive if it occurred five times or more. Only productive utterances were accounted for in the grammars. Third, several unique utterances turned out to be 'stereotype' holistic phrases.

QUESTION: Do you mean if it occurred one time during all the protocols you took, or one time during an hour, or what?

BLOOM: In the entire sample of approximately eight hours obtained over a few days.

QUESTION: Did you take only intelligible responses?

BLOOM: Yes. No responses that were partially or wholly unintelligible were included.

QUESTION: You have identity between the number of times something occurred and your willingness to call it productive. But do you intend something else by the term "productive"?

BLOOM: To be sure, the notion of *productivity* implies an underlying rule system that accounts for some utterances and not others. The criteria for productivity that I spoke of was a methodological decision for attempting to say something about underlying productivity.

QUESTION: How do you analyze your data? Might you analyze it in such a way as to bring the unique utterances into conjunction with what you call the productive ones?

BLOOM: I saw unique utterances as having three potential sources. They were either (1) mistakes that the children often self-corrected, that is, "performance" errors, (2) stereotype utterances such as everyone has observed in young children, or (3) forms that anticipated structures that were productive in later samples.

QUESTION: Do you have evidence that the three-term string was a function of linguistic capacity and not a performance limitation? Could it require three terms, but for some performance reason the child could not produce three words in a row?

BLOOM: The admissible evidence was the actual utterances that occurred and judgments or inferences about the semantic intent underlying those utterances. I concluded that the actual utterances that occurred were often reductions of more complex underlying structures. In the actual derivation of sentences the three-term strings did not occur, and there was a limitation to two terms. Although subject-verb-object strings were not produced by the children, these grammatical relationships were postualted in the underlying structure of utterances to account for the inferred interpretation of two-term utterances that occurred, and to account for the fact that all combinations of subject-verb-object were productive.

QUESTION: Did the child understand a three-term string when spoken?

BLOOM: I did not study comprehension at all.

QUESTION: How does the structure you predicated here account for "Mommy pigtail," in the example you gave? It seems there is one other thing implied there—"Mommy make a pigtail for me," with "for me" implied.

BLOOM: There was no occurrence of direct object-indirect object in the data, and therefore no evidence in their speech that the children had knowledge of the dative relation.

QUESTION: Once you postulated that this reduction can go on, is there no theoretical limit to what can be reduced?

BLOOM: It's true you could go on indefinitely. You can say "Mommy make pigtail," "Mommy make me a pigtail," or "Mommy makes a pigtail," or "Mommy makes a pigtail for me," or "I see that Mommy makes a pigtail for me," or "I tell you that I see that Mommy makes a pigtail for me." The potential expansion of that utterance is different from what I have attempted to do in simply accounting for the relationship between the two constituents that actually occurred.

QUESTION: Suppose Mommy did have pigtails. Would the child say, "Mommy wears pigtails?"

BLOOM: It could be "Mommy's," the possessive, in relation to "pigtail"—a genitive relationship rather than subject-object, but Mommy did not have pigtails.

QUESTION: Some of the descriptions of the grammars are in error because they don't account for the functional relationship between the terms that are used. Don't you feel that we must look at how children meet functional needs in relating with their environment?

BLOOM: What you are talking about is important, but I see those functional notions as being superimposed on the grammatical functions that I am talking about here.

QUESTION: Could you clarify the distinctions you make between grammatical relations and functional relations?

BLOOM: In grammatical relations, substantive words such as "Mommy" and "sock" occur with variable grammatical meaning in relation to other substantive words. This variable grammatical meaning depends on the fact that there is a reciprocal relationship between the substantive words that occur in a string or utterance. The child needs to learn an essential notion of "Mommyness." He then needs to learn that not only is there an essential notion of "Mommyness," but that Mommy is subject, Mommy is object, Mommy is possessor.

Children also learn other kinds of relational expressions. I have called these functional relations in an effort to distinguish them from grammatical relations. These are not reciprocal in the same way. Function words such as "more" and "no" operate in linear one-to-one relationship with substantive words to specify a particular relational notion (such as recurrence, or nonexistence). The substantive word gives nothing to "no" to account for the inherent relationship between them.

So substantive words such as "Mommy" and "sock" enter into relationship with other words, they are not in themselves relational terms, in that they can stand alone. In the sense that "Mommy" distinguishes certain classes of animate, human, female beings from certain other classes of animate, human, female beings, the form "Mommy" is "relational." But it is not a relational term in that it does stand alone to represent a particular state of affairs or a particular aspect of experience. Even though "no" and "more" can occur as single-word utterances, "no" and "more" mean nothing unless you know what "no" and "more" relate to. They have an inherent relational attachment to some apsect of experience that may or may not be expressed in the utterance.

QUESTION: Did you find that using your own child as a subject had any particular advantages or disadvantages?

BLOOM: When she started to talk I made the very righteous decision that I was never going to talk about her language development. First of all I wasn't even going to record her. I wasn't going to make notes. I was just going to enjoy her, because I had just spent three years of my life studying children's language. That just wasn't possible. I was teaching a research seminar with some very bright students and the proximity of a subject was irresistible. What really interested us was that she wasn't developing at ages 10 through 18 months as I had expected. For example, she did not imitate, and her vocabulary acquisition was not cumulative. (I have since discovered that Leopold made similar observations of Hildegard at the same time.) We went back to look at the literature on single-word utterances and discovered that no one has really studied single-word utterances in young children. All the accounts are anecdotal, or they are vocabulary studies. We realized that the beginning of grammatical competence, the origin of the child's knowledge of grammar, exists in the way he uses single-word utterances. To study the origins of grammatical competence, it is necessary to have some really well-documented, well thought-out studies of how children use single-word utterances. But this is by no means easy to get. Children don't rapidly spit out single words as they talk. You can follow them around all day long before you hear six or seven words. Because I lived with Allison, I was able to make several observations about the kinds of words she used, and how she used them before the appearance of syntax in her speech. And, I must say, the seminar provided an excellent sounding board as well as being a valuable source of informed questions and comments.

QUESTION: What types of stimulation were you giving her at this time? How were you interacting?

BLOOM: I talk to her, and I expand, and I model. I'm very conscious of what she says. In fact, someone once said to me, "How is she ever going to talk? You just sit and think about what she says." This is true. I'm very attentive to what she says and how she says it.

I also have a tendency to interact with Allison much as I interacted with Kathryn, Eric, and Gia. This was a specialized interaction in which I waited for them to respond or waited for them to talk, rather than questioning or prompting.

QUESTION: Were you concerned about when she would learn substantive words?

BLOOM: No, because she was using substantive words all the time—but most occurred only a few times. Between 17 and 18 months I counted more than 150 different words that came out in the appropriate situation consistently and repeatedly. Most often these words functioned simply to name or point out a referent in the environment. However, at the same time she began to produce sequences of two or more single-word utterances that were related to the same state of affairs, the same phenomenon, the same speech event. The words were said in succession, but they were clearly single-word utterances. They were not syntactic construction. I have a number of examples of sequences of single-word utterances that have gone to four and five words. For example, we were taking a walk in the airport last week and she pointed to a man sitting on a chair and said, "man, coat, chair, case." The man was wearing a coat and sitting in a chair and had a suitcase.

QUESTION: What do you think was the semantic intent of the string?

BLOOM: She was noticing or realizing different related aspects of a referent without being able to state the relationships among them. I do not think she was saying, "That man sitting on a chair is wearing a coat and has a suitcase." I think that far exceeded what she knew about syntax. She knew very little about using syntax in her speech, even though she appeared to understand syntactic relationships in the speech she heard and even though she recognized more than one aspect of a referent.

QUESTION: How do you know those are related words? You were in the airport. There are other suitcases around and other men.

BLOOM: She pointed to the man. He was wearing a coat and had a suitcase.

QUESTION: What is the relationship between the linguistic code and the underlying semantic intent or cognitive notion?

BLOOM: From what I observed in the four children I have studied, it seems that they learned a linguistic code, learned the syntax of language in order to say something about the world, the nonlinguistic states of affairs they were talking about. There are serious limitations on the extent to which you can extrapolate from three or four children to all children learning language. There are also serious limitations on the extent to which you can take this information and simply apply it to children with language disorders, but I have tried to begin to ask the kinds of questions that might lead to such application.

REFERENCES

Bloom, L. *Language development: Form and function in emerging grammars.* Cambridge: MIT Press, 1970.
Bloom. L. A. comment on Lee's developmental sentence types: A method for comparing normal and deviant syntactic development. *J. Speech Hearing Dis.,* 1967, *32,* 294–296.
Braine, M. D. S. The ontogeny of English phrase structure: The first phase. *Language,* 1963, *39,* 1–13.
Brown, R. and Fraser, C. The acquisition of syntax. In N. Cofer & B. S. Musgrave (Eds.), *Verbal behavior and learning.* New York: McGraw-Hill, 1963.
Chomsky, N. *Aspects of the theory of syntax.* Cambridge: MIT Press, 1965.
Chomsky, N. *Language and mind.* New York: Harcourt, Brace and World, 1968.
Lenneberg, E. *Biological foundations of language.* New York: Wiley, 1967.
Leopold, W. F. *Speech development of a bilingual child.* Vol. 3. Evanston, Ill.: Northwestern University, 1949.
McCarthy, D. Language development in children. In L. Carmichael (Ed.), *Manual of child psychology.* New York: Wiley, 1954.
McNeill, D. Developmental psycholinguistics. In F. Smith and G. A. Miller (Eds.), *The genesis of language.* Cambridge: MIT Press, 1966. Pp. 15–84.
McNeill, D. Explaining linguistic universals. Unpublished paper.
Miller, W., and Ervin, S. The development of grammar in child language. In U. Bellugi and R. Brown (Eds.), The acquisition of language. *Monograph of the Society for Research in Child Development,* 1964, *29.*
Piaget, J. Language and thought from a genetic point of view. In J. Piaget, *Six psychological studies.* New York: Vintage Books, 1968.
Schlesinger, I. M. Learning grammar from pivot to realization rule. Unpublished, 1968.
Schlesinger, I. M. Production of utterances and language acquisition. In D. I. Slobin (Ed.), *The ontogenesis of grammar.* New York: Academic Press, 1971.

SYNTACTIC STRUCTURE
AND LANGUAGE DEVELOPMENT IN RETARDATES

WILBUR A. HASS
Shimer College

SARAH K. HASS
Dixon State School

WILBUR A. HASS received his B.A. from the University of Nesbraska and his Ph.D. from the University of Michigan (in 1965, in Clinical Psychology). His major interest is in language development, on which he has published articles in several psychology and speech journals. After teaching at the University of Chicago, he is now on the faculty of Shimer College, Mt. Carroll, Illinois.

SARAH K. HASS received her B.S. from Loyola University (Chicago) and her Ph.D. from the University of Chicago (in 1970, in Clinical Psychology). She is interested in perceptual development, learning disabilities, and language pathology. Her current position is as a Psychologist III at Dixon State School for the Retarded, Dixon, Illinois.

"Grammar" for many of us involves deciding whether "none" takes a singular or plural verb, puzzling over declining German adjectives, or worrying about dangling participles. We are not dealing with such issues of literary cosmetology in this chapter. Such problems have their place, but that place is far from the point of maximal concern for the mentally retarded.

Neither do parameters such as sentence length, type-token ratios, and part-of-speech proportions, handy though they may be, get directly at the problem. Although some professionals in the field hold that psycholinguistics is typified by such parameters (Webb and Kinde, 1967), we do not subscribe to that. We feel that "grammar" should show how closely syntactic structure is bound to basic features of communicative acts. We belive that this view carries implications for research and intervention into the language development of retardates.

THREE FACES OF SYNTAX

As Spradlin (1963) pointed out, data in the area of language typically deal with the over- and under-occurrence of certain forms, either in general or in specific settings. We are therefore concerned with why a mentally retarded individual fails to use, or why he over-uses a certain grammatical construction. Some perspective on this question may be gained by considering why that grammatical construction exists (in

---

Preparation of this paper was partially supported by the U.S. Office of Education, through the Early Education Research Center of the University of Chicago.

English or another natural language). Why does any grammatical construction exist? Why do we not talk in one-word sentences or random strings of words? At whatever level of generality one deals with these questions, three kinds of answers appear (Hass and Wepman, 1969; Hass, 1970b). These are the "three faces of syntax."

The first is surface structure. Syntax facilitates the "mechanical" processing of language to hierarchical organization, a sensorimotor "outline" with binary, yes–no decisions wherever possible. Such organization allows a combination of flexibility and directness. The sentence is divided into constituent clauses of ever-smaller size, until individual meaning-units are reached.

With respect to this aspect of syntax, a given individual should prefer constructions which fit the level of "pattern-making" he has attained. This reflects his ability to store "syntactic footnotes" in immediate memory while producing and receiving sentences. There is no direct correspondence here to the number of words in a sentence, although some relation no doubt exists.

Semantic representation is the second aspect of syntax. Syntax allows a person to talk about the world. To some extent there is a parallel between the way we organize the world into "chunks," and the way we use referential language. The relations and structuring of language may serve as the dimensions along which we organize our picture of reality. There is a good deal of ferment about the best way to discuss cognitive structure. From a Piagetian point of view, the kinds of shifts involved in the attainment of concrete and formal operations will be reflected in the organization of what we represent in language.

Transformations comprise the third aspect of syntax. Language fits referential content, whatever that may be, into the context where individuals are communicating. Many features of language relate the sentence as structured-sound to the world as structured-representation. It is not enough for us to know that "dog" may refer to any canine creature; we want to use language (e.g., "dog") in patterns which say something (e.g., about such a creature). Sentences "make a point." In Skinner's terms, verbal operants are seldom pure tacts, but their "impurities" (if you choose to look upon them as impurities) often deal with quite lawful characteristics of interaction. It is this feature of syntax with which this chapter is mainly concerned. We wish to indicate some ways in which communicative features are inherent in syntactic structures, to show that examination of syntax leads to insights into how communication-via-language works—and how it may fail to work.

CONTRASTS WITH OSGOOD'S "MONSTER"

To give some notion of the implications of the above trichotomy, we will contrast it with Osgood's "monster" model (Osgood, 1957a, 1957b). This model is the basis for two highly successful research procedures, the Illinois Test of Psycholinguistic Ability (ITPA) and the Semantic Differential (SD). The model has three levels: projection, integration, and representation. We may take projection for granted, as does Osgood, who says little beyond that it is "wired in." This would not be the case if we were concerned with sensory-modality deficits.

Integration corresponds to our surface-structure feature. There are, however, important differences. Integration is described as a one-level process. We emphasize that surface-structure is hierarchical. Hierarchical organization has more recently been recognized by Osgood (1963), but he does not say where it comes from, or if he thinks it is peculiar to language. Osgood states that integration reflects stimulus redundancies (S-S associations) and response redundancies (r-R associations) as a direct function of frequency of pairings. Recent work on perception and motor skills shows that a better description involves reference to feedback loops of the kind used by analysis-by-synthesis programs (Wathen-Dunn, 1967) and mechanisms of differentiation as well as integration (Gibson, 1969). Also, Osgood makes no reference to the fact that phonological structure, although also hierarchical, differs in some formal respects from surface syntactic structure. For these reasons, success on the items in ITPA's Auditory-Vocal Automatic subtest are interpreted by us differently than in the typical Osgoodian rationale.

Comparing Osgood's representational level to our semantic-representation feature would require a whole new discussion. Briefly, the key difference lies in the isolated nature of Osgood's signs, as compared to our conception of linguistic referential elements as forming organized groups, both with respect to paradigmatic contrast and syntagmatic co-occurrence. In our view, the meaning of "dog" is not primarily the result of pairing a certain word with a certain furry stimulus (or with other meaningful words), but a process involving construction of the notion of what a dog is (which, in turn, involves the related notion of what a living animal is, and what it is to use class-names). We happen, additionally, to view this process as following an inherent sequence in terms of organization, namely, a Piagetian one (cf. Piaget, 1967). Similar points could be made from quite different perspectives (Quine, 1960; Weinreich, 1966; or McCawley, in press). Again, Osgood (1963) has more recently opted for semantic dimensions, which is a start in our direction.

Osgood's "monster" has nothing which corresponds to our transformational feature. As an example of the trouble this produces, consider how he could deal with the learning of the word "here." This word, for him, could be paired with a number of scenes, in fact all the scenes in which the growing child hears the word. Given just this, unfortunately, the child should have a fantastically difficult time differentiating "here" from, say "there," since every "here" becomes a "there" with a change in locus of communication, and vice versa. (The same sort of trouble occurs, by the way, in an operant variant, since any locus of communication can serve as a discriminative stimulus for "here.") Somehow the nature of the communicative acts of which "here" is a part must be specified if the different "here's" are not to fuse together into an unenlightening "everywhere." The same remarks are true of "now," "me," and whatever other deictic signs are learned (cf. Weinreich, 1966, pp. 154-158, for a general survey of deixis).

The point is not that Osgood is unable in principle to formulate a model incorporating them, or that this could not be accomplished by other associationistic learning theories. Whatever doubts we have on that score have been voiced quite sufficiently

SOME TRANSFORMATIONAL SYNTAX

Studies of syntactic structure which use transformations and strive toward a complete ("generative") account have spread far beyond the seminal work of Chomsky (1957; 1965). But before we turn to newer issues, perhaps it is well to stress that the whole enterprise has rested on the insight that the same "content" may receive different syntactic patternings. Compare sentences (1) through (5), spoken with usual intonations in a suitable context:

(1) Bill is rocking back and forth.
(2) Rock back and forth, Bill.
(3) Is Bill rocking back and forth?
(4) What is Bill doing?
(5) Bill is not rocking back and forth.

What is at issue in these sentences is Bill's rocking back and forth, which may be asserted, ordered, questioned in any of several ways, or denied. That these transformational variants are related to differences in communication is obvious. This insight cannot be gainsaid, but it can be enlarged upon. Note that (a) "Bill is rocking back and forth" or "Is Bill rocking back and forth?" may sometimes be used to give orders, in polite (or otherwise special) circumstances: (b) different stress and intonational patterns may alter the function of such sentences; (c) these sentences may have other communicational functions not marked in their overt sentence structure.

It is enough that these sentences which indicate fundamental transformations serve as general cues to the stance taken by the speaker and interpreted by the listener. The same is true, but perhaps less obviously, for patterns of conjunction. We would not deny that it is convenient to say, "I got milk, bread, and beer at the grocery store" rather than the three noncompound sentences which correspond to it—"I got milk at the grocery store," "I got bread at the grocery store" and, "I got beer at the grocery store." In addition, compounding serves to indicate what the speaker thinks is related. Imagine a scene where a boy named John has just thrown a brick through a window. Some of the things one could say about it are:

(6) John broke the window.
(7) John broke the window with the brick.
(8) The brick broke the window.

Sentences (6) and (8) look alike, in terms of surface syntactic structure. They both have a noun-phrase subject, a transitive verb, and a noun-phrase object. But they are not in fact completely parallel, since one would not use (9) as a compound for (6) and (8):

(9) John and the brick broke the window.

This is not caused by surface structure features, since the following sentences sound quite natural:

(10) John attended class.
(11) Mary attended class.
(12) John attended class with Mary.
(13) John and Mary attended class.

There you can do the conjunction.

Neither can the difference between (6) and (8) be simply reduced to the fact that "John" is animate and "the brick" in inanimate, since (14) and (15) can occur if you imagine a sufficiently wild setting:

(14) John broke the window when Gargantua flung him through it.
(15) Gargantua broke the window with John.

This is a good example in which to make a distinction between semantic and syntactic features. And it is not parsimonious to blame the difference between (6) and (8) on different senses of "broke," since parallel constructions exist for many verbs. And there is no need to add dictionary items for each verb when a general syntactic principle is involved. That conjunction does more than indicate that a person has experienced the conjoined items in similar sentence slots. There are ways of making the relationship marked by conjunction more prominent:

(16) Susan is a brunette, but she has lots of fun.
(17) Susan is a blonde, and Jean isn't so smart either.
(18) Susan is a blond, and gentlemen prefer Jane too.
(19) Susan is a blonde, and only her hairdresser knows for sure.

These examples reveal presuppositions that:

For (16) blonds have more fun.
For (17) blondes are dumb.
For (18) gentlemen prefer blondes.

And for (19) it is possible to be a natural-looking blonde by artificial means. It goes without saying here that one must refer, not to individual meanings of "but," "either," "too," and "only" in isolation, but to the syntactic patterns of conjunction in which they figure.

Another stronghold of transformational analysis has been the noun phrase. How is "communicational relevance" applicable to "the cup on the table?" This is a perfectly good noun phrase in a sentence like:

(20) The cup on the table has a nick in its rim.

This looks like an "unvarnished fact" if there ever was one. In a sentence like "The cup on the table has a nick in its rim," the "communicational varnish" becomes readily apparent. Let's contrast it with (21):

(21) The cup with a nick in its rim is on the table.

Since both (20) and (21) would apply to the same states of affairs, the difference must lie in how one wants to talk about them. Any speaker of English shows (although he may not be able to tell you in so many words) that in (20) the speaker is assuming that the cup is on the table and is concerned with its having a nick, while the converse is true for (21).

If I don't see a cup on the table, I have a hard time responding to (22), which corresponds to (20):

(22) Does the cup on the table have a nick in its rim?

But (23), which corresponds to (21), is easy.

(23) Is the cup with the nick in its rim on the table? This is how you get "when did you stop beating your wife?" kinds of questions.

The difference between (20) and (21) can be summarized by pointing to the difference in topic/comment division between them.

The same topic/comment issue arises in analyzing the familiar passive, which is also a transformational classic. We may use (24) as opposed to (25) when dealing with a certain cup rather than a certain puppy.

(24) The cup was broken by the puppy.

(25) The puppy broke the cup.

In the first case you are taking for granted the cup and what you are doing is asserting the puppy's breaking of it. In the second case you are taking for granted the puppy did something, and what you are asserting was that what he did was break the cup. Other factors may also, of course, be involved in given active/passive contrasts.

The topic/comment distinction may be found in other major sentence types as well:

(26) There are a lot of psycholinguists at Shimer.

(27) A lot of psycholinguists are at Shimer.

These sentences make reference to the same fact, which in this instance happens to be fictitious. The sentences use almost the same words, except for the dummy, "there" (which has been a puzzler for referentially oriented accounts). Sentences (26) and (27) tend to be used in different situations, and be understood to "make different points." Sentence (26) is focusing on the number of psycholinguists, in the context of a Shimerian locus. In (27), it is the location at Shimer of the already recognized individuals which is at issue. The same contrast comes up in this syntactic pattern:

(28) Shimer College has a lot of psycholinguists.

(29) The college that has a lot of psycholinguists is Shimer.

Again, stress patterns can serve to emphasize or nullify these relations if you like.

One last set of examples may demonstrate that even innocent-looking, simple noun-phrases are tied into syntactic patterns for their interpretation:

(30) Ralph says that Nancy wants to marry a Norwegian.

Leaving aside a crucial ambiguity concerning the indefinite article (a specific Norwegian, or any Norwegian may be indicated), one still has at least a triple ambiguity for "a Norwegian." Consider the following continuations of (30):

(31) . . . but the Norwegian she has in mind is a confirmed bachelor.

(32) . . . but that she thinks he's a Dane.

(33) . . . but Ralph thinks he's a Dane.

That is, the referent male's "Norwegian-ness" may be from the point of view of Nancy alone, as in (32) or Ralph alone, as in (33), or generally accepted (31) by Nancy, Ralph, and the speaker of (30). Even more complicated cases may be found by permuting and combining an elaborate superstructure for any of these examples of still more ambiguities.

Such "point of view" contrasts in themselves occur quite often. They may be cleared up by the syntactic pattern, the nonlinguistic context, or left indefinite. When one sees a videotape of a man listening to a tape recording of a voice saying, "This tape will self-destruct in five seconds," one takes for granted that the five seconds are measured from the point of playing the tape recording, not from the point of making the tape recording or the point of playing the videotape. We take it for granted as a sophisticated modern communicator. What a less sophisticated person does needs study.

This section has presented, in a casual way, the view of syntax arising out of generative-transformational linguistics (cf. Hass [1970] and Feldman and Hass [in preparation] for more detail). The enormous technicality, variety, and divergence of the specific linguistic formulations have been completely ignored. They can be found in various texts and papers. The problem with published literature is that most papers do not get published for two or three years, and by that time they are out of date.

In summary, consider the following points:

1. Examination of sentences which "sound right" and "are speakable" in a language reveals certain regularities in structure (i.e., in the patterning of meaningful units).

2. These regularities can be formulated by a body of transformational rules which relate surface syntactic structures to semantic representations. One can speak of a sentence in terms of various levels of "deep" (or "underlying") structure, depending on how close one is to the semantic representation of that sentence. It may be noted that the wording and the intonation of the sentences are both described transformationally in the view I am presenting, and that for any content there are various surface structures in which it can be expressed. For example, the concept of ownership may be reflected in "John has a boat," "John's boat," "the boat belonging to John," "the boat John owns," and many others. The listener cannot determine the surface structure from knowing what is talked about, but maybe he can make a guess from knowing a certain language.

3. The transformations relate to: (a) the communicative stance of the speaker toward the content expressed; (b) the interrelations along different parts of the message; (c) what the speaker wants to take for granted and what he wants to focus on; (d) a codification of referential elements from one point of view.

4. Such a grammar represents what an ideally sensitive and knowledgeable person recognizes in his language. There is no implication that the ordered transformations "generate" any sentence in the way a speaker goes about producing it or a listener goes about understanding it. Ordering rules may be taken as an *indication* of the relative centrality of a process in those who know the language, just as number of rules may reflect differentiation of functioning (cf. Hass, in Binnick et al. [1969]). If one memorizes a single sentence in a foreign language, one does not thereby acquire the transformations that are relevant in understanding what a native speaker may "have in mind" when producing or interpreting that sentence. The same probably holds for interpretation of ritualized sentences, like "How do you do?," even when spoken and heard by sophisticated native speakers.

CAN COMMUNICATION BE DEVELOPED?

So much for language at its best. We now turn to possible means for facilitating the development of transformationally marked communicative operations. Compare the plights of the following individuals:

1. An American college student in France for the summer, who finds that his school-acquired French is not adequate for him to "get across what he wants to say."
2. An anthropologist discovering a New Guinea culture never before encountered by Western man.
3. A severely retarded ten-year-old who has been institutionalized several years.

The college student has all the semantic representation and communicational skills he needs, except for minor details. He lacks only the mastery of some surface features.

The anthropologist expects, on the basis of his theoretical stance, that there may be significant novelties in the form of representation and interaction of the culture.

The retardate may be aware that people say and do puzzling things to him and that many of the things he tries to say and do go wrong. It is not his task to discover linguistic variants nor a new Weltanschauung, but rather to construct the whole organization of experience in which linguistic or cognitive variation may occur.

Unfortunately, we have more ready insight into the problem of the college student, or even the anthropologist, than into that of the retardate. We know the sequence normal children go through in the construction of syntax. As to the determinants of this sequence, we know the following things: there is no necessity for speaking at all (Lenneberg, 1967); and that direct imitation of adults is only minimally involved (Ervin, 1964), as is contingent approval of parents (Brown, 1966). There is a study which reveals that for two ordinary Madison, Wisconsin, families, direct approval, like saying "That's good," accounted for, respectively, one utterance out of a thousand of the parents to the child, and in the other case under one utterance in a thousand to the child. Some forms of dialogue may result in facilitation (Cazden, 1965; Brown, 1966). However, little is really known about how children are led to recognize their patterns of speaking and listening in the course of growing up.

There is no question that retardates are deficient in communication skills in general (cf. Schiefelbusch, Copeland, and Smith, 1967). Those aspects of communication which are prominently coded in English syntax are probably also deficient, although more specific documentation is needed on this point. Thus, retardates typically make low scores on the ITPA Auditory-Vocal Automatic subtest (Mueller and Weaver, 1964; Bateman and Wetherell, 1965; Bilovsky and Share, 1965). Also, Lenneberg's (1967, pp. 309–320) investigation of a group of mongoloid children, for instance, includes the observation that "Peter likes small cookies and red lollipops" was easier for his subjects to repeat than "Peter wants one and so does Johnny." For although the two sentences have the same number of words, the former involves deletion and conjunction while the latter requires mastery of a pro form and subject-verb transposition as well.

Facilitation of retardates' syntactic development might start at attending to where the child stands with respect to the normal sequence (as well as to his other diagnostic characteristics).

Does this hold implications for *methods?* Can we improve on Schiefelbusch's description of the best speech teacher as "simply an adult who takes an interest in the child and gives him rewarding experiences that go beyond those currently available" (1965, p.7)? The best direct application is still to use a mixture of whatever seems reasonable (as has in fact been presented by, e.g., Smith, 1962, and Wiseman, 1965).

This fairly well characterizes the published intervention programs. For purposes of increasing our knowledge, however, some attempt must be made to weigh the contribution of various practices. We will comment on four, in terms of the issues raised above:

1. Verbal bombardment, sometimes called "language bath." This method consists of having caretakers talk to the child as much as possible, preferably about ongoing matters of concern. An example:

Psychologist: "Hello, Bernard. Come along upstairs. Let's go upstairs. Up we go. Up we go. Up. Up." Progress up the numerous stairs would be slow as Bernard places both his feet on each tread and often stops to wipe his nose.

Psychologist: "Up we go. Now we're nearly up." "Oh, yes," says Bernard at this point.

Psychologist: "Up we go. Now we're at the top."

Bernard: "Oh, yes." (Sampson, 1964, pp. 90–91).

Here the child is exposed to a number of syntactic patterns (although this is not deliberately stipulated, it is the usual consequence of asking an adult to talk; and the usual quality of such a monologue is of "theme and syntactic variations."

There is a certain in-built break from topic to comment, from topic to comment. On the other hand, one does not really believe that retardates lack exposure to samples of ordinary English, certainly not in the days of TV and radio. No provision is made for involving the verbalization of the child. And more pointedly, there is no safeguard that all the stimulation isn't just "going in one ear and out the other" (as seems to have happened for Rigrodsky and Steer, 1961).

2. Labeling (tacting) in its most usual form is presented to the trainee with pictures or objects to get him to say "their names." The "names" are usually single nouns or adjectives, or sometimes short noun phrases. One may get taciturn retardates to use common words in this way. But more has been claimed for it. In the work of Jim McCarthy, "Labeling is the first developmental step of language; its foremost position in language learning is testament to its importance (1964, p. 92)." One of the authors doubts that normal children's early language is in fact best described as "labeling." This is despite the fact that some researchers have noted periods of 18 months or thereabouts in which some children like to go around getting labels for things.

Be that as it may, the procedure does need a "bridge" to more typical language use. How often do we, in ordinary language, use single words and phrases in this directly referential way? Perhaps in commenting on the weather ("nice day"), or teaching someone a new vocabulary item ("nematode"), or when we have information we think the other would like in a structured situation (calling out a bus stop: "57th Street"). For most purposes the referential factor in language is subordinated to some larger function, somewhat as single "names" are embedded in sentences. Although we might expect to get some use of words and phrases learned as labels for general functions, this is too much to simply take for granted, particularly if the child's only contact with the referent is to label it. And it is precisely the skill of shaping the same referential content in different ways that seems most relevant to syntax.

3. *Grammar drills.* How about just getting the child to memorize the basic syntactic patterns of English? This might consist of drilling the child on standard constructions—more or less the way one goes through taped foreign-language drills in high school. Here the trainee is praised or otherwise rewarded for sentences that are good basic English or good basic intermediate steps in language development of English, and ignored, corrected, or punished for divergent sentences. This can be combined with modeling (Odom, Liebert, and Fernandez, 1969), echoic or intraverbal control of verbal behavior, repetition drills, or drills in which the task is to make a declarative out of a parallel interrogative, etc. It would be surprising if they were very productive, since the problem for most retarded children is not mainly in the management of surface structure per se (despite greater incidence of speech defects that most people have noted), but rather in knowing what the sentence means and when one would say it that way, as in the contrast between "There ball" and "Ball there." Even improved scores on the ITPA Vocal-Auditory Automatic subtest would not necessarily indicate that generally beneficial results have been obtained, although such data would be interesting to have.

4. *Structured communication* is the best way to get someone to use syntactic patterns in a communicatively productive manner. The objective is to communicate with him via syntactically organized language, or to monitor his communication with others with an eye toward syntactically-relevant aspects.

An example: When the child entered the playroom he usually found it bare, all the toys being in the cupboard.

Psychologist: "Well, what do you want today?"

"Telephone," might come the answer, or if the child did not answer he would probably go to the cupboard and look in.

Psychologist: "What are you going to get? What are you looking at?"

Child: "Jigsaw."

Psychologist: "Bring it over here."

The child would then sit down at the table with the psychologist. Converstation in which he asked for guidance ("Where this go?" etc.), or 'regulated' his own attempts as he worked ("Where's his tail?" "This go in here") or announced success, would be likely to follow.

"Put it away; bricks now," from the child would lead on the next activity. (Sampson, 1964, p. 91).

Note that the trainer must actually relate his behavior to the statements, requests, questions, and focusings, of the child he is interacting with. One could probably increase the value of such interaction through two tactics.

1. Arranging for reciprocity of roles, so that what the child does at one point as a listener he can do at another point as a speaker. This was in fact found by Clawson and Schlanger (1968) to be of value for adolescent retardates in a referent-centered setting.

2. Arranging for juxtaposition of varying syntactic forms to point up their different communicative value. Again, this could be done in conjunction with the type of referent-centered interaction situation that Krauss and Rotter and other people have used, but it would require a richer referent world and fewer constraints of speaker-listener interaction. Such a situation would necessarily expose the child to surface structures. This would allow him to find out things about the workings of the world, and it would confront him with different social-interaction structures.

In conclusion, in order to understand where one wants to go in language training, one must attend to the roles a person plays in communication with others. These roles may be suggested by examination of the function marked or left ambiguous in the sentences we use. These roles may also suggest ways to get to where we want to go in the language development of the mentally retarded.

SUMMARY OF DISCUSSION

QUESTION: You state that "the problem for most retarded children is not mainly in the management of surface structure per se, . . . but rather in knowing what the sentence means and when one would say it that way." Could you give me a reference for a statement of that import?

HASS: I can give you an example. I have seen many retardates whose only language is a memorized set of sentences which they will say on appropriate cues. For instance: "Hi, I'm Ronnie." Or they will go along saying, "WOC-TV, Davenport, Iowa," which means nothing except that they have been watching television.

QUESTION: But aren't there many children around who have some tremendous deficit in surface structures?

HASS: I think there may well be among groups of children who are diagnosed as retarded. But there are many others for whom that might not be true.

QUESTION: We have no sophisticated descriptions of retarded children's speech to say whether or not it is, as people have been saying for many, many years, the process of normal development which is somehow slowed down. One of the main questions we have right now is "What will a sophisticated analysis of retarded children's speech reveal with respect to the kinds of language they use?"

HASS: Children who look like the only thing wrong with them is in surface structure are labeled with something like aphasic, or, if you prefer, "specific language disabilities," or something like that. Those labels are specifically reserved for children who have trouble with the mechanics of language. They are not necessarily retarded. The child may just have difficulty managing the speaking and hearing of language. Or the organization of what he wants to talk about may be eluding him. Or he may not be clued in communicationally. Or any combination of these three.

QUESTION: Isn't there something else to be said about the things you are bringing up? We talk about the retarded as though there is one kind of retardation. It is not as simple as saying some of these kids are called aphasic, or whatever. Some of them who, in every significant social way, function as retarded children are found in institutions for the retarded or classes for the retarded. Although they may not really be retarded they have no area in which they are actually functioning normally. How do we know whether they have real deviance in language or simply a lag in development of language?

HASS: Having one handicap doesn't preclude having something else wrong. I hope I haven't given that impression because I don't believe that.

QUESTION: Returning to the question as to whether or not retarded language develops qualitatively differently or just at a slower pace, it doesn't seem to me there is any adequate way of characterizing normal language development.

BLOOM: I think we can answer it in two ways. You can look at retarded children's speech and compare it with what appears in the literature with respect to normal children's speech. You can also begin to replicate some of the studies that have to do with the way people communicate certain facts about the world around them.

HASS: We are also starting to get cross-cultural data on normal development in children from non-Indo-European language settings. This is very important because what happens in English surface structures or transformations or deep structures may be quite different with Mayan children.

BLOOM: I want to add something else. I wonder to what extent we can accept the information about normal children coming in the literature? I sometimes get the impression that the whole world thinks children start out talking about pivot-open grammars. I don't believe it. There is much more you can say about young children's language. I don't know whether or not the descriptions we have at this point about normal children learning to speak are directly applicable to studying retarded speech. Do we know enough about normal language to make that comparison at this point? Or can we make this comparison knowing at the same time that we are still asking questions about what normal language is?

HASS: It depends on your tolerance for wishy-washiness. I would state as a fact that children do not clean up one aspect of their phonology or one part of their grammar before going on to another. What is involved is a process of sorting out everything in one giant, systematic approach to wherever they are in language at that time. Whatever claims you might have for a program which drilled a certain syntactic construction, you could never make the claim that that's the way a child goes about establishing satisfactory construction.

QUESTION: What kind of referents from the real world do we have in terms of transformations as they develop? Is there much information on any order in terms of the transformations?

HASS: Order in development?

QUESTION: In syntax. Yes. Where are we in terms of behavioral or observed referents for the development of transformation in children?

BLOOM: What is the sequence in which syntactic structures are learned? Some people feel they have answered it. For example, Paula Menyuk has recently published a book in which she describes children's language from the ages of three to seven years in terms of the adult rules they use and do not use, the kinds of sentences they use, and the mistakes they make on their approximations of adult structures. The best-documented work is Roger Brown's description of the development of "wh" questions. Ursula Bellugi has described the development of negation. And I have described the development of negation. Most researchers say passive and yes–no questions develop before "wh" questions develop and negation, which is probably not a transformation at all, develops before that.

QUESTION: Do we have the evidence yet to view these in a developmental frame rather than to see them as two different things that can be related logically but not necessarily developmentally?

HASS: It is impossible to answer the question the way you have stated it. Transformational processes change radically as a child gets concrete operations and formal operations. You should not think of a pre-operational child as having transformations in the same sense as a concrete operational child. So to ask at what time a transformation occurs makes sense in a limited way only if you are speaking within a range of pre-operational thought or concrete operational functioning or formal operational functioning.

BLOOM: I would agree with that. I don't think there is an answer to that question. I think we have used the term "generative" and "generate" to the point where the words have really lost their meanings. Essentially, a grammar is generative if the rules are interrelated in a very special way, which means that any one rule of grammar implies antecedents and consequences so that a transformation as the rule of grammar implies rules that have gone before. So that we can't simply use transformations as rules for labels for the kind of sentences children use. Children don't learn a particular rule. They learn the grammar, and they learn the rules in the process.

QUESTION: I wonder if something can't be said in defense of studying retarded children even though the state of affairs in the study of normal children is a pretty difficult one? I doubt that we are going to take the methods developed with normal children and just transfer them wholesale to retarded children. There undoubtedly are going to have to be all kinds of changes made. But it may be necessary to work out the problems involved with normal children, unless we start all over again. In any case grammar is never going to be a completed study. We will never study retarded children's grammar if we wait for complete normal knowledge.

BLOOM: That's what the MIT linguists said about children's language, too. How can you study children's language until you have a grammar of English?

QUESTION: The approach to study of language has been to look for the frame of reference to understand the communication pattern. I wonder about this sort of approach to the communication pattern among the retardates, simply to make inference by observing the response of retardates. Do you see any merit in this type of approach?

HASS: Yes, I think it's very fine. Can you explain what they are doing?

NIHIRA: It's a very basic phenomenological approach. They record conversation among retardates and try to come up with some rule or basic frame of reference so they can understand what seems to be going on from that instead of judging or analyzing conversation from the grammar rules of adults.

HASS: I have never seen that applied to straight syntactic issues. I just don't know how it would work there.

QUESTION: Do these observations include parallel linguistic descriptions or data such as nonlinguistic physical cues?

NIHIRA: That's right. It includes the actual language, the facial expressions, the tone of conversations, and also a recording of how frequently they laugh at certain remarks.

SCHIEFELBUSCH: This hasn't crept into our discussions up to now, but there are quite a few studies indicating that children acquire a kind of physical code that has communication structure roughly the same way that they acquire the linguistic codes.

ROSENBERGER: It certainly happens. Shortly after the token economy was established in Fernald School, one boy was observed standing at the door in typical boss fashion with one hand out and the other one raised and fisted. Each boy who had just received his token as he went out that door either handed all of them or some of them to this fellow.

SCHIEFELBUSCH: It may not have the same kind of information or the same kind of structure for communication, but such a physical code may still be regarded as language.

QUESTION: In the distinction you made in the beginning when you spoke of surface structure and semantic representation and transformations, do you mean them in a sense of the generative grammar, transformation of grammar? Do you see transformations primarily as focus transformation?

HASS: I see transformations primarily as focus, lexical insertion, and the sort of general-purpose ones that used to be called "singular."

QUESTION: Is that what you mean by referential content?

HASS: No, by that I mean semantic representation, what one talks about.

QUESTION: Is that transition?

HASS: It doesn't represent anything like a temporal sequence of psychological processes. A person doesn't think what he wants to say in terms of a pure, abstract, platonic world and then transfer it into the fact that he is talking to another person at this point in time. The point is that we generally distinguish between the referential implications of a sentence and the fact that the sentence occurs between two people who are communicating.

QUESTION: Then you feel the former is semantic, the latter transformational?

HASS: The use of the word "transformations" is only a label. You could say that your semantic representation really included both aspects, meaning referential ones and some footnotes which indicated what transformations would occur. In that case the difference would be between the referential content and the dummies that cued off the transformations, whichever formal way you want to indicate that difference.

QUESTION: Back to the cup with the nick in the rim. As you add additional characteristics to the cup, don't you begin to exceed the capacities of the mentally retarded to use that type of syntactic structure?

HASS: Certainly. Children don't start out with noun phrases elaborated in subject position. Adults don't talk that way in ordinary speech either.

QUESTION: Doesn't this get back to the issue raised earlier about whether the speech of the retardate is a slower version of normal children or whether you are really dealing with certain imposed ceilings resulting from limited comprehension and the other associated processes that are involved that perhaps make it impossible for it to be slowed up version in its fullest dimensions?

HASS: You can distinguish between the slowness of a process and the ceiling that it gets to at its end point, so that as a process is slowed up, it might or might not reach a lower ceiling where it eventually stops, or asymptotes. Again the point is that there could be three kinds of reasons for asymptoting or slowing, or both asymptoting and slowing, or any partial combination of these in the language of the retarded.

REFERENCES

Bach, E., and Harms, R. T. (Eds.), *Universals in linguistic theory.* New York: Holt, Rinehart and Winston, 1968.

Bateman, B., and Wetherell, J. Psycholinguistic aspects of mental retardation. *Ment. Retard.*, 1965, *3*, 8–13.
Bellugi, U. The development of interrogative structures in children's peech. Symposium on the development of language functions, University of Michigan, 1965.
Bellugi, U. Linguistic mechanisms underlying child speech. In E. M. Zale (Ed.), *Proceedings of the conference on language and language behavior.* New York: Appleton-Centruy-Crofts, 1968.
Bellugi, U. Simplification in children's language. In R. Huxley and E. Ingram (Eds.), *CIBA conference on mechanisms of language development.* New York: Academic Press, 1970.
Bellugi, U., and Brown, R. (Eds.), The acquisition of language. *Society for Research in Child Development Monograph*, 1964, *29*(1).
Bilovsky, D., and Share, J. The ITPA and Down's syndrome: An exploratory study. *Am. J. Ment. Deficiency*, 1965, *70*, 78–82.
Binnick, R. I., et al. Papers from the fifth regional meeting of the Chicago Linguistic Society. Chicago: Dept. of Linguistics, 1969.
Brown, R. The dialogue in early childhood. Mimeographed paper, Harvard University, 1966.
Brown, R., and Bellugi, U. Three processes in the child's acquisition of syntax. *Harvard Ed. Rev.*, 1964, *34*, 133–151.
Brown, R., Cazden, C., and Bellugi, U. The child's grammar from 1 to 3. In J. Hill (Ed.), *Minnesota symposia on child psychology.* Vol. 2. Minneapolis: University of Minnesota, 1969.
Cazden, C. Environmental assistance to the child's acquisition of grammar. Unpublished dissertation, Harvard University, 1965.
Chomsky, N. *Syntactic structures.* The Hague: Mouton, 1957.
Chomsky, N. *Aspects of the theory of syntax.* Cambridge: MIT Press, 1965.
Chomsky, N. *The acquisition on syntax in children from 5 to 10.* Cambridge: MIT Press, 1969.
Clawson, W. B., and Schlanger, B. B. Oral vocabulary responses of educable mentally retarded adolescent boys in a dyadic situation. *Exceptional Children*, 1968, *34*, 761–762.
Darden, B. J., et al. Papers from the fourth regional meeting of the Chicago Linguistic Society. Chicago: Dept. of Linguistics, 1968.
Dixon, T. R., and Horton, D. L. (Eds.), *Verbal behavior and general behavior theory.* Englewood Cliffs, N. J.: Prentice-Hall, 1968.
Ervin, S. M. Imitation and structural change in children's language. In E. H. Lenneberg (Ed.), *New directions in the study of language.* Cambridge: MIT Press, 1964.
Feldman, C. F., and Hass, W. A. *Sentence meaning: A psycholinguistic theory of communication*, in preparation.
Gibson, E. *Principles of perceptual learning and development.* New York: Appleton-Century-Crofts, 1969.
Gruber, J. S. Topicalization in child language. *Foundations of Language*, 1967, *3*, 37–65.
Hass, W. A. On the heterogeneity of psychological processes in syntactic development. In C. S. Lavatelli (Ed.), *Language training in early childhood education.* Urbana: University of Illinois, 1970.(a)
Hass, W. A. Why we can't say what we mean in transformational theory. Papers of the regional conference of the Chicago Linguistic Society, April, 1970. (b)
Hass, W. A., and Wepman, J. M. Surface structure, deep structure and transformations. *J. Speech Hearing Res.*, 1969, *34*, 303–311.
Jacobs, R. A., and Rosenbaum, P. S. *English transformational grammar.* Waltham, Mass.: Blaisdell, 1968.
Jacobs, R. A., and Rosenbaum, P. S. *Readings in English transformational grammar.* Waltham, Mass.: Blaisdell, 1969.
Klima, E. S., and Bellugi, U. Syntactic regularities in the speech of children. In J. Lyons and R. J. Wales (Eds.), *Psycholinguistics papers.* Edinburgh: Edinburgh University Press, 1966.
Langacker, R. W. *Language and its structure.* New York: Harcourt, Brace and World, 1968.
Langendoen, D. T. *The study of syntax.* New York: Holt, Rinehart & Winston, 1969.
Lenneberg, E. H. *Biological foundations of language.* New York: Wiley, 1967.
McCarthy, J. J. The importance of linguistic ability in the mentally retarded. *Ment. Retard.*, 1964, *2*, 90–96.
McCawley, J. D. Semantic representation. In P. Garvin (Ed), Cognition: A multiple view. New York: Spartan Books, in press.
McNeill, D. Developmental psycholinguistics. In F. Smith and G. A. Miller (Eds.), *The genesis of language.* Cambridge: MIT Press, 1966. (a)

McNeill, D. The creation of language by children. In J. Lyons and R. J. Wales (Eds.), *Psycholinguistics papers*. Edinburgh: Edinburgh University Press, 1966. (b)

Menyuk, P. *Sentences children use*. Cambridge: MIT Press, 1969.

Mueller, M. W., and Weaver, S. J. Psycholinguistic abilities of institutionalized and non-institutionalized trainable mental retardates. *Am. J. Ment. Deficiency,* 1964, *68,* 775–783.

Odom, R. D., Liebert, R. M., and Fernandez, L. E. Effects of symbolic modeling on the syntactic productions of retardates. *Psychonomic Science,* 1969, *17,* 104–105.

Osgood, C. E. A behavioristic analysis of perception and language as cognitive phenomena. *Contemporary approaches to cognition*. Cambridge: Harvard University Press, 1957. (a)

Osgood, C. E. Motivational dynamics of language behavior. *Nebraska Symposium on Motivation,* 1957, *5,* 348–424. (b)

Osgood, C. E. On understanding and creating sentences. *Am. Psychologist,* 1963, *18,* 735–751.

Piaget, J. *The child's conception of the world*. Totowa, N.J.: Littlefield, Adams, 1967.

Quine, W. V. O. *Word and object*. Cambridge: MIT Press, 1960.

Reibel, D. A., and Schane, S. A. *Modern studies in English*. Englewood Cliffs, N.J.: Prentice-Hall, 1969.

Rigrodsky, S., and Steer, M. D. Mowrer's theory applied to speech habilitation of the mentally retarded. *J. Speech Hearing Dis.,* 1961, 26 *26,* 237–243.

Sampson, O. C. The conversational style of a group of severely subnormal children. *J. Ment. Subnorm.,* 1964, *10,* 89–100.

Schiefelbusch, R. L. A discussion of language treatment methods for mentally retarded children. *Ment. Retard.,* 1965, *3,* 4–7.

Schiefelbusch, R. L., Copeland, R. H., and Smith, J. O. (Eds), *Language and mental retardation*. New York: Holt, Rinehart and Winston, 1967.

Smith, J. O. Group language development for educable mental retardates. *Exceptional Children,* 1962, *29,* 95–101.

Spradlin, J. S. Language and communication of mental defectives. In N. R. Ellis (Ed.), *Handbook of mental deficiency*. New York: McGraw-Hill, 1963.

Steinberg, D. D., and Jakobovits, L. A. (Eds.) *Semantics: An interdisciplinary reader in philosophy, linguistics, anthropology and psychology*. London: Cambridge University Press, in press.

Walthen-Dunn, W. (Ed.) *Models for the perception of speech and visual form*. Cambridge: MIT Press, 1967.

Webb, C. E., and Kinde, S. Speech, language, and hearing of the mentally retarded. In A. A. Baumeister (Ed.), *Mental retardation*. Chicago: Aldine, 1967, Chap. 5.

Weinreich, R. On the semantic structure of language. In J. H. Greenberg (Ed.), *Universals of language*. Cambridge: MIT Press, 1966. (2nd ed.)

Wiseman, D. E. A classroom procedure for indentifying and remediating language problems. *Ment. Retard.,* 1965, *3,* 20–24.

THE DEVELOPMENT OF REFERENTIAL SKILLS IN CHILDREN

SEYMOUR ROSENBERG
Rutgers University

SEYMOUR ROSENBERG, Professor of Psychology at Livingston College, Rutgers University, received his undergraduate degree from The Citadel in 1947 and did his graduate work in psychology at Indiana University, receiving his Ph.D. in 1952. He worked as a research psychologist for the Air Force from 1952 until 1958 on problems of aircrew compatibility and team performance. He then joined the Bureau of Child Research at the University of Kansas as Field Director of a project on language and communication of retarded children. In 1959 he moved to Bell Telephone Laboratories where he pursued his research interests in language and social interaction. In 1965 he was visiting professor at Columbia University. He decided to stay with academia and joined the faculty at Rutgers University. He is now in his second year of a five year research scientist award from NIMH. His current research and teaching interests include semantics, the psychological processes associated with communication between speakers and listeners, personality perception, and mathematical models of social behavior.

This chapter is concerned with the referential processes which underlie human communication and with the development of these processes in children. Referential processes, as used here, refer to how a *speaker* selects from his repertoire of names, descriptions, and gestures in order to communicate with his listener about certain objects, events, or relationships. Referential processes also refer to how a *listener* correctly or incorrectly identifies his speaker's referent from his speaker's utterance.

The first part of the chapter describes a research paradigm which has been developed and elaborated during the last several years in order to study referential processes empirically. This is followed by a summary of a theoretical formulation proposed in previous papers (Rosenberg and Cohen, 1964, 1966, 1967) and used both to organize certain empirical findings and to guide us to new, and we hope worthwhile, research questions.

The main part of the paper is concerned with the problem of determining how and when children, in the speaker role, learn to *take the viewpoint of the listener.* This is an important skill in human communication and social interaction generally. The empirical problem is to disentangle the development of this skill from the development of other component skills that the young child acquires in order to communicate effectively. Previous research into these problems, as well as some very recent work in our laboratories with a novel research methodology, is described.

This work was supported in part by NIH Research Scientist Award #1-K5-MH-29,326-03 and in part by NSF Grant GS-2552. The research program on referential processes at Rutgers, part of which is described in this paper, as well as the ideas on which this program is based, are the result of a long and very congenial collaborative effort with Bertram D. Cohen.

Finally, a brief description is included of our current work on communication about referents removed in time and place from the immediate environment of the speaker and listener. In such situations, the actual objects, events, and relationships being referred to are not present and we denote whatever implicit representation of the referents that the speaker and listener may have as *surrogate referents*. One of the distinctive features of human communication is that people talk about referents which are not in their immediate environment and which may even be imagininary. Animals, by contrast, communicate exclusively about the here-and-now, as do children when they first begin to talk. In the course of normal development, of course, the ability to communicate about remote and imaginary referents emerges in the child.

There are interesting and important communication functions in conversation, auxiliary to and supportive of the referential function, which are not covered in this chapter. The anatomy of a conversation typically includes a fair proportion of *metareferential* acts (Jakobson, 1960; Rosenberg and Cohen, 1966) by both speaker and listener. These acts are essentially sources of feedback that are particularly indigenous to human communication. For example, a speaker may seek information from his listener about whether an utterance is incomplete or inadequate in some way ("Do you know what I mean?"). With or without prompting from the speaker, the listener may provide his speaker with feedback about the adequacy of an utterance ("I understand," "Tell me more about it," "Do you mean the *blond* girl?"). Nonlinguistic and paralinguistic forms, e.g., head nods, pauses, etc., may also have a metareferential function. A cataloging of the various metareferential acts which occur in ordinary conversation and the way they function in referential communication was recently the subject of a thesis study completed in our laboratories (Mueller, 1970).

RESEARCH METHODOLOGY

The basic communication situation for studying referential behavior is as follows: A speaker is presented with a set of stimuli and is asked to provide a description of one (or more) of these stimuli that will enable his listener to make correct selections from the stimulus set. The listener's task is to identify the referent in the stimulus set using the speaker's response.

This communication paradigm has been used by several investigators with a variety of stimulus objects; for example, color chips, abstract designs, words (concepts), odors, geometric forms, facial expressions, and familiar, everyday objects (e.g., Krauss and Weinheimer, 1964, 1967; Maclay and Newman, 1960; Pascual-Leone and Smith, 1969; Rosenberg and Cohen, 1966; Rosenberg and Gordon, 1968; Triandis, 1960; Werner and Kaplan, 1963). Speaker names and descriptions in these various studies were sometimes restricted in some way (e.g., length or type of response) and sometimes completely unrestricted. Some of the variation in materials and speaker forms is illustrated in the three examples which follow.

The first example, which shows the use of the paradigm in a relatively simple form, is provided by the materials being used in a number of our current studies with children and adults. In these studies, a speaker is shown a series of stimulus sets, each consisting of two photographs of different facial expressions. The two poses may be of the same or of different persons. The speaker is asked to give a description of the "mood, feeling, or emotion" expressed by one of the faces (the referent) designated by the experimenter. Thus, the speaker's description is restricted in this work as to length and type of content. The listener's task is to identify the referent face in each set on the basis of the speaker's description. Figure 1 is an example of two faces and the set of speaker descriptions given for the referent face to distinguish it from the nonreferent. As the example illustrates, a group of speakers typically gives a variety of descriptions; the particular ones chosen for subsequent presentation to the listener(s) depend on the nature and purpose of the study.

The second example is one in which we allowed speakers to give descriptions unrestricted in any way. Figure 2 shows two sets of three snowflakes presented to a group of listeners, one set at a time (Rosenberg and Markham, 1971). The description of

ANGRY	14	AFRAID	1	ILL	1
EXCITED	3	AGGRESSIVE	1	INFURIATED	1
VIOLENT	3	AGITATED	1	INSANE	1
ENRAGED	2	CRAZED	1	MAD	1
FIERCE	2	DISGUSTED	1	MEAN	1
FRIGHTENED	2	DISTURBED	1	NAUSEOUS	1
FURIOUS	2	FEARFUL	1	STRUGGLING	1
PAINFUL	2	HORRIFIED	1	THREATENING	1
SCARED	2	HUNGRY	1	UPSET	1
SHOCKED	2				

Fig. 1. Descriptions given by 52 adult speakers to distinguish the expression on the referent face from that on the nonreferent face. The number of speakers who gave each descriptive term is shown to the right of the term.

the referent (left-most flake) given with the first set was:

> "This is a six-sided figure with each side as the top form sides of a hexagon [sic]. In the center of this figure there is a small hexagon with another one just inside it. In the center of it is a starfish-like object."

The resulting distribution of guesses as to which of the three snowflakes was the referent, as obtained from 115 listeners, was 0.652, 0.035, 0.313, respectively. The description of the referent (right-most flake) given with the second set was:

> "A square-cornered triangle with an external overlay that follows the same shape pattern to the three seeming corners where it takes on the shape of huge, bulbous nodes."

The resulting distribution in this case was 0.254, 0.254, and 0.491, respectively. The lack of agreement among listeners is typical when the stimuli within a set are similar. The theory described in the next section provides a good account of listeners' choice behavior under such referentially ambiguous circumstances.

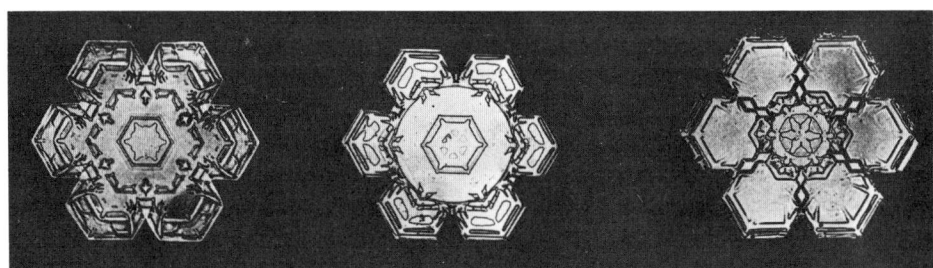

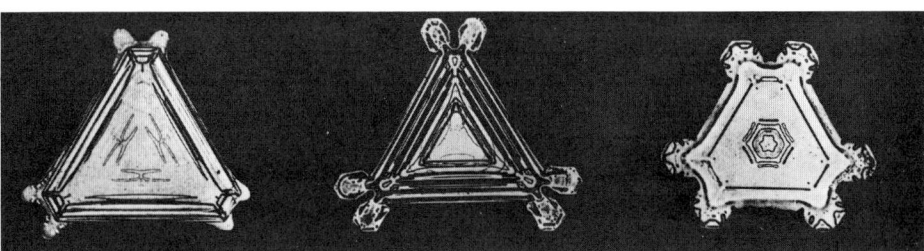

Fig. 2. Two sets of three snowflakes, used by Rosenberg and Markham (1971) as stimulus materials in a study of referential processes.

A third example of the paradigm, with gestures instead of names and verbal descriptions, recently appeared in a study of referential behavior in children (Pascual-Leone and Smith, 1969). In this study, the investigators put a child in the "speaker" role by showing him pairs of common objects, e.g., an apple and a ball, one pair at a time and asking him to "make a movement" so that the experimenter could guess what he was thinking of. In the listener role, the child was simply asked to pick out one of two objects from an experimenter's gesture—e.g., the experimenter pretended to eat something to refer to the apple and not the ball.

These examples illustrate some of the versatility of the paradigm. Other elaborations have been made in order to analyze certain details in speakers' and listeners' communication processes, to study language development, metareferential behavior, and referential behavior associated with surrogate referents. Some of these elaborations will be described later in the chapter.

THEORY OF REFERENTIAL PROCESSES

The essential notions of a formal theory of referential processes developed by Rosenberg and Cohen (1966) along with more recent theoretical ideas, are summarized here. The exposition is divided into a subsection on the speaker process and a subsection on the listener process.

Speaker process

The speaker's referential process is a concatenation of two hypothetical psychological stages: *sampling* and *comparison*. Both stages are assumed to be probabilistic. That is, the process begins with a sampling stage in which a name or description is randomly selected from the speaker's repertoire of linguistic units associated with the referent. For any given referent, it is assumed that the speaker's repertoire contains a number of such names or descriptions, each of which may be more or less adequate as a linguistic cue for the listener. In the comparison stage, which follows sampling, the relative *associative strength* (or *descriptive strength*) of the sampled response to referent and nonreferent stimuli determines the probability with which the speaker will emit the sampled response. If, as a result of the comparison stage the sampled response is rejected as an inadequate communication, the sampling-comparison cycle is repeated. Ultimately the speaker emits a response, thus terminating the process. A diagrammatic representation of the two-stage process is given in Figure 3.

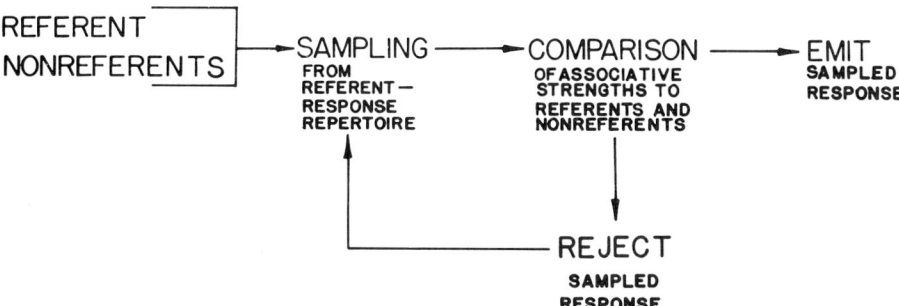

Fig. 3. Sketch of the speaker's referential process conceptualized for normal adults.

Intuitively, one may think of the speaker's comparison stage as one in which the speaker implicitly "tests" the adequacy of the sampled response to distinguish the referent from the nonreferent(s). That is, he takes the role of the listener. In fact, the speaker's comparison stage and the listener's choice process are formally similar in this theory.

In a modified conceptualization (suggested by Sam Glucksberg, Princeton University) of the speaker's comparison process, the speaker not only tests the adequacy of each sampled response but also "stores" in short-term memory, some or all of the responses that he samples and rejects. Then at some point, whether because of self-induced or external pressures to communicate, the speaker stops sampling and selects from among the sampled responses that have been stored. This type of formulation is intuitively appealing. It incorporates the fact that a speaker may know that his actual utterance is not adequate, but that he cannot do better at the moment. An engaging example in this connection is the case of the immigrant who attempts to communicate in the language of his adopted country and finally, in desperation, reverts to his native language even though he knows he probably will not be understood by his listener.

In any case, the comparison stage is imperfect among normal adult speakers in naturally-occurring communication for reasons in addition to the time pressures to communicate; for example, the speaker may not have adequate information about the linguistic skills of his listener or he may not be aware of all the objects which his listener is considering as the possible referent. An additional source of imperfect comparison, recently discovered in our laboratory, is the presence of a speaker bias in the comparison stage. This is essentially a tendency by the speaker to overestimate the associative or descriptive strength of a sampled response to any stimulus designated as a referent; that is, the speaker evaluates his sampled response as better for listener identification than it really is.

Listener process

When the alternatives being considered by a listener are well-defined, his choice of an alternative as the referent is the result of a one-stage process resembling the speaker's comparison stage (without storage). Imagine a listener being shown the two faces in Figure 1, for example, with any one of the words in the list as the speaker's description. It is assumed that he compares the associative strength of each of the two faces to the description and chooses one as the referent on the basis of which strength is the larger.

This comparison process may be conceptualized in terms of a number of existing choice theories. An important distinction among these choice theories is whether they treat the choice process as probabilistic or deterministic (Luce and Suppes, 1965). We favor a probabilistic formulation based on Luce's (1959) choice axiom, although we have also tested certain deterministic theories. The axiom, which will not be discussed here, has been tested with a variety of data and is fully described elsewhere

(Rosenberg and Cohen, 1966, 1967; Rosenberg and Donner, 1968; Rosenberg and Gordon, 1968).

One theoretical issue is, however, germane to studies of listener behavior in children and will be discussed here. The axiom does not describe the detailed psychological processes associated with a single act of choice, as for example, how a person inspects the alternatives in order to come up with a choice. One type of inspection process is a random walk process (Atkinson, Bower, and Crothers, 1965). This is a "pathological" process because it states that a listener may choose an alternative as the referent without ever examining the other alternatives, particularly if its associative strength to the speaker's utterance is high. The random walk process is similar to answering a multiple-choice question by choosing the first alternative that seems correct without necessarily inspecting all the alternatives. Such a process may characterize what goes on in young children and in certain pathological groups. As the normal child develops, however, a more "rational" process is likely to be involved in his choice behavior.

We have developed one model of such a rational process termed a "suspended judgment" model. This model describes the choice process as one in which a listener inspects the alternatives sequentially and makes a separate "yes–no" decision about each (with probabilities that depend on associative strength). If there is one and only one "yes," he chooses that alternative as the referent—otherwise he inspects again. Since the "yes–no" decision is a probabilistic one, he will eventually come up with one and only one "yes," at which point he makes an overt choice.

It can be shown that Luce's choice axiom can be derived *both* from certain random walk models *and* from the suspended judgment model. However, the two types of models make very different and testable predictions about decision time as a function of associative strengths. Consider a situation in which the speaker response is equally associated to each of two stimulus objects, x and y. In such a case, the probability of choosing x will be 0.5 regardless of how the listener makes his choice, whether rationally or pathologically. Now, if the associative strengths are high as well as equal and if the listener is choosing according to the rational (suspended judgment) model, he will be prone to make repeated comparisons, hence his *latency* will be slow. Indeed, his choice latency in situations involving high but equal associative strengths will be as slow as in situations in which the associative strengths are both extremely low, but equal. In contrast, if the listener chooses according to the pathological (random walk) model, the latency when the associative strengths are equal and *high* will be considerably faster than when they are equal but *low*, since the act of choosing depends only on the associative strength linking the speaker response to whichever object the listener is considering at the moment. That is, he does not engage in any true comparison of the alternatives.

Another possible way of differentiating the two models is by observing directly the way a listener visually inspects the alternatives. The main limitation with the latter method is that he may, after one or more inspections, remember some or all of the alternatives without looking again. In that case, the suspended judgment model might not appear to hold when it is in fact correct.

REFERENTIAL PROCESSES IN CHILDREN

Studies of language acquisition were, until recently, concerned almost exclusively with prelanguage vocalizations, phonemic composition of children's speech, degree of conformity to a prescriptive grammar, vocabulary growth, and ability to imitate (see reviews by Ervin and Miller, 1963; McCarthy, 1954). While these topics continue to concern researchers, other investigators influenced by the *Zeitgeist* of comtemporary psycholinguistics have turned their attention to structural analyses of children's grammar (e.g., Bellugi and Brown, 1964; Smith and Miller, 1966).

Another contemporary research trend, this one traceable to certain traditions in child development, social psychology, and cognitive psychology, has focussed on the acquisition of referential skills—or more broadly, communication skills (e.g., Cohen and Klein, 1968; Flavell et al., 1968; Glucksberg, Krauss, and Weisberg, 1966; Krauss and Glucksberg, 1969; Pascual-Leone and Smith, 1969; Rosenberg and Cohen, 1967).

Interest in a child's increasing ability to communicate with others actually dates back to one of Piaget's (1926) earliest research concerns. Piaget concluded, on the basis of certain observations of children's language, that young children (particularly, from six to seven years old) do not communicate effectively because they are unable to take the role or viewpoint of the listener. The speech of older children (eight years and beyond), on the other hand, contains less idiosyncratic references, less *egocentric speech* as Piaget termed it. Taking the viewpoint of the listener, Piaget thought, was part of a more general social-cognitive skill that the child acquires during this period.

These Piagetian notions, as well as Mead's (1934) conception of the "generalized other" and its development in children, are closely related to our conception of the speaker's comparison stage, as outlined in the previous section. It is clear that a sampling process alone, even with a sizeable vocabulary, does not provide the child (or adult) with the means to distinguish, for his listener, *referents in novel stimulus sets where the nonreferents in the set may be called by names similar to the referent*. In short, the comparison stage is a necessary filter for referentially ambiguous utterances. What is not clear is the extent to which inadequate communication in young children may be caused by a small vocabulary and to what extent it may be caused by a comparison-stage deficit.

Recent studies, much more controlled than those of Piaget, still do not provide an unequivocal answer to this question. With older children, that is, third, fifth, and seventh graders, the evidence seems to favor the hypothesis that it is the size of the child's vocabulary and not the absence of a comparison stage that may limit his communicative effectiveness (Cohen and Klein, 1968). Effective communication by preschool children, on the other hand, seems to be limited not only by a relatively small vocabulary but also by a weak (or nonexistent) comparison stage (Glucksberg et al., 1966). The use of idiosyncratic or familial references by preschool children in communicating with strangers, has been and still is one of the main bases for this conclusion. (Of course, adult speakers also attempt to communicate even when they know they will probably not be understood, as the example given earlier of the immigrant illustrates.)

There is another consistent bit of evidence that is relevant to our understanding of the way speaker skills develop in young children. Several studies, including those cited above, have shown that a child, at a given age, is less adequate as a speaker than he is as a listener. That is, presented with a name or description from an older child or adult, a young child is often able to use it effectively to identify the referent even though the young child may not have been able to generate the name himself. If the comparison stage in a speaker functions similarly to that in a listener, as we have conjectured, then the problem seems to be either (1) a vocabulary deficit, or (2) a failure by the young child to utilize his comparison skills when he functions as speaker—comparison skills that he is able to use as a listener.

The problem has been, and still is, to examine separately the functioning or lack of functioning of each of the two stages in children—a difficult problem when information about the linguistic history of the child is unavailable to the investigator. A possible solution, then, is for the investigator to create a bit of linguistic history for the child and to bring this history into play in a communication task. This is what we have done on a modest scale in our laboratory.

The procedure as used by one of our students in a doctoral dissertation (Saunders, 1969) is first to teach a child a small *probabilistic* vocabulary for a set of objects and then to use these objects in a speaker task. There is good evidence that this type of procedure, when used with adults, yields data which parallel certain effects found in naturally-occurring language (Rosenberg & Donner, 1968; Rothberg, 1970).

Saunders paired each of two fictitious animals (drawings), which I will denote by A and B, with a different name and with a third name common to both A and B. One repertoire was as follows:

A is named "goo" on 80% of the trials
A is named "tum" on 20% of the trials
B is named "goo" on 80% of the trials
B is named "bop" on 20% of the trials

A second repertoire, with two different drawings and with three different nonsense names was also used. This repertoire involved a 50–50 schedule instead of the 80–20 schedule shown above.

Test trials, interspersed between blocks of ten learning trials, consisted of asking the child to give the names of A and of B. After an initial set of 20 trials additional blocks of ten learning trials were discontinued as soon as a child correctly gave the two names paired with A and the two names paired with B. Learning rates differed considerably for children of different ages, as Figure 4 shows.

Immediately following learning, the child was given a speaker task in which A was the referent and B the nonreferent, or vice versa. The instructions, which helped make the communication task naturalistic and understandable to the child, are as follows:

> "Now let's pretend that you are going to tell a story about one of these animals to a friend. We'll pretend that your friend is sitting here

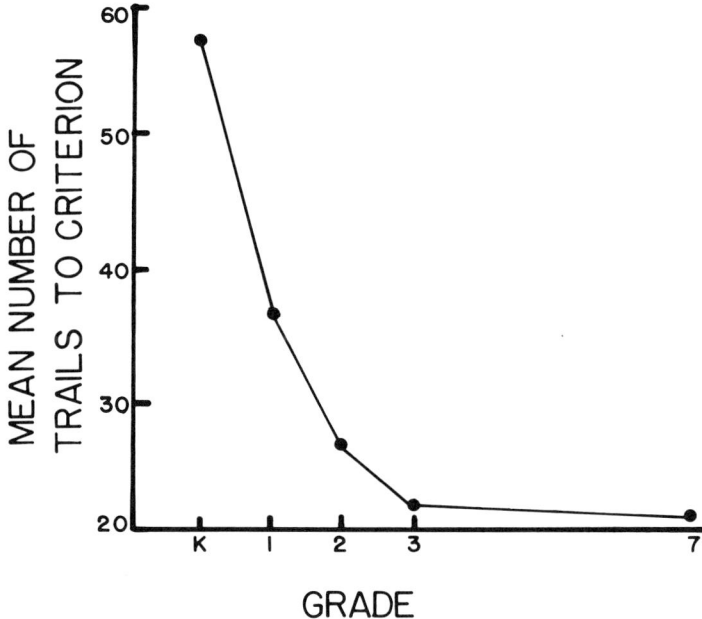

Fig. 4. Mean number of trials required for children at different grade levels to learn the probabilistic vocabulary in the Saunders (1969) study.

[experimenter points to the side of the table opposite the child] and that he sees *both* of these animals in front of him. Just like any story, you would say 'This is a story about an elephant,' for example, if the story was about an elephant, so that your friend would know which animal the story was about. Now, I will point to one of these animals, and I want you to *say one of the animal's names so that your friend would know which one of the animals the story is about*."

The experimenter designated the referent object and recorded the child's response and latency. The same procedures were repeated on the second session with the same child, but with different objects, responses, and learning schedule (50–50 or 80–20, depending on which the child didn't have in the first session).

It is clear that there is an optimal way for the child to name the referent. If the referent is A, he should use the name "tum" in the 80–20 example above; if the referent is B, he should use the name "bop"; "goo" is ineffective. The same would be true for the 50–50 schedule. In short, both schedules provided a name that was invariably associated with one and only one object, and all the objects used had their own name—the use of this name is optimal.

Now as to predictions from the speaker theory. First of all, the theory does not predict optimizing. That is, the better response may not be given by all speakers, even if each follows the theory. The basic reason for this prediction is that the process is assumed to be probabilistic and with a 80-20 schedule, there is a much greater probability of sampling the ineffective response instead of the optimal one; this coupled with probabilistic comparison results in a greater than zero probability that a speaker will emit the poorer response. Second, according to the speaker theory, the presence or absence of a comparison stage does make an important difference in the relative proportion of good responses. Thus, if the comparison stage develops during the age range studied, a trend toward increasingly good responses should be observed.

The results are shown in Table 1. Both predictions held up. First, even seventh graders do not optimize: 15 of the 40 seventh graders did not use the optimal name. Second, when the data from the two schedules are combined, the proportion of speakers giving the optimal name increases systematically with grade level. The somewhat erratic trend observed for each schedule separately is probably caused by the rather small numbers of subjects involved. Our experience in previous research on speaker processes suggests that N's of 20 are too small for dramatically demonstrating most effects.

TABLE 1

Number of speakers at each grade level who gave the optimal name for the referent
(From Saunders, 1969)

Grade level	80-20 schedule ($N = 20$)	50-50 schedule ($N = 20$)	Both schedules ($N = 40$)
K	5	10	15
1	9	7	16
2	10	9	19
3	8	12	20
7	11	14	25

The paradigm used by Saunders does not tell us, of course, how a child develops speaker-comparison skills but only (and we are not yet sure of this) when he does. Studies on the "how" question should consider at least two possibilities:

    1. The child acquires these skills by observing adult speakers and modeling his speaker comparison after theirs. While this is a likely hypothesis for the acquisition of a vocabulary (i.e., increasing his sampling repertoire) and other observable aspects of speech, the modeling notion does not seem likely for the development of such a relatively inaccessible process as speaker comparison.

    2. The child first acquires listener-comparison skills in response to other speaker's utterances and then transfers these skills to the judgment of his own utterances. This hypothesis is consistent with the empirical finding that a child develops listener skills before speaker skills.

A study related to this question is currently being conducted by Bertram Cohen and one of his students. Handicapped children, all within normal intelligence limits but with physical or psychological problems that prevent normal school progress, are being studied using the communication paradigm. It is planned, first, to identify deficits in these children's speaker and listener skills; and second, to use the communication situation as a teaching device to facilitate skill development. For example, the problems that some of these children manifest can be construed as failures in speaker comparison, or egocentric speaker comparison. They will attempt to modify this behavior by systematically shifting the child's role from listener to speaker in an attempt to facilitate his acquisition of speaker-comparison skill.

SURROGATE REFERENTS

In all the research discussed in the previous sections, whether with children or adults, the speaker was able to look at (or more generally have some direct sensory contact with) the referent and the set of objects from which the listener would have to choose the referent. The listener, in turn, made his choice directly from a set of objects. This feature of the research paradigm, that is, having the referent and nonreferents present in the communication situation, has seemed necessary in order to make the psychological analysis of referential behavior an empirically tractable problem.

Yet a considerable amount of naturally-occurring human communication contains references to objects and events removed in time or place from the communication setting of the speaker and listener, e.g., a telephone conversation between two people in which they agree to meet at a particular time and place. Moreover, references are frequently made to a class of objects or events, all members of which cannot be present in the immediate environment of the speaker and listener; consider, for example, the impossibility of assembling all members of classes such as "presidents of the U.S.," "cats," "money," "sentences." To retain the concept of the referent, we have postulated the notion of a surrogate referent in the form of some implicit representation of the referent itself.

In the method we have developed for studying communication about surrogate referents, each of a set of objects is first paired with a different arbitrary symbol until the subject has learned all the object-symbol pairs perfectly. For example, in several of our studies the photographs (faces) of different persons are paired with different forenames, e.g., Alice, John, Mary, etc. Two of the faces we have used in this work are those shown in Figure 1. In one condition, the subjects learned the man's name as "George" and the girl's name as "Mary." (Other conditions consisted of using other forenames for counterbalancing purposes.) The method is of course applicable to almost any set of objects used by us and others in studies of referential behavior.

Following the pairing of objects and symbols (or members of object classes with symbols), the subject can be given either the speaker or listener role within the communication paradigm already developed. For example, as speaker the subject is asked to describe George's expression so as to distinguish it from Mary's expression for a listener. Neither speaker nor listener has the actual photographs in front of him and the speaker cannot use the name itself as the reference term, i.e., "George." Otherwise the procedure is the same as the one used for the photographs themselves. The listener is then given the names, George and Mary, along with the speaker's description of one of them, and asked to pick out the name (surrogate referent) of the person whose expression was best described by the speaker.

In general, we have found that the referential processes associated with surrogate referents are similar to those found for the referents themselves. The quality of speaker descriptions diminishes significantly, however, when he communicates about a facial expression from memory. The effect on the listener of having to choose from memory is noticeable also; his choices contain more errors.

I shall describe briefly the main results from a study of listeners which exemplify the type of difference obtained between referent and surrogate-referent communication. In this study, photographs of eight different persons were used. After pairing the faces and names, half the subjects were given sets of two and three names, one set at a time, with a speaker description; for example: *Mary–Alice–Susan; "This person's face looked happy."* The other half of the subjects were given the corresponding sets of *faces* along with the same speaker description. In the first case, the listeners were asked to pick out the surrogate referent (the name) on the basis of the speaker's description and in the second case, the referent (photograph) itself.

The results are summarized in Figure 5. The abscissa is the proportion of choices predicted from our application of Luce's choice axiom; the ordinate is the observed proportion of choices in the two-alternative sets. Figure 5A was obtained from the surrogate-referent condition and Figure 5B from the referent condition. The fit, in

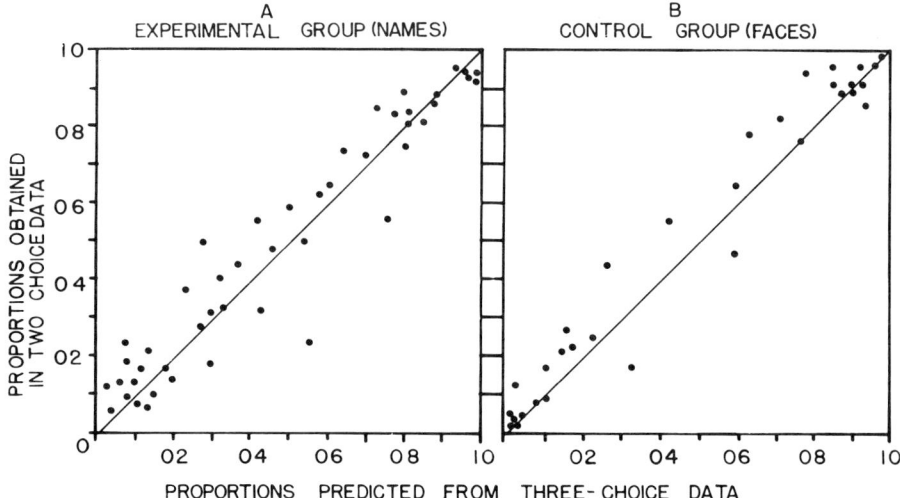

Fig. 5. Scattergrams of proportions predicted from three-choice data using Luce's choice axiom versus proportions actually obtained in the two-choice data. *A*, data from listeners who chose from surrogate-referents (i.e., names); *B*, data from listeners who chose from referents (i.e., photographs).

both cases, is excellent. That is, the choice process in the two conditions conforms to the theory. What is different is the degree of certainty of the choice. This difference can be seen in the way the points cluster in the two conditions. With surrogate referents, the predicted (and obtained) proportions distribute themselves more uniformly over the range of values. With the actual referents, these proportions tend to cluster more closely to the extreme (0 to 1) of the range.

Although our current analyses of surrogate referents are with normal adults, extensions to children would appear to be very worthwhile since surprisingly little *empirical* attention has been given to the emergence of this important ability in children. These extensions to children would probably require relatively minor modifications of the research paradigm used with adults.

SUMMARY OF DISCUSSION

QUESTION: Do you give the subjects no vocabulary at all for describing, for example, the photographs of the faces? They just generate that freely?

ROSENBERG: We give them no vocabulary.

QUESTION: Do you give them any instruction as to techniques or tactics?

ROSENBERG: We impose some limits on them, depending on the materials. With the faces we ask them to limit their descriptions to the mood, feeling, or emotion in the face rather than saying, "It's the man, not the little girl." We specifically give them a sentence frame. "This face looks" is the sentence frame. In the case of the snowflakes, their descriptions are unrestricted. Anything they want to say is fine. With colors, in some cases we have restricted their descriptions in length. Subjects naturally restrict things, too, depending on the stimulus materials.

QUESTION: What about time and space separation between speaker and listener?

ROSENBERG: In some experiments the speaker and listener are separated in time and place. That is, we have speakers whose listeners are given their descriptions later and the listener subjects try to identify the pictures from the descriptions.

Another situation is where the speaker and the listener are visually separated, but they can hear each other. The speaker can say whatever he wants to, again limiting his description to the affect on the face rather than the enduring features.

QUESTION: Why do you have these two different situations?

ROSENBERG: They allow us to study some interesting features of a conversation. We really get to see the basic anatomy of a conversation, including the use of meta-referential skills by speaker and/or listener.

QUESTION: How about the speed with which they are expected to respond to the snowflakes? Are they given time to study the photographs?

ROSENBERG: Yes.

QUESTION: What about feedback on correctness?

ROSENBERG: We vary that, too.

QUESTION: Do you only use one speaker-listener combination?

ROSENBERG: It depends on the kind of research. We use both a unique speaker-listener combination, and we also take a distribution of speaker responses and give them to a number of listeners. These questions about variety in procedure are difficult to answer in the abstract, because they are always connected with some psychological question. If you are interested in the anatomy of a conversation, then a speaker-listener pair is what you need. If you are interested in other features of the speaker process—the thinking process, the cognitive process—then you are more interested in getting a number of listeners to respond to some particular description or subset of descriptions.

QUESTION: Are you suggesting that comparison occurs at two levels? First, do you dip into your repertoire of vocabulary items that are even grossly relevant to the task, then compare which ones seem to bear any relationship to that stimulus object at all? Then do you make still another set of comparisons in terms of your knowledge about the other end of the configuration, the listener? Does the first comparison have to grow out of the whole range of vocabulary items that might be grossly related which are indeed accurate representations of your sense or feeling about that object?

ROSENBERG: Yes. But I doubt that a speaker really has access to the relevant vocabulary all at once.

QUESTION: You imply that as the speaker samples from his vocabulary, he makes certain decisions. In making his first decision, he is sampling, which means he is selecting one. Could it be a comparative or comparison process with the others which he chooses not to sample?

ROSENBERG: Yes. He chooses not to sample, but he has sampled them in some sense or other. But there is another notion about what goes on here. If a sample is found to be inadequate, it may not be dropped, it may be stored. The sampler may collect three or four and then pick the best of those.

QUESTION: Your comparison here is with respect to the two different referents?

ROSENBERG: Right. Two different objects.

QUESTION: In one case you are comparing the effect of different contrast objects and in the other you are comparing the features of whatever you think of that repertoire of vocabulary items. So if you compare whatever you measure about this task, as in the one case as a function of what the comparison objects are, and the other case as a function of what kind of repertoire or vocabulary people generate, don't you then have the comparison of the two aspects?

ROSENBERG: Yes.

QUESTION: You don't really mean that the comparison always follows the sampling, do you? In some cases you can set up the pair of objects so the person compares them first and says, "This one is happier, this one is bigger or brighter."

ROSENBERG: It is possible to build alternative models. We construct to try to understand what is going on.

QUESTION: Is there any sense in thinking of the comparison as following the sampling?

ROSENBERG: There is some sense to it. If you rearranged it you would have to rearrange your ideas about sampling, too. That's all right. I'm not opposed to that at all. But, if you want to rearrange the processes to come up with ways of differentiating this model from others, that's difficult. Even the storage notion, which seems like an important addition or change in this model, is difficult to test—that is, whether it is a useful idea or just a gratuitous appendage to theory.

QUESTION: Does the editing process work the same way over time if you separate it from memory? Will the same child or adult tend to choose the same word if he is tested over time, and memory is sort of cancelled out?

ROSENBERG: Yes, this is a probabilistic process. In sampling, it is like the person reaching into an urn and pulling out a word with the probability being different for different words. There is no strict hierarchy in which he always pulls out the strongest association or description first, followed by the next strongest, and so on.

QUESTION: Is the probabilistic function similar for children and adults?

ROSENBERG: The precise data on the probabilistic nature come from adults. The work with children is not so precise, so I cannot answer that question.

QUESTION: Is it a sort of a hierarchy with a child?

ROSENBERG: I don't know. Most of the people who work with children have really not been interested in quantitative issues. The probabilistic versus deterministic hypothesis ends up as a quantitative problem, as a math model problem.

QUESTION: What are you testing in Saunder's study?

ROSENBERG: The setup pits vocabulary prowess of a word against its effectiveness from the standpoint of the listener. That fictional animal A has been called a "goo" most of the time. It is more likely to be sampled than the other word. If the process stops there, then the child will use "goo" as a way of describing animal A, and it will be completely ineffective. If the process goes further, that is, includes editing or taking the role of a listener, then the child will realize in some sense or other that "goo" is not good as a description because it doesn't differentiate animal A from animal B.

QUESTION: Is it possible with the younger children there is a memory function? If

DEVELOPMENT OF REFERENTIAL SKILLS

you wrote the two words out for them, would that redress that tendency to revert to the more frequent word "goo"?

ROSENBERG: Yes, I would say that the more likely thing to be remembered is the nonoptimal word. But the task, as it is, is like ordinary communication where the alternative words are not written out for the child.

QUESTION: Did you attempt to match the variables or to examine the successes from the nonsuccesses on a post hoc basis?

ROSENBERG: No. The subjects were randomly drawn from classes in the same school. There was no matching, and there was no post hoc.

QUESTION: I wonder about the stimulus materials, and whether or not they were distinct enough, whether there were differences sufficient in the figures that those things could be attached to the differential nonsense materials?

ROSENBERG: The researcher checked the children after a certain number of training trials. She asked the child, "Now, what is this called?" If the child said "goo," she would say, "Well, what else is it called?" If the child didn't come up with the correct response, she'd go through another set of trials.

QUESTION: Are you still building in the acquired equivalents by giving them the same nonsense syllable name? Are the animals different enough to make a difference for the child? Is there some distinctive feature about the picture?

ROSENBERG: Yes. They really do look different.

QUESTION: Couldn't your verbal labels wipe out any difference? We have a lot of situations, you know, where we could name two things, a horse or a cow, and in another situation one becomes a mare or a stallion or a palomino or something else.

ROSENBERG: Yes, but that's the way it is, isn't it? We call things horses and then sometimes we call certain horses palominos to distinguish them from other horses. But they are both horses.

QUESTION: Yes, they are both horses. But 20 per cent of the time we are calling one palomino and the other simply a horse.

ROSENBERG: But that's the way language is. I thought we did a good job of representing the natural state of affairs.

QUESTION: Yes, but why do you say, "I don't understand why all these seventh graders call them horses?"

ROSENBERG: Because they have been overwhelmed by both of them being called horses.

QUESTION: Was any reinforcement used? Couldn't both speaker and listener get paid off if communication is achieved?

ROSENBERG: That might make a difference. It might just raise the performance level at each grade.

QUESTION: Could you speculate for us where you line of work might go? Where will you go with this in subsequent research? How will this relate to people who are concerned with children, how they learn to talk, and how mentally retarded children learn to talk? We know approximately when a child comes to take into account the facts of a listener, the needs of a listener, but we don't know how this happens. And there is a related point that is especially interesting to me. How does the child move away from his dependence on context and behavior to talk about things that are not immediately apparent to him? Isn't this something children also need to learn? Do you have any ideas as to how children move in this direction?

ROSENBERG: No, I don't. I talked about surrogate referents because I felt that the research in communication was missing that important ingredient. It is obvious that something needs to be done with children, but we have not yet developed this. It's clear that animals communicate. Many of the things that we think of as being communication are things animals do. One thing that differentiates people from animals is that animals seem to communicate about the here-and-now exclusively, as do very young children. Adults are not restricted that way. To answer the first part of the question I have to refer to students who have become interested in actually doing the work. I mean it's easy to have ideas and talk about things, but someone has to do the work on these things. Some students are studying how to teach children to take the role of the listener in the speaker function. That's one direction. And the most obvious approach is to put children in a listener role in some communication task and then see to what extent that changes the way they function as speakers. We have data which show that children are better listeners than they are speakers. They can respond appropriately to some descriptions they can't produce themselves. If they can do that, why can't they take that skill and plug into it when they are functioning as speakers? Maybe it's as simple as really taking a communication task, having them function as listeners. Maybe it will be more obvious to them that that's what they should be doing when they are in the speaker role.

QUESTION: If you consider the child's instructional experience, isn't much of this communication experience actually with an adult or an older person? He probably gets a great deal more experience as a listener than he does as a speaker. How can we develop instructional procedures to give a child more of this experience? Wouldn't that help give him a sort of a maximum skill, at least for what he needs in many kinds of contexts?

ROSENBERG: Yes. But it takes a very patient adult to really give a child that experience. Some teachers talk as much as 95 per cent of the time. And when the children talk, they are talking to the teacher, who can interpret much more easily what the child is saying and reduce the ambiguity in whatever the child says.

REFERENCES

Atkinson, R. C., Bower, G. H., and Crothers, E. J. *An introduction to mathematical learning theory.* New York: Wiley, 1965.
Bellugi, U., and Brown, R. (Eds.), The acquisition of language. *Society for Research in Child Development Monograph,* 1964, *29*(1).
Cohen, B. D., and Klein, J. Referent communication in school age children. *Child Development,* 1968, *39,* 597–609.
Ervin, S. M., and Miller, W. R. Language development. In H. W. Stevenson, et al. (Eds.), *Child psychology: 62nd yearbook for the National Society for the Study of Education.* Chicago: University of Chicago Press, 1963. Pp. 108–143.
Flavell, et al. *The development of role-taking and communication skills in children.* New York: Wiley, 1968.
Glucksberg, S., Krauss, R. M., and Weisberg, R. Referential communication in nursery school children: Method and some preliminary findings. *J. Exp. Child Psychol.,* 1966, *3,* 333–342.
Jakobson, R. Closing statement: Linguistics and poetics. In T. A. Sebeck (Ed.), *Style in language.* New York: Wiley, 1960. Pp. 350–377.
Krauss, R. M., and Glucksberg, S. The development of communication: Competence as a function of age. *Child Development,* 1969, *40,* 255–266.
Krauss, R. M., and Weinheimer, S. Changes in reference phrases as a function of frequency of usage in social interaction: A preliminary study. *Psychonomic Science,* 1964, *1,* 113–114.
Krauss, R. M., and Weinheimer, S. The effect of referent array and communication mode on verbal encoding. *J. Verb. Learning Verb. Behavior,* 1967, *6,* 359–363.
Luce, R. D. *Individual choice behavior.* New York: Wiley, 1959.
Luce, R. D., and Suppes, P. Preference, utility, and subjective probability. In R. D. Luce, R. R. Bush, and E. Galanter (Eds.), *Handbook of mathematical psychology.* Vol. 3. New York: Wiley, 1965. Pp. 249–410.
Maclay, H., and Newman, S. Two variables affecting the message in communication. In D. Willner (Ed.), *Decisions, values and groups.* New York: Pergamon Press, 1960. Pp. 218–228.
McCarthy, D. Language development in children. In L. Carmichael (Ed.), *Manual of child psychology.* (2nd ed.) New York: Wiley, 1954. Pp. 492–630.
Mead, G. H. *Mind, self and society.* Chicago: University of Chicago Press, 1934.
Mueller, D. R. Referential and metareferential communication in continuous discourse with varying degrees of referent-nonreferent similarity and with direct-stimulus and surrogate-stimulus presentations. Unpublished Master's thesis, Rutgers University, 1970.
Pascual-Leone, J., and Smith, J. The encoding and decoding of symbols by children: A new experimental paradigm and a neo-Piagetian model. *J. Exp. Child Psychol.,* 1969, *8,* 328–355.
Piaget, J. *The language and thought of the child.* New York: Harcourt, Brace, 1926.
Rosenberg, S., and Cohen, B. D. Speakers' and listeners' processes in a word-communication task. *Science,* 1964, *145,* 1201–1203.
Rosenberg, S., and Cohen, B. D. Referential processes of speakers and listeners. *Psychol. Rev.,* 1966, *73,* 208–231.
Rosenberg, S., and Cohen, B. D. Toward a psychological analysis of verbal communication skills. In R. L. Schiefelbusch, R. H. Copeland, and J. O. Smith (Eds.), *Language and mental retardation.* New York: Holt, Rinehart and Winston, 1967, Chapter 4.
Rosenberg, S., and Donner, L. Choice behavior in a verbal recognition task as a function of induced associative strength. *J. Exp. Psychol.,* 1968, *76,* 341–347.
Rosenberg, S., and Gordon, A. Identification of facial expressions from affective descriptions: A probabilistic choice analysis of referential ambiguity. *J. Personality Soc. Psychol.,* 1968, *10,* 157–166.
Rosenberg, S., and Markham, B. Choice behavior in a referentially ambiguous task. *J. Personality Soc. Psychol.,* 1971, *17,* 99–106.
Rothberg, M. A. Tests of a two-stage "speaker" communication model using induced response hierarchies. *J. Exp. Psychol.,* 1970, *84,* 204–212.
Saunders, P. S. An experimental analysis of egocentrism in children's communication. Unpublished doctoral dissertation, Rutgers University, 1969.
Smith, F., and Miller, G. A. (Eds.), *The genesis of language.* Cambridge: MIT Press, 1966.
Triandis, H. C. Cognitive similarity and communication in a dyad. *Human Relations,* 1960, *13,* 175–183.
Werner, H., and Kaplan, B. *Symbol formation.* New York: Wiley, 1963.

Language Training

A SYSTEMATIC APPROACH TO LANGUAGE TRAINING

WILLIAM A. BRICKER
George Peabody College for Teachers

WILLIAM A. BRICKER was formerly director of Research and Training at Parsons State Hospital and Training Center in Parsons, Kansas. He is currently Kennedy Professor of Psychology and Special Education at George Peabody College for Teachers in Nashville, Tennessee. The major focus of Dr. Bricker's research is on methods for establishing verbal behavior in the repertoires of severely and profoundly retarded children.

During late 1969 and early 1970, the Bureau of Child Research and its researchers developed and proposed a language-training program project. The language system that formed the basis for that proposal provides the substance for this chapter. The use made of it there, plus what it generated in terms of what are now called procedural lattices, provide a description of how various language processes can be shaped into the repertoires of severely retarded children.

In developing a language training model we synthesized what we could from linguistic and psycholinguistic theory and data from past research using the operant approach. We then put together, much like an engineer, a system of training events sufficient to facilitate the development of language. We defined a series of terminal states or sub-terminal states which represent a developmental hierarchy.

To a large extent, the absence of or deficiency in language production defines retardation. This relationship between language and retardation is pronounced in the behavior of children and adults who are classified as severely or profoundly retarded. Most of these low-functioning persons are unable to respond to or emit verbal behavior. Consequently, they do not learn a complete language system with great speed and in the absence of formal instruction. Certainly, the failure to acquire language may be attributable to damage in the nervous system which interrupts the normal learning processes. Such an assumption, if taken together with the description of the linguist's Language Acquisition Device (LAD), would lead to the conclusion that language training for such children is a well-intentioned but futile gesture. Fortunately, this conclusion establishes a challenge rather than an epitaph for behaviorists working in language.

Several of the chapters in this publication reflect the efforts of investigators who literally enjoy the opportunity to meet this challenge. The language training model presented here represents an organizational scheme into which some of these efforts fit.

The language acquisition model presented in the previous chapter establishes a pattern of normal language development that is rapid, complex, and occurs in the absence of formal instruction. The implications of this model, and especially of the presumed hierarchical mental mechanisms associated with language learning, have challenged traditional learning theory. Chomsky's (1959) review of Skinner's *Verbal Behavior* established a battleground among psychologists and reawakened the issue of mentalism. The concepts of "base structures" and "competencies" are clearly constructs that are assumed to be isomorphic with the operations of the nervous system but not descriptions of the nervous system. To the linguist and the psycholinguist such inferences about the nervous system are necessary in a complete account of verbal behavior. The defense of this clearly mentalistic view has been given by a number of linguists and psycholinguists including Chomsky (1965), McNeill (1966), Fodor (1966), and Lenneberg (1967). The purpose of this chapter is not to argue with these formulations of language and language acquisition, but to present a behavioral alternative in the form of a language training model and to evaluate the extent to which current linguistic theory contributes to a technology of language instruction. However, it should be pointed out that the language training of retarded persons is a valid area in which to evaluate the relative contributions of behavioristic and linguistic approaches.

The language-acquisition model presented in the previous chapter hits on a process through which normal children rapidly develop language. They acquire a very complex repertoire in a matter of four years. No formal instruction is apparent. There is no careful, systematic manipulation of contingencies in order to bring language into being. As long as we describe and focus exclusively on the normal child, we can be pretty safe in certain assumptions about innate structures, intrinsic processes, and what the child brings to the language learning process.

When we look at retarded children we have a different situation, one that requires formal instruction and the systematic manipulation of contingencies. We work backward from a set of terminal states, or forms of behavior that seem to approximate a complex repertoire. We begin by talking about associative processes, memory processes, then cognitive states that can be defined. Going back further, social use of language must be normalized, and before that we have to get the social use of language established. This in turn depends upon meaningful sentence production preceded by a conceptual productive vocabulary and verbal imitation, and a conceptual receptive vocabulary which depends upon a functional hearing level.

The lattice in Figure 1 contains the general areas of our language training model mentioned earlier. The boxes above the ascending diagonal represent the sequence of terminal behavior to be established as a consequence of the training programs underlying them. In turn, the program boxes under the diagonal contain phrases that were generated following the statement: "Program for training in . . . ." Along the bottom of the lattice are those programs which are continued throughout the entire span of language training specified by the model. Looking first at the terminal state boxes, it is evident that they represent a sequential arrangement of increasing developmental capability moving from simple controlled behavior to social and cognitive uses of complex verbal behavior. There is little reason to describe these in any detail since the definition of each is dependent upon the programs that generate it.

The program boxes are placed to represent hierarchical sequences in both the vertical and horizontal dimensions. Consequently, reinforcement occurs before the attention-to-task program. Both are necessary for repertoire assessment. However, in the structure of this lattice, repertoire assessment seems somewhat misplaced. The implication of this specific program is that children who are new have to be assessed in order to establish the form of training they need. Thus, a child is first tested for hearing level, then discrimination among words, imitation of words, naming objects, sentence production, answering questions about actions, events, and locations, using nonverbal language, and, finally, using language as a cognitive tool. These areas are represented by the seven program boxes immediately below and attached to the terminal state boxes. The implication of this is that the programs in each of these seven areas contain assessment procedures for operationally establishing the extent to which the current repertoire approximates the defined terminal states. Failure in any area specifies where training should begin. Consequently, the repertoire assessment program establishes the training a child will receive in the beginning. Training need not begin at simple response learning for all children as implied in the lattice. However, once training is started, all programs to the right and above the starting point should occur in sequence.

The lattice contained in Figure 1 is only the beginning of our language training model because each program box contained in the lattice is only a marker for another more complex system that is called a "procedure lattice." The procedure lattice specifies the content and methods of instruction necessary to produce the behavior described in the covering program box. An example of one procedure lattice is contained in the following figures. This lattice specifies the sequence of training that is potentially sufficient to establish pivot-open phrases. There are four steps in the procedure to establish the initial pivot-open phrase: (1) assessing the repertoire to establish the level of pivot-open training, (2) establishing the pivot-open phrase as an imitative response (these two phases are represented in stage 1 contained in Figure 2), (3) establishing the appropriate motor response in the presence of the salient discriminative stimulus (SD). The term salient SD refers to a question or situation that establishes the appropriateness of a particular pivot-open response such as the question, "Where is the ball?" (see Figures 3 and 4) establishing both the motor response and the emission of the pivot-open phrase in the presence of the salient SD (see Figure 5). The next step is to generalize the use of the initially selected pivot across the specified open words, and, subsequently across the other pivots. This latter training procedure is outlined in Figure 5 and indicates a basic recycling of the previous programs across these new forms. Although this program has never been tested empirically, it is not unlike the generalized imitation programs by Baer, Peterson, and Sherman (1967), Metz (1965), and others.

An example of this training procedure would be the pivot "there" in combination with open words such as "ball," "mamma," and "cup." The salient discriminative stimulus would be either the phrase "Where cup?" or "Where is the cup?" depending on the training decision concerning the salient SD. The former approach is supposedly unlike the manner in which adults speak to children but it does minimize the number of discriminations the child must make among the elements of the controlling stimulus. The initial response form to be trained is the echoic response "There

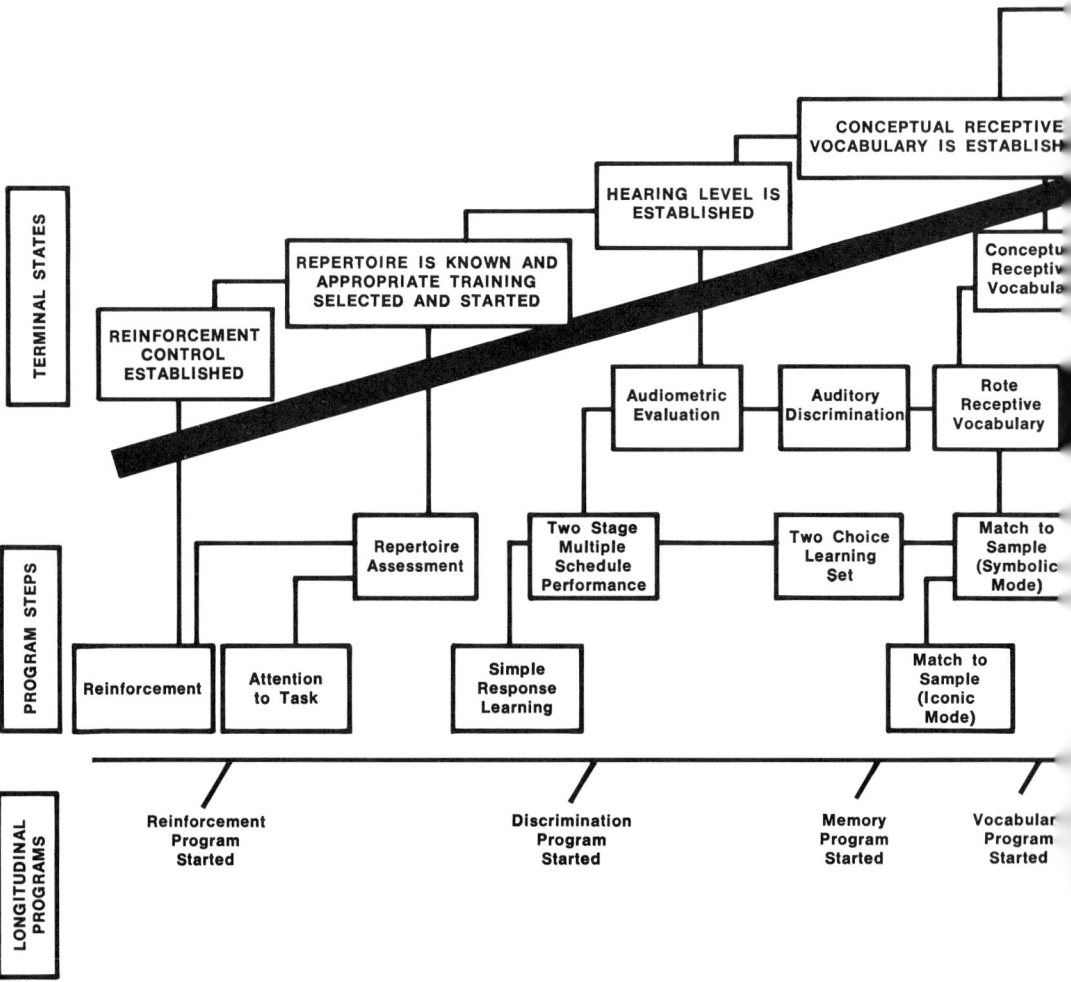

Fig. 1. Lattice of language

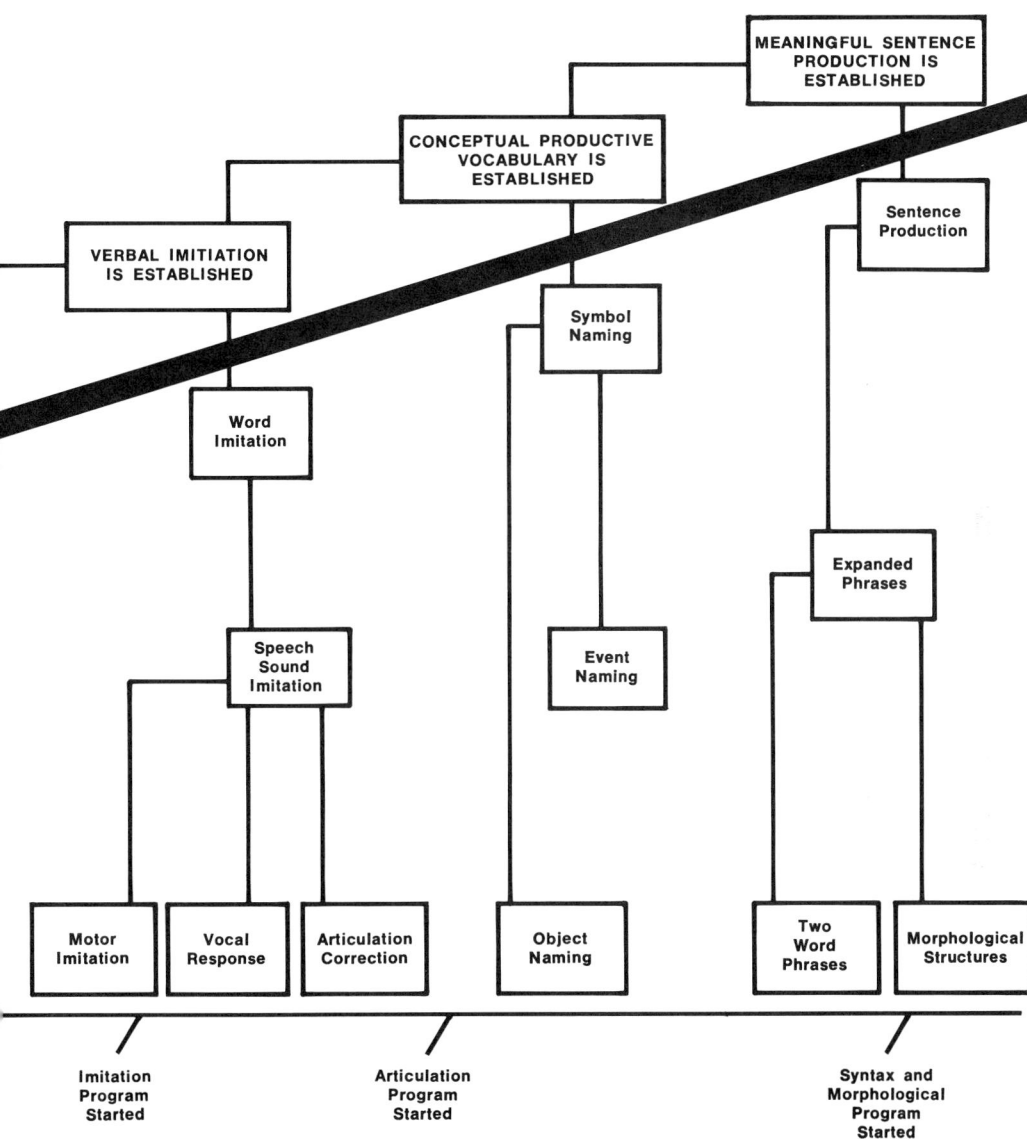

training model.

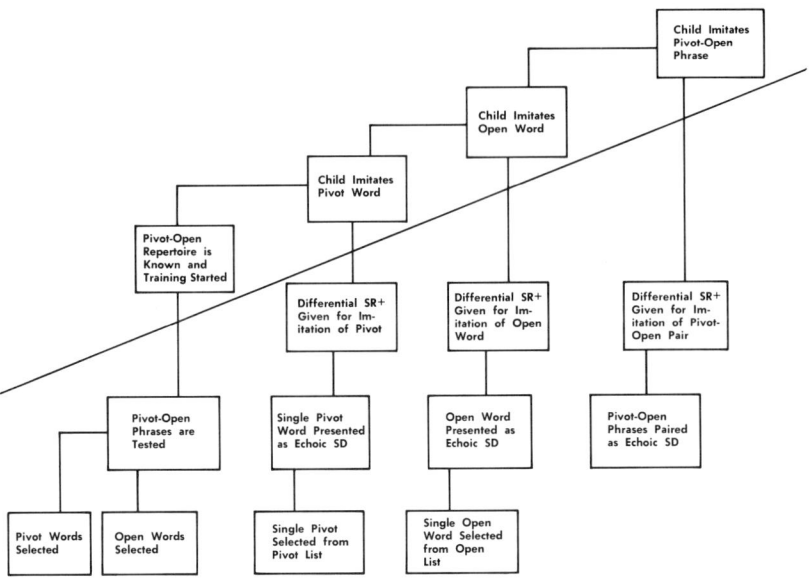

Fig. 2. Stage 1, Pivot—Open Training Procedure.

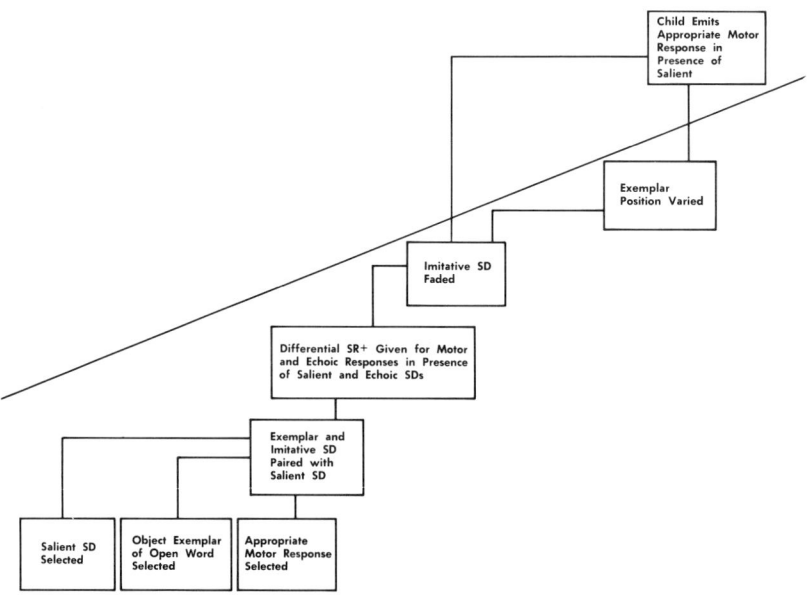

Fig. 3. Stage 2, Pivot—Open Training Procedure.

SYSTEMATIC APPROACH TO LANGUAGE TRAINING

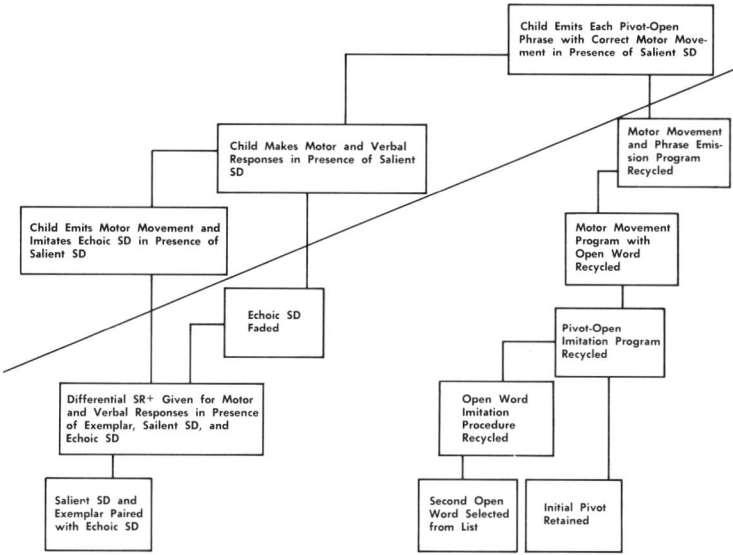

Fig. 4. Stage 3, Pivot—Open Training Procedure.

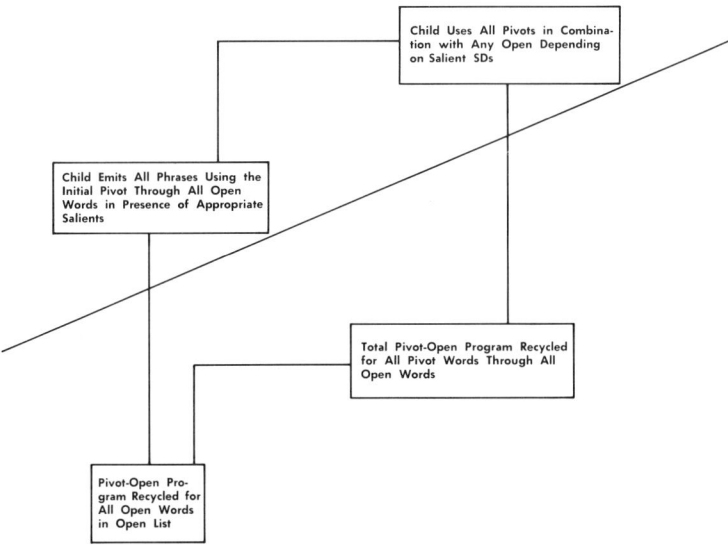

Fig. 5. Stage 4, Pivot—Open Training Procedure.

cup" which is established as a consequence of an echoic stimulus and a differential reinforcement operation. Next the child is shaped to point in the direction of the cup, again using imitation and differential reinforcement. The cup position is varied so that the pointing response is generalized across such variations. Then the pointing response and the verbal response are trained in combination so that in the final step the child says "There cup" and points at the object when the question "Where is the cup?" is asked. To generalize this particular phrase, training is then given with each of the other open words in approximately the same way until the child correctly uses the phrase "There ———!" across open words in response to the question "Where is the ———?" A contrast pivot could then be trained which would increase the number of SDs to which the child would have to be made sensitive. For example, in the contrast responses "Here cup!" and "There cup!" the additional SD would be the distance from the child. Distance could be made discriminative by using "here" when the object can be directly touched and "there" when the object is at a distance that does not allow touching.

This illustration provides some major clues to the relationship between the operant paradigm and the competence position described in the preceding chapter. Each specific outcome of the pivot-open phrase training can be represented as an SD-response-reinforcement chain. Taken alone, this fact is of little importance in language training since any parrot can be trained to perform in this manner. The key feature of this model is that as the training progresses, each subsequent step involves a change in the antecedent stimulus, the reinforced response, or both. Such changes are critical if a generative terminal state is to be achieved. These changes also appear to have a structure which must be followed. For example, if the pivot words are changed too frequently, additional training may be required to maintain the full repertoire. If they are changed too infrequently, the control of the antecedent stimuli may be lost. In the first variation, we are straining the memory capabilities of the child, while in the second we have established only an undiscriminated free operant in which the child emits the key phrase (i.e., "There ball!") without regard to the question being asked. Knowing when a second pivot should be introduced as a contrast has relevance to the learning of the full set of pivot-open phrases. In most areas, a given moment of training can be best understood and managed as an operant contingency structure. The sequence of changes contained in the training must be specified by the structure of the content being taught.

The area of speech sound development offers another example of this structure-training relationship. Imitation is one of the more frequently used mechanisms to establish repertoires. It is difficult to get a child to emit behavior if it is necessary to always pick out approximations and reinforce them. If use can be made of the very powerful tool of imitation, it is possible to speed up the performance aspects of learning as opposed to the competence aspects. One means for training speech-sound imitation is to select a specific sound and reinforce it in the presence of a physically similar model. This procedure is continued until the model becomes discriminative for the occurrence of this sound. A second convenient sound that is discriminable from the first is then selected and the process is repeated, followed by some rehearsal of the initial sound. As the procedure is continued and new sounds are added, the acquisition process becomes increasingly more rapid until the child imitates new sounds immediately following the first presentation of a novel model. This terminal state basically defines generalized verbal imitation or echoic behavior (Skinner, 1957). However, several procedural alternatives are available to training this class of behavior, depending on the view of imitation held by the investigator-trainer. For example, Baer, Peterson, and Sherman (1967) originally maintained that the similarity between the modeled and imitated responses became discriminative for reinforcement to the subject. In this light, the order in which responses were trained or the structure of the responses used in training does not matter. Responses that teach the discrimination of similarity are adequate. Another view presented by Gewirtz and Stingle (1968) assumed that imitation involved a class of responses under the control of intermittent extrinsic reinforcement. Here again the order or content of training does not influence either the attainment of the defined terminal state or the efficiency of training. However, a third approach to imitation based on a linguistic account of speech sound development does affect order and content of training. This is seen in the distinctive feature model of phonology initially presented by Jakobson, Fant, and Halle (1963) and elaborated more recently by Chomsky and Halle (1968). The assumption in this position is that speech sounds are compounds or bundles of component features. When a child learns or is taught one of these compounds which contain all relevant features he will be able to generalize to all novel responses constructed from those features, thus acquiring a generalized repertoire. There is some descriptive data available to support this approach, including the work of Miller and Nicely (1955) and Bricker (1967). While there may be no differences among the three approaches in terms of how a single stimulus-response form of behavior is trained, there are variations in the sequence and structure of content to be taught. These variations may relate to the validity and efficiency of training.

From these two illustrations it is apparent that procedural lattices are structured on the basis of a behavioral technology and some integrated assumptions about the structure of behavior in each area. Some of these assumptions about structure can be derived from sources such as the language acquisition model presented in the preceding chapter, and from linguistic, psycholinguistic, and cognitive theory. When there are different assumptions about the behavior in question, then different procedural lattices can be constructed to represent these variations and to then compare them empirically. This brings us into model evaluation. There are four major ways in which models as procedural lattices can be evaluated—validity, generality, efficiency, and facility.

Validity pertains to the extent to which a given procedure can be used to approximate the defined terminal state regardless of the methods and materials used or the number and characteristics of the persons being trained. The bulk of the behavior modification literature is at this stage in model building. For example, Wolf, Risley, and Mees (1964), Sidman and Stoddard (1966), Bijou (1968), and Lovaas (1968) presented descriptions of procedures that were tested on only a few children over a long period of time and with continual modification of the training structure to accommodate the behavioral characteristics of the children being trained. These modifications ultimately led to valid procedures in each of the behavioral domains investigated by these researchers. Small numbers of subjects and flexible shaping designs are both logical and desirable in the development of a procedural lattice. Conversely, if we do not know how to precisely train in a given domain of behavior, it seems senseless to use rigidly fixed procedures and large groups of subjects in the research. However, a demonstration of procedural validity does not represent a complete test of a training model.

One criticism of behavior modification research (Bricker, 1970) is that the children on whom procedures were tested were not randomly selected from a defined population and, in the absence of this control, replications of procedural validity with four out of four children not randomly selected do not represent procedural generality. To properly index this parameter, one needs to select an adequate random sample of children from a defined population and test the procedure in a prescribed way. The probability of success in terms of the proportion of children who reach the terminal state as a consequence of the procedure will provide an estimate of generality.

The third model-testing procedure is in the area of efficiency. It is here that cognitive and linguistic theory have an important place. An analogy may help to clarify the relation of this procedure to the two previously discussed. A procedural lattice can be viewed as a path along which behavior is moved to a well-defined destination. However, in many cases of retarded development, we are exploring a wilderness between the child's current repertoire and the defined terminal behavior. The research problem resembles trail blazing in which the validity of the map (i.e., the procedural lattice) can be assumed if even a single person reaches the destination. The replicability derives from the extent to which others may follow with a stated probability of success. The problem of efficiency is dependent upon whether someone else can find an easier or quicker path to the same destination. Continuing with the linguistic theory can be viewed as a few potentially helpful landmarks that might facilitate the task of developing more efficient paths. For example, does the use of the pivot-open phrase structure produce a more efficient approximation to sentence production than a procedure that assumes children should be learning adult grammatical forms from the beginning, thus focusing on training of pronouns, adjectives, and functor words as well as nouns and verbs? Does an assumption of distinctive features in speech-sound development produce a more efficient procedure than one that assumes that speech sounds are equipotential? These are questions which, if answered, should evaluate and improve the efficiency of the training model.

Procedural efficiency also brings into focus some major variations between the language acquisition model presented and discussed in the preceding chapter and the language training model discussed here. Reinforcement and imitation are critical to the application of the language training model but are not held in high repute in the language acquisition model. Fodor (1966) has discussed this distinction between the two models. The importance of imitation and extrinsic reinforcement in normal language acquisition is an unanswered question, but for those who work with retarded children, the alternative methods cannot be derived from the acquisition model. Imitation is the most efficient means for establishing a verbal repertoire, and reinforcement is necessary for modifying and maintaining it. A second distinction between these two models is the order of training. However, there are surprisingly few differences. Discussion in the previous chapter did indicate that the language acquisition model leads to articulation correction and speech sound development in the context of words, while the training model calls for the inductive construction of words out of speech sounds. Fortunately, these are procedural variations that can be checked experimentally.

The final test of a procedural lattice is facility. The importance of a language training model is the extent to which it can be used by relatively untrained parents, teachers, or cottage aides. There is a strong possibility that a valid, replicable procedure can only be used by highly trained personnel. This limits the number of children who can benefit. The process of assessing the facility of a program actually involves recycling the three preceding processes. First a small number of representative persons are selected and given the necessary training to use the procedural lattices. Then they are watched closely as they apply the techniques to determine where alterations in procedure have to be made to accommodate problems. As the procedures gain validity in the hands of these relatively untrained persons, they are checked for generality with a larger group. Finally, these two sets of data can be combined and used to suggest additional variations to improve efficiency. Such aspects as the unit of behavior selected for measurement, the methods of measuring rate, use of differential reinforcement, and techniques of fading may have to be made less precise and less technical in order to increase the facility of the procedure.

One feature of this approach to language training is most important. A system of language training that contains a description of hierarchically arranged terminal states, programs necessary to attain those terminal states, and a set of procedural lattices that define the methods and content of instruction becomes a theory of the target behavior. In the final form, such a system can be used to predict, control, and explain human behavior. In addition, the system becomes a behavioral microscope for looking at damaged organisms and specifying the form and severity of the disability. Both of these prospects are highly speculative, but the concept of a program as a theory is perhaps consistent with what Skinner had in mind when he stated: "Beyond the collection of uniform relationships lies the need for a formal representation of the data reduced to a minimal number of terms . . . It will not stand in the way of our search for functional relations because it will arise only after relevant variables have been found and studied. Though it may be difficult to understand, it will not be easily misunderstood, and it will have none of the objectionable effects of the theories here considered" (1959, p. 69).

SUMMARY OF DISCUSSION

QUESTION: Have you tried any of this?

BRICKER: Our first attempt was with reinforcement control; simple response, simple stimulus. We took a group of 40 severely retarded children and went through four different procedures for establishing generalized tone control over a simple response. We then moved into discrimination learning and discrimination learning set. We used this response repertoire as the basis for receptive vocabulary training so the child could use consequences differentially as an information base and make decisions about word-object associations.

We are in verbal and motor imitation now, trying to study the component structure as opposed to randomly selected responses in training. We select responses according to the component structure they may have as I explained during the presentation. So we have worked with verbal imitation, motor imitation, receptive vocabulary, and operant audiometry.

Consequently, parts of it have been tried. On the other hand, the part I emphasized in the presentation is something that hasn't been tried. But there is nothing magical about these proposed extensions; they follow logically from work done in imitation.

QUESTION: What is this receptive vocabulary?

BRICKER: You use words as an SD for choice. In other words, words are trained to operate as discriminative stimuli for choice in a two-choice situation.

QUESTION: They are not linked to any kind of referents?

BRICKER: Yes, they are. The child is presented with objects, and the objects are varied. If you want to deal with rote receptive, you deal with 25 objects. If you want to deal with concepts, you establish a set of stimuli that carry on irrelevant dimensions and maintain relevant dimensions. The discouraging thing about working with really low-functioning children is that we haven't found very much evidence for generalization. We found a bit in tone generalization in that we were able to get responses across the variations in tone. But when we moved into words the receptive vocabulary didn't generalize.

QUESTION: What other concept are you teaching?

BRICKER: Dog, cat, spoon, lady, man, and other common word clauses.

QUESTION: Will the children spontaneously emit these? If you had the children in a room for a while and some of these objects were around, would they spontaneously emit the words?

BRICKER: Some of them would. Of 50-some children with whom we have worked some of them do have that kind of repertoire.

QUESTION: But as a result of what you do, would they emit the words?

BRICKER: Yes, we set it up so the aides are doing things on the ward consistent with what we were doing in the laboratory.

QUESTION: I assume you have a pointing response or reaching response for building this receptive vocabulary.

BRICKER: Yes. It's actually moving an object in some cases, and we go to a two-dimensional "press panel" system in others.

QUESTION: It's built into your program where you establish pivot-open? You also establish pointing response?

BRICKER: That was an optional procedure, but it is not necessary. If we want the pivot "Here cup" and "There cup," we would probably establish touchability as the SD for the response "here" and "there."

QUESTION: Would you pick your pivot-open words to use from this vocabulary in the receptive level that you have established?

BRICKER: Yes. We would be working with a critical receptive vocabulary. We would work on the same vocabulary with expression or production. We would also work with the same words when we move into reading. So we really have to index the vocabulary early to determine useful concepts and superordinate classes.

QUESTION: To follow through on a previous question, did you find that the environment supported what you did in your choice task? And were there other places in the environment where you could see the effects of what you did?

BRICKER: We didn't index them. However, many such questions have been asked in our laboratory, one to one, and with our own definition of what generalization is.

QUESTION: Do you expect generalization to a new object from learning "lady"? Would you expect an acquisition process to take place? Do you plan to test to see if the child is generalizing an ability to acquire new pivots, pivot-opens from this experience?

BRICKER: Yes. I don't know what to expect, since it has not been done, but we would hope for generalization in the sense that the child would combine all the pivots with new open words. That is the one that would be most anticipated. The second would be that he selects out new pivots and varies that system across open words.

QUESTION: Is this the most efficient way to get even the one child to reach that terminal state, applying your other criterion of efficiency?

BRICKER: I don't think we have really developed our training programs in explicit fashion so we can say what their procedural structure is. The systems analysis approach, this particular one, makes explicit what the procedures are so we can contrast two approaches to find out why one might be working for one out of 20 children, and another is effective for 8 out of 20 of the same defined population. We have a lot of the validational data to keep us going, but we have not yet systematized our approach toward more efficient procedures.

QUESTION: Is this not a pitfall you can fall into? If you find the procedure valid for a child or even for a group of children, you may make the assumption that this is a valid procedure. If it is then incorporated in teacher aide training or in parent training, they may find that it is not really the most efficient way to reach the terminal state.

BRICKER: There are cases of this. But the point is that we have two contrasts that may have different efficiencies. The environments may determine the effectiveness.

QUESTION: Do you test these on the same children?

BRICKER: They can be tested on the same children, or we may take a group of children and divide them in some legitimate way. Our work has been based on multiple group comparisons.

QUESTION: How do the experimenters or the training people relate to the people in the natural environment? Is there some point in your program where a child is introduced to the environment so that environment itself can take over and the child finds himself in the same position as a child who didn't need special training in the first place? Would these children normally be fed back into the environment itself? In a training procedure would you normally keep a child outside the environment while building in the successive stages?

BRICKER: The kinds of environments I hope to have contact with in the next few years are natural in the sense that every environment is natural—an institutional environment and a community environment where you can deal with the parents in the home and the teacher monitoring the child's behavior in the classroom. My view is that you take a child aside only for individual tutorial work to establish a repertoire that doesn't seem to be establishable in the more complex setting. Perhaps we can look to some of our teaching machines to do some of this for us. As we make the processes of instruction explicit, persons who are less well-trained should be able to use them.

QUESTION: Are there periods of time at least in some cases where children are left alone in their natural environment to see if there is any regression, loss, or even acquisition?

BRICKER: Yes, we need to know if we can expect the child to start looking for examples of a new response form. And we need to know if what we do in training makes it more probable that he will, in fact, seek out new uses of a learned structure.

QUESTION: Don't you have a potential confounding effect with respect to what happens in the ward when you are using objects that are very likely to be present in the ward? Suppose you used objects they did not normally encounter. Would this perhaps make your conclusions about the effects of training a little more valid?

BRICKER: Yes, it would have an impact on us. Some of the examples contained in our training manual were the same as those we were researching in the laboratory. So while we did use a pretest-post test design, we also had imbedded individual analyses, so if anything irregular happened, we could see it.

QUESTION: I would take issue with such validity as far as it seems to place all of the power in your training procedures. The assumption is that if the child makes it through the program his success is somehow a function of the training procedure. That may be true in one sense, but there has to be interaction between certain status characteristics or whatever the child brings with him to that situation. It may be that the training procedure you have devised is capable of moving one child you selected through. It may also have relevance to no other children. So your validation ought to be matching a particular training procedure to particular assessed characteristics that the child brings with him.

BRICKER: This can be done automatically through generality and efficiency designs.

QUESTION: I think you pose interaction questions which are different than the search for methods. You search for methods as a function of characteristics, starting with that as a preconception. I think that's a different sort of model.

BRICKER: Yes.

QUESTION: Just one other comment in relation to this imitative repertoire. Even in the Baer, Peterson, and Sherman article which has been referred to, they brought their subjects to high levels of imitative proficiency, then moved into the language realm. My recollection was that in every instance they had to drop way, way back. With one subject, for example, after getting the child to chain off very, very long imitative responses, four or five movements, they had to drop back and start into manipulation, physical manipulation of the face, to get the sounds P and T. So it was clear that they weren't teaching an imitative repertoire. It breaks down at some point, at least between vocal and nonvocal dimensions. Do you have any reactions?

BRICKER: I remember in one of the earlier studies that Baer did, they had the motor responses going pretty well and so they started with just doing /ah/ as a response. You recall they couldn't get that. It didn't have immediate novel production. And so they got up, turned a circle, and at the end of turning around a full circle they went /ah/ and the child got up, went full circle, and imitated that, but when it got to specific speech sounds, they had to go back to prompts.

But this again would reinforce the idea of a distinctive feature model, that the child's repertoire at the moment or imitation level did not imbed the features associated with sound production. That's why I am so interested in distinctive features.

QUESTION: There is one aspect of imitation that is implicit in everything you discuss but you don't make it explicit in this discussion. You talk about imitation as a stimulus mode for getting a response in a repertoire, and certainly that is one major function. But it is quite clear, too, that as you go through your various programs you are also using imitation as a stimulus control to get certain responses emitted at an appropriate time in terms of the training and context and the association context that you are getting. You are using imitation in different functions, one as a basic topography-oriented stimulus and another simply as an efficiency measure to get certain responses emitted at certain times when you can manipulate things you want to control. It is a powerful way of evoking a specific response at a specific time. And it functions quite a bit differently than it does when you use it early to create a new response topography.

BRICKER: Yes, we have the salient stimuli operating. The echoic is a second-order stimulus to get that response going in the presence of the salient.

QUESTION: It is clear how you use the procedures to assess validity, but how do you assess the validity of the terminal states or sequence of terminal states that you have?

BRICKER: We attempt to get motor imitation before we train verbal imitation, so if a child is not imitating motor responses we can test the extent to which he will learn verbal imitation without motor imitation as a prerequisite or precursor. Or we may take the same child and probe with motor and then verbal-motor then verbal. We have to look at the left-to-right and bottom-to-top structure as an empirical question, too. We don't know what is necessary in there. Our guess is that we are talking about an approximate language training sequence which in many cases is based on evidence we have in the literature.

QUESTION: Back to generalization. If you define a terminal state as something the child can use in his environment, you have to think of generalization. If you are teaching receptive vocabulary that is one thing. But if you are going to get the child to respond receptively in the ward, that is another thing.

BRICKER: That is not the way I was using generalization. I was talking about a set number of training events which are varied in some specific way.

QUESTION: Are you doing nothing about the other kind?

BRICKER: As a person trying to deal with the retarded and trying to get improvement in performance, I am interested in the kind of training event it takes to get him to use language in another location where it is more practical for him to do so than in a laboratory room speaking into a tape recorder. Once we get the form of behavior and it is pretty well controlled, it seems to me it is possible to make it functional, so I don't have any qualms about that. My concern is whether I can establish the repertoire and whether it has a good, flexible characteristic or capability. If I can't get it in a laboratory, I doubt I am going to be able to get it on a ward, but I am not sure of that.

QUESTION: Regarding pivot-open training. You are arbitrarily selecting words that children have used as pivot words before. One of the striking things about this is that these words are different for different children. Therefore, you can assume there is nothing inherent in the word itself which makes it a pivot word. Suppose the stimulus is "Where cup?" You're looking for the response "There cup." Would you also reinforce "Cup there," or would you tend to try to inhibit that response?

BRICKER: I would make some training adjustments to get the response in the other order.

QUESTION: If you started with "Cup there" and then you tried to introduce "Is it," "Cup, is it there?" wouldn't make a lot of sense in communications. But if you insisted on putting these in proper order, then you introduce the additional vocabulary to be grammatically correct.

BRICKER: If we want the variations to be "There is the cup," "The cup is there," we start with one of those forms first and build in a second form.

QUESTION: You are apparently choosing the most difficult point to work—namely with children who have a generalized learning difficulty. In many instances you apparently don't get learning at all. Wouldn't you have a better test if you use children at least somewhat up the line?

BRICKER: That's a question I've asked myself every day for the last four years. I started working with autistic children in Oregon some years ago. They gave indications of very rapid change. So we got a little bit carried away with our success. We thought we could probably work with many severely retarded children in the same way. We quickly learned that wasn't true. So I am interested now in going up the scale into trainable mentally retarded (TMR) children with some language functions already operating and with younger children. We find though that about 20 to 25 per cent of our mute children seven years and older do learn language, but it is still a pretty small percentage in terms of the amount of effort we expend.

REFERENCES

Baer, D. M., Peterson, R. F., and Sherman, J. A. The development of imitation by reinforcing behavioral similarity to a model. *J. Exp. Anal. Behavior,* 1967, *10,* 405–416.

Bijou, S. W. Studies in the experimental development of left-right concepts in retarded children using fading techniques. In N. R. Ellis (Ed.), *International review of research in mental retardation.* Vol. 3. New York: Academic Press, 1968. Pp. 66–96.

Bricker, W. A. Errors in the echoic behaviors of preschool children. *J. Speech Hearing Res.,* 1967, *10,* 67–76.

Bricker, W. A. Identifying and modifying behavioral deficits. *Am. J. Ment. Deficiency,* 1970, *75,* 16–21.

Chomsky, N. Review of Skinner's *Verbal behavior. Language,* 1959, *35,* 26–58.

Chomsky, N. *Aspects of the theory of syntax.* Cambridge: MIT Press, 1965.

Chomsky, N., and Halle, M. *The sound pattern of English.* New York: Harper and Row, 1968.

Fodor, J. A. How to learn to talk: Some simple ways. In F. Smith, and G. A. Miller (Eds.), *The genesis of language.* Cambridge: MIT Press, 1966.

Gewirtz, J. L., and Stingle, K. G. Learning of generalized imitation on the basis for identification. *Psychol. Rev.,* 1968, *75,* 374–397.

Jakobson, R., Fant, C. G., and Halle, M. *Preliminaries to speech analysis: The distinctive features and their correlates.* (2nd ed.) Cambridge: MIT Press, 1963.

Katz, J. J. Mentalism in linguistics. In L. A. Jakobovits and M. S. Miron (Eds.), *Readings in the psychology of language.* Englewood Cliffs, New Jersey: Prentice-Hall, 1967.

Lenneberg, E. H. *Biological foundations of language.* New York: Wiley, 1967.

Lovaas, O. I. A behavior therapy approach to the treatment of childhood schizophrenia. In J. P. Hill (Ed.), *Minnesota symposia on child psychology*, Minneapolis: University of Minnesota Press, 1967. Pp. 108–159.

Lovaas, O. I. A program for the establishment of speech in psychotic children. In H. Sloane and B. MacAulay (Eds.), *Operant procedures in remedial speech and language training*. Boston: Houghton Mifflin, 1968.

McNeill, D. Developmental psycholinguistics. In F. Smith and G. Miller (Eds.), *The genesis of language*. Cambridge, Mass.: The M.I.T. Press, 1966.

Metz, J. R. Conditioning generalized imitation in autistic children. *J. Exp. Child Psychol.*, 1965, *2*, 389–399.

Miller, G. A., and Nicely, P. A. An analysis of perceptual confusions among some English consonants. *J. Acoust. Soc. Amer.*, 1955, *27*, 338–352.

Sidman, M., and Stoddard, L. T. Programming perception and learning for retarded children. In N. R. Ellis (Ed.), *International review of research in mental retardation*. Vol. 2. New York: Academic Press, 1966. Pp. 152–208.

Skinner, B. F. *Verbal behavior*. New York: Appleton-Century-Crofts, 1957.

Skinner, B. F. *Cumulative record*. New York: Appleton-Century-Crofts, 1959.

Wolf, M. M., Risley, T. R., and Mees, H. I. Application of operant conditioning procedures to the behavior problems of an autistic child. *Behavior Res. Ther.*, 1964, *1*, 305–312.

ADVENTURES IN SIMPLISTIC GRAMMAR

DONALD M. BAER
University of Kansas

DOUG GUESS
Kansas Neurological Institute

JAMES A. SHERMAN
University of Kansas

DONALD M. BAER earned his Ph.D. in psychology at the University of Chicago in 1957. Since that time he has taught courses in human development, conducted research, and published extensively in fields related to psychology and child development. He is currently a research associate in the University of Kansas Bureau of Child Research, and a professor of human development and psychology. At the time this work was reported he was associate editor of the Journal of Experimental Child Psychology, *a member of the board of editors of the* Journal of Experimental Analysis of Behavior, *and associate editor of the* Journal of Applied Behavior Analysis.

Consider the case of an average toddler who has begun to use words. Many of these words he imitates, having heard his parents use them repeatedly. This toddler in addition is something of a thrower, and in consequence he has often heard mother explain that a plaything is broken because he "threw it." This fact, together with the distinctiveness of his throwing response and its close correlation with despairing cries of "Don't throw it!" has produced unusually early stimulus control of these verbal operants: throwing by the child now is often accompanied by his comment "throw it," and queries about the whereabouts of past missiles yield a smug "threw it!" from him.

In recent years, wandering teams of psycholinguists and tape recorders have noted such early interactions, pointed to the childish but correct organizations of the present and past tense forms of an irregular verb, and cannily waited for more to happen. And indeed as a few months pass, a variety of other verbs do appear in the child's repertoire, in both present and past tense forms. However, most of these verbs indicate past tense by ending in /d/, /t/ or /əd/. And so there comes a day when the tape recording displays not the familiar and correct "threw" of the child's earlier speech, but a new utterance—"throwed."

Should students of language development argue that language is merely another form of operant behavior, and thus exists primarily because of its relevant conditioning history (Bijou and Baer, 1965), then should they not be thrown by "throwed"? In the simple view, "throwed" has no direct conditioning history. That is, no one has directly shaped "throwed" into the child's repertoire, nor has anyone in his environment even used it for him to imitate. Instead "throwed" appears to be his own invention rather than a passive acquiescence to reinforcement and imitation. However, the child's "throwed" is not an invention without precedent. In fact, he has merely rearranged his "throw" to fit the other verbs he is now using, which most often take the past tense form by adding the /d/ morpheme. Thus, in essence he is a creature of rules, rather than of responses. That is much to be applauded, of course. But the question then becomes, where do these rules originate? Do we teach them, or merely admire them?

Sometimes it is argued that the child is inherently a creature of intrinsic rules, most especially so in the matter of language development—that he is biologically constructed to use such rules (Lenneberg, 1969). Consequently, given minimal exposure to the forms or morphemes his culture uses to exemplify these rules, he should then gallop into a similarly grammatical organization of everything further that he may hear or invent. Thus, our persistent thrower had early acquired his correct "threw" merely as a response, prior to sufficient experience with verbs and time to activate his intrinsic sensitivity to a present tense/past tense rule. Given that experience, however, the rule was catalyzed. It seized upon the morpheme forms usually embodying it, thereby acquired a shape, and promptly reorganized the prior mere-response ("threw") into the same shape ("throwed"). We celebrate the child's acquisition of a grammatical rule, of course. But we recognize a small teaching problem at the same time: we must free "throwed" from the morphemes exemplifying the usual rule in favor of other morphemes ("threw"), which we recondition in the child's repertoire as an exception to the rule, one that he may correctly extend to other verbs such as "blow" and "grow," but not to "snow." We will of course respond to "snew" by conditioning an exception to the exception's rule, in a minature replication of the same basic process we had just completed. Nevertheless, we emphasize that these conditioning adventures are exceptions, and continue to celebrate the fact that language has rules.

Whether rule-bound language is seen as a development biologically ready to emerge under slight environmental urging, or as a development slightly predisposed by biological structure to emerge under the massive contingencies of the language-speaking social environment, becomes a matter of emphasis. However, some emphases are more practical than others. Particularly in the case where a child has had considerable exposure to the language-using social environment but has failed to develop language of his own, emphasis on social contingencies may suggest different action than will emphasis on biological structure. Considerations of biological structure typically lead to the conclusion that this child is structurally deficient. Sometimes that conclusion is tautologically identical to the fact that he does not have much language, rather than a description of his structure. In any event, institutionalization is a likely action. It is an action which recognizes the deficit rather than remediates it. By contrast, emphasis on the role of contingencies in the development of language suggests that we apply better contingencies to the language-deficient child. To do so requires that we know what the appropriate contingencies are, or can be. If we do not know what they are, we need to find out. Fortunately, that is an eminently practical assignment, and it has been pursued with some success this past decade. It needs further pursuit, particularly in the direction of establishing language rules whereby the child will continue to develop, invent, and use his own language in ways that we will understand.

Rule-bound behavior is not a new target of contingency-bound research techniques. The animal laboratory has known for some time that it is possible to teach infrahuman organisms that a triangle is discriminative for reinforcement and that a circle is discriminative for extinction; and it has found that if it teaches this lesson with enough exemplars, there will result positive response to all triangles, and no response to all circles. It is fair to call this rule-bound behavior, in that the resultant pattern of behavior is uniform across triangles and circles never involved in the original training contingencies. It is also reasonable to doubt the extreme significance of this demonstration, in that one circle is much like another, and triangles similarly are not particularly diverse, whereas language is much more complex than a matter of curves and angles. Nevertheless, it is apparent that simple rules can be accomplished by a program of simple contingencies. Such a conclusion reinforces a researcher for asking whether complexity can be analyzed into simplicity, and inevitably he will ask whether somewhat greater complexity can also be analyzed that way, too.

A conservative, unimaginative, or lazy researcher may even approach that greater complexity with the same techniques used before on the lesser complexity. Thus Baer, Peterson, and Sherman (1967) showed that it was possible to teach severely retarded nonimitative children to imitate, simply by teaching them a series of different imitations. Imitation embodies a rule apparently more complex than the one discriminating triangles from circles, for to imitate, you must do as the model does, and the model may do considerably more diverse things than be three-sided or round. Furthermore, imitation seems essential to the establishment of the morphology of language; hence, it is not only respectably complex, it is also relevant. In particular, Baer, Peterson, and Sherman found it possible to teach retarded children to imitate so thoroughly that they would reproduce immediately upon the first demonstration new performances never before involved in their repertoires, and continue to perform these new imitations even though no reinforcement for them was ever offered. Only when reinforcement for all imitations was discontinued did the children's imitations cease, and they were all promptly recovered, previously reinforced and unreinforced alike, when reinforcement was resumed for only some of the child's total repertoire of imitations.

If a child will imitate new demonstrations without direct instruction or shaping, and if he will continue to do so without reinforcement, so long as at least some other imitations are reinforced, then much of the significance of our precocious thrower disappears. If a variety of his verbs earned reinforcement by taking their past tense with /d/, /t/, or /ə d/ endings, then unreinforced instances of the same practice could well appear, and "throwed" should qualify as an unreinforced instance. What is different about the "throwed" case is that a prior usage ("threw") had already been established, and that the behavior was not simple imitation, but was a labeling of actions and answering questions about actions. In the language of operant conditioning, the child was not imitating, but *tacting;* and he had a prior reinforcement history for a different tact in that situation.

Fortunately, to proceed beyond the deliberate establishment of widely generalized imitation into tacting is not an unsolved problem. Research by Lovaas (1967), Risley and Wolf (1965), Bricker and Bricker (1966), and Baer, Peterson, and Sherman (1967) suggests diverse methods for the development of tacting from an imitative base. In brief, these methods reinforce motor imitation and generalize it to a reasonably comprehensive range of performances. Then, those performances are gradually programmed to become head and mouth responses which more and more involve breathing, blowing, and vocalization components, until simple, isolated vocal imitations are well established. Alternatively, with motor imitations well established, simple vocal performances are chained to longer, more complex motor sequences, and commonly will occur in such positions even though they do not occur in isolation. The surrounding, enhancing motor sequence then is gradually diminished over a series of trials, until isolated vocal imitations occur readily without other motor involvement. Given reliable vocal imitation, it is expanded according to the standard techniques of chaining until imitative vocalization of a length and variety suitable to language are being reinforced. At that point, transfer of stimulus control from the experimenter's demonstration to an object to be labeled is programmed. Typically, a verbal prompt by the experimenter is coupled with the visual presentation of the object to be labeled. The child responds in imitation of the experimenter, but through a series of trials, the verbal prompt becomes quieter, briefer, and later. If this fading of the prompt is done gradually enough, with consistent reinforcement for correct performance, the child continues to give the correct vocalization, and finally is producing it simply in answer to the visual presentation of the object to be labeled. Thus, he possesses one topographical label, or tact. The process is repeated for one object after another, and as various labels are mastered, they are evoked in quick but unsystematic alternation, until the child responds reliably to all the objects he has been shown with their corresponding labels. At the end of the process, the child may well acquire new labels for new objects in a single trial, not necessarily reinforced, and will maintain the new label in his repertoire about as well as a college student learning another word of a foreign language for similarly isolated reasons.

Thus, the question becomes: can vocal tacting behavior—specifically, labeling—be given a rule-bound grammatical organization, such that child will use this rule to produce new instances of language which have not been directly trained, nor previously modeled, yet exemplify the rule? And the question continues: will the rule so produced have such organizing power that it will overturn or preempt any prior behavioral organization to which a label might have been subject? These outcomes have been demonstrated in a recent study by Guess, Sailor, Rutherford, and Baer (1969), working with a ten-year-old institutionalized severely retarded girl, Janet, who had exhibited no linguistic behavior since her second year of life. She was successively taught imitation, vocal imitation and labeling, and her labeling was then subjected to a simplistic but nevertheless superordinate organization—the grammatical production of plurals. Guess and his colleagues describe the necessary procedures in these terms:

Janet sat at a table beside the experimenter. Various reinforcers and objects to be used in the study were placed behind a partition near the experimenter but out of Janet's sight. An observer stationed in the observation room recorded data, as did the experimenter.

Stages. Experimental sessions were conducted twice daily and ranged in length from 15 to 45 minutes. Stimuli for the study consisted of various small objects which were placed on the table in front of the subject. The order of object(s) presentation followed a daily, three-stage sequence.

In Stage 1, Janet was shown a single object and asked, "What do you see?" If the object was correctly named in its singular form within 20 seconds of its presentation, she was given a bit of food (ice cream, jello, chocolate or plain milk, or mixed fruit). If she failed to respond within 20 seconds, the experimenter correctly labeled the object, withdrew it from sight for ten seconds, and then presented it again. This was repeated until Janet named the object correctly. (Janet seldom required more than one correction.) If Janet labeled the object incorrectly on its first presentation, the experimenter said "No," and repeated the same procedure. Criterion performance for this stage of the training required three consecutive correct responses.

In Stage 2, Janet was presented with two of the same objects and asked, "What do you see?" Reinforcement was contingent on a plural response. If Janet said the singular, the investigator said "No," stated the correct plural label, and withdrew the objects for 10 seconds. Again, criterion performance was three consecutive correct responses.

A random sequence of single and multiple (two) objects was presented in Stage 3 of the training session. Criterion performance for Stage 3 required a sequence including three correct singular responses intermixed with three correct plural responses, without intervening errors.

Criterion for each stage was to be reached before the next stage was begun. Completion of the third stage constituted the end of a session. Each session was devoted to the training of the singular and plural labels of one item, and each session involved a new item not used before . . .

These three stages with their associated criteria were repeated for each item presented throughout each of the experimental conditions described below . . .

Conditions. In Condition I, Janet was trained to respond correctly with singulars or plurals when presented with single objects or pairs of objects, respectively. In Condition II, the reinforcement contingencies were reversed, such that she then was required to give a plural response to single objects and a singular response to pairs of objects. Condition III returned to the normal contingencies originally used under Condition I . . .

Irregular and different plurals. During Condition III, Janet was shown five objects whose labels are governed by irregular or different plural rules than her training had embodied (e.g., man–men, leaf–leaves, glass–glasses).

These probes were conducted to determine if her experimental plural training would control her production of normally irregular plurals, and thus substantiate the original observations that she did not have a prior plural usage. These probes were conducted at the ends of five consecutive sessions late in Condition III, one object per session. Correct responses to single object presentations were reinforced; responses to pairs were never reinforced.

The results of these procedures are shown in Figure 1. This graph represents the percentage of trials performed correctly by Janet in meeting the three successive criteria of each new label presented to her. It is apparent that she accomplished errorless production of plurals of each new item, and maintained perfect use of those plurals during interspersed use of their singular forms, starting with the third word taught during Condition I and continuing for the seven words programmed thereafter. Thus, Janet displayed several of the criteria characterizing a grammatical child. She produced novel language items; specifically, the untaught plurals of new labels presented to her only in the singular; and she produced these novel items according to a rule which had exemplified her first teachings. Thus, in this simplistic way, she was organizing her own language repertoire, but in accordance with the grammar

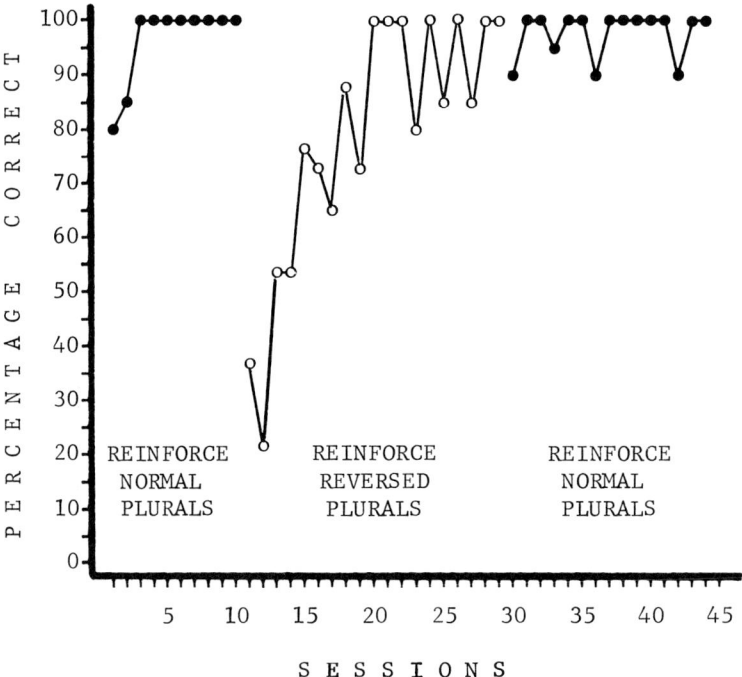

Fig. 1. Percentage of trials performed correctly by Janet in meeting the three successive criteria of each new label presented to her.

specified by her teachers and understandable by them. It would seem likely that she could continue doing this indefinitely into the future.

This graph also shows that Janet's rule was what the experimental contingencies defined it to be. For when those contingencies were reversed during Condition II, Janet reversed her rule, achieving errorless performance on the tenth word. That is, she labeled single objects in the plural, and pairs of objects in the singular. Of the nine words which followed during this condition, three showed some errors, but none of these errors involved the correct (i.e., singular) labeling of a pair of objects on their first presentation. When Condition III returned to the familiar contingencies for singular and plural labels of Condition I, Janet promptly returned to her typically perfect production of new plurals. Of the 15 words involved in Condition III, four showed some errors, but none of these involved errors in labeling the first pair of any new item with the plural form.

Much later in this study, when Janet was still proceeding according to the standard pluralization rule of English, she was presented with four words she had learned during Condition II and had not used since. That is, in the midst of a series of words being pluralized in the standard way she was shown items which she had learned some days earlier, according to a reversed pluralization rule. When she had last labeled each of these objects, she had answered its single presentation with its plural label, and its presentation as a pair with its singular label. Now she labeled them, without hesitation or error, according to the *current* rule. In other words, the rule exemplified in current training completely overrode the reversed organization originally taught to her for those words. Thus, Janet simulated the performance of the precocious thrower with whose case this argument began. Just as he had abandoned a directly taught "threw" in favor of a generalized "throwed," so Janet had abandoned a directly trained pluralization for its generalized opposite.

We argue that Janet's performance merited the labels "generative" and "grammatical" for these reasons. There can be no argument but that these accomplishments by her represent the most simplistic case of grammar, and of surface grammar at that, in the terms that Chomsky (1967) and other psycholinguists have made common. Consequently, we have repeated this study, and have readily obtained the same effects. Thereupon, we have attempted slightly more complex developments of surface grammar, with essentially similar designs. Our data demonstrate simplistically generative grammatical accomplishment in the case of adjective-noun phrases, noun suffixes, present tense/past tense usage, and the receptive transpositional use of comparative and superlative forms of adjectives. Our subjects uniformly have been drawn from the ranks of institutionalized retardates who for many years previously had shown little or no linguistic skill or organization. Thus, Janet's study proves to be typical and prototypical. As a group, these studies then contribute to the context with which this argument opened: a rule-bound organization of language can be achieved in language-deficient children by techniques no more complicated than reinforcement and imitation applied to a sequence of items which are no more than ordinary exemplars of the desired rule. In following these rules, the subjects of our studies develop, expand, and invent their own small language, but do so in ways that are constantly understandable by us, their relevant language community. To the extent that they can do so, they relieve us of further direct teaching of every organizational detail of future instances of the grammatical cases they now know. Thus, to that extent, they represent an experimental analysis of generative surface grammar.

Whether or not they can represent an experimental analysis of the complete language of the normal speaker remains to be seen. The linguistic analysis of language appears to be aimed at the statement of a more profound grammar, one located in the abstract "depth" below surface grammar, and meant to account for the production of every sentence variation any of us are capable of emitting. However, surface grammar accounts for some fraction of the sentences we emit; obviously, the more surface grammar that proves subject to experimental analysis as described here, the more of the totality of normal language will have been analyzed for a possible (but not necessarily typical) acquisition process. So far, that experimental analysis has repetitively pointed to the adequacy of simple, reiterative application of imitation and differential reinforcement techniques to a simple series of exemplars of the (surface) grammatical rule under study. Possibly, more complex cases of surface grammar will prove amenable to the same simple analysis. If so, a highly pertinent question will become, *what* fraction of our complete sentence-emitting behavior thereby is analyzed? If the fraction is large enough, the role of a deeper grammatical structure, while not denied, becomes at least less pressing to know, and the developmental analysis of language acquisition may, to whatever extent the fraction testifies, become integrated with behavioral processes clearly involved in many other learned repertoires of human capability.

SUMMARY OF DISCUSSION

QUESTION: Have you given any thought to why the studies of imitation produce generative stimulus control whereas in most studies of stimulus control generality is not achieved?

BAER: Perhaps the fact that we are dealing with a complex stimulus dimension—that is, one which has many dimensions within it—is critical here. I can teach a child to do what I do (that is one way to describe imitation). If what I do is extremely diverse, and yet he learns, across that diversity, to do virtually anything I do, then I have very complex stimulus control, compared to the usual case in which stimulus control is examined.

QUESTION: Isn't it possible that you've been able to direct their attention to something more specific rather than something more complex so that they can pick out that specificity from all the different situations in which it occurs?

BAER: The specificity of imitation *could* be put this way: The results of what the model does, and the results of what the imitator does, considered as stimuli, have only minimal difference between them. But since the stimuli which are to be minimally different are so diverse, then the imitator's appreciation of minimal differences has to be correspondingly diverse.

QUESTION: Could you give us a better picture of this child's language skills before you got her? I gather from what you said that she was able to say words.

BAER: Her records show that at the age of two she had begun to display the kind of language two-year-olds do, but it had stopped abruptly. She was institutionalized a few years thereafter. In the institution she had shown no *language* behavior of any sort during the past four years. When we first started with her she would scream and make the usual mechanical vocal sounds—burps and what not—but we heard nothing from her we could call language.

QUESTION: You went from that to singulars and plurals? I don't understand.

BAER: No, we went to motor imitation; then vocal imitation; then labeling; and *then* singulars and plurals. At the point at which this singular-plural study started, I would say the child represented an investment of between 50 and 100 experimental hours. Many of those hours were devoted to the simultaneous enhancement of her vocal imitation and the suppression of a tantrum skill (which she possessed to a beautiful degree.)

QUESTION: Isn't the much more impressive thing seen in getting her to the labeling point, never mind the singulars and plurals?

BAER: Yes. But in that, we were not breaking new ground. Lovaas, Risley and Wolf, and Bricker and Bricker, among others, had shown already how to accomplish that. We were following the Risley and Wolf and Lovaas paradigms. The fact that the third word taught to her as a singular-plural case produced perfect behavior and the seven words following that produced perfect behavior should always be understood in the context of the preceding 50 to 100 hours of experimental training.

QUESTION: For someone who has almost no linguistic skills, 50 to 100 hours really doesn't seem like much. Is that your idea of what she was like before you got her—absolutely nothing or almost nothing?

BAER: When we started with her, we attempted to evoke language and particularly plurals. We failed. That is, of course, a weak statement. Perhaps we didn't try hard enough or in the correct way. But no one who knew her in the institution ever described her as having any language capabilities. She was essentially a screamer.

QUESTION: Do you think you could indiscriminately pick children and invest 50 hours in them and do this?

BAER: Let me have up to 200 hours and I'll spot you nine out of ten.

QUESTION: In your answer to the question about generalized imitative behavior, did you mean that to be a *different* animal from stimulus generalization?

BAER: Warren Steinman at the University of Illinois is pursuing (1970) work which will show that instances of generalized imitation, those which are never reinforced, are discriminated by the child as nonreinforced. The child will show (to put it loosely) that he knows these are to be nonreinforced, yet he will continue to imitate them. For example: give him a choice of two responses, one of which in past history always has been reinforced, and the other which in his past history never has been reinforced, instruct him he may imitate either of the two, and (Steinman reports) he will imitate the one which in the past has been reinforced. Similarly, latencies to perform when there is no choice will be pretty clearly differential between those previously reinforced and those previously unreinforced. That can be taken as evidence that there is no lack of discrimination as to whether performance will or won't be reinforced. Yet the unreinforced performance maintains.

QUESTION: Does this generalize to other forms of behavior, too, or just to the verbal imitation? If you did something else, nonverbal, would they imitate it?

BAER: There is some interaction between ordinary instructional control of the explicit form, "Do X," and imitative control of the implicit form, "Do what I do." Some training devoted to one appears to contribute substantially to the other. So, the best guess may be that there will be some induction from imitative training to other kinds of generalized response classes.

QUESTION: You haven't tested her for that?

BAER: No. In this case, I don't have a test I could present with confidence to prove the point. I'm generalizing from other studies.

QUESTION: About this little girl, how do people describe her now in this institution or wherever? Does she still scream?

BAER: Whether or not she screams depends on whom she's with. With the experimental crew, no screams, no tantrums. With ward staff, screams and tantrums as ever. But then, they reinforce her for that, and we don't.

QUESTION: In that case isn't it true that the schedules that you set up are not so much good as the schedules that the institutions set up are bad?

BAER: Perhaps both.

QUESTION: Did the little girl imitate each new person?

BAER: Yes. No problem there. You can evoke imitation readily from other models as well.

QUESTION: Did you try it with the ward personnel?

BAER: No, with other personnel. It's easier to secure their help.

QUESTION: If you have certain behaviors which the child imitates but which in fact are never reinforced, do they drop out over time or are they maintained indefinitely?

ADVENTURES IN SIMPLISTIC GRAMMAR

BAER: The only way to find that out, finally, is to run throughout the life span of the child. In my experience, across 100 experimental hours and probably 100 to 500 repetitions, they don't drop out.

QUESTION: In dealing with nonresponsive behaviors which the experimenter has modeled but which belong to a separate response class not reinforced, isn't it likely that eventually discrimination will be formed to allow some kind of distinction?

BAER: One would think so—eventually. Simply running with the consistent contingencies I have described, hasn't produced it yet. And Steinman's data indicate discrimination is there, although the performance remains more or less uniform across both classes.

QUESTION: What about longer latencies? It's not response dropping out but longer latencies to response and various topographies coming in.

BAER: Yes. If you run a while more, you may yet see the two repertoires diverge.

QUESTION: Isn't it possible that this behavior is being reinforced in other ways or in other places?

BAER: I couldn't testify to what happens in other places, but in these particular demonstrations, I would bet against it. These ward evironments are fairly stable. They're not places where behaviors are modeled and imitations of them are reinforced.

QUESTION: If you are talking about nonreinforced imitations, aren't they being reinforced by being members of this whole sequence? Which could be why they imitate even though they recognize that they are nonreinforced.

BAER: Yet, you can program changeover delay between their performance and the next presentation of a model, and they still will survive that. Perhaps it's not a sufficiently long changeover delay. At any rate, ordinary precautions against simple chaining have been taken, and yet the performance persists.

QUESTION: If you found that the nonreinforced imitation did not drop out, wouldn't that be a difference between what you would ordinarily expect to find from these procedures, and wouldn't it be something to wonder about?

BAER: Yes.

QUESTION: What is the verbal behavior of this child in the ward now?

BAER: In the ward it is not much different than before. In the canteen is where you see the delightful anecdotes. She will ask for cookies and candies, in the singular or plural, appropriately.

QUESTION: In your Condition II, when you reverse the contingency, was the form of the plural the same as in the other two conditions? Did you move from an inflectional ending to a different form of plurality in Condition II?

BAER: No.

QUESTION: It was the same in all three conditions?

BAER: Yes. There can be some small variation in the kind of word preceding the plural: for example, whether it ends with a consonant or an open-mouthed vowel. We believe we detected some very small change in the probability of correct pluralization associated with whether the word did end in a consonant or a vowel, but it was a slight effect. I'm not perfectly certain of it.

QUESTION: Would it be wrong to conclude from the results of your comparison study between two imitative behaviors (Steinman's) that the child knows one is not going to be reinforced? Wouldn't absolute preference also be shown with a difference in two possibly reinforced behaviors?

BAER: But the preference at least is testimony to a discrimination between the classes.

QUESTION: Even if there is a discrimination in reinforceability of the two, might not the one reinforced less still be reinforced by something we don't know about?

BAER: I don't know what. Perhaps the reason these children are retarded is bound up with the success of these techniques in producing that outcome. They are not a random sample of children. They are obviously a very different sample of children.

QUESTION: Certainly you have done this with young normal kids, haven't you?

BAER: No. We tried to find some children with verbal labels, but no plurals, and we failed. Any child we found with a few labels had some plurals to go with them—although we found a lot of parents who were positive their child had labels but not plurals.

QUESTION: Isn't there some reaction to this—that the rule-governed issues really revolve around sentences and not the morphological rules so much? I don't know anybody that has made really much issue about morphological rules. But I don't think it is reasonable to generalize the statement about this being applicable only to retarded kids. Any procedure which produces a certain bit of behavior is not necessarily the procedure that occurs in nature. If I can produce schizophrenia in the laboratory, that doesn't mean that's how schizophrenia is produced elsewhere.

BAER: That's right. I reiterate the point, though, made at the end of my presentation: I think the question is how much of the language-using behavior of the speaker you can account for, by demonstrations of the control of tense of verbs, superlative form of adjectives, plural or singular usage of nouns, etc. We are doing a study now in which the child is taught to label the 26 letters of the alphabet presented to him in three-dimensional form (the kind children put on a magnetic tack board.) The child is taught to label them accurately. He is then taught six verbs, which can be exemplified with any pair of letters, for example, A touches B, C covers D, E pushes F, etc. And he is trained to use the verbs so that we can take any letter and exemplify any verb in action against any other letter and get an accurate sentence from the child. That is, he will say, "F replaces G," if that's what you did. Now you have there very simple sentence structure. First of all, it is perfectly trainable. No problem there. And it generalizes nicely. You don't have to teach the child every letter-verb combination. You teach him enough of them, and he will produce the rest himself. We are now having the child run through such exercises and we're trying to teach the use of a passive verb voice, but with only one of the verbs. Every time the child says accurately what has just been shown—for example, H touches M—the experimenter at first says, "Right," hands over the reinforcer as usual, and as he does so says, "M is touched by H." In other words, he models the passive. We do that for a series of trials, and so far, nothing happens: the child never produces the passive. We have now introduced a second "child," actually a research assistant, who is asked the same question. We are prepared to explore whether or not we can produce use of the passive voice in our sentence-emitter, simply by running through some of the possible variations in modeling including discontinuing the child's reinforcement for the active voice while reinforcing the model for use of the passive voice.

I can't tell you if any of these things will work, yet. We're still on our first subject. But you did raise the point about sentence structure being the important thing. I suggest this model of research can be applied to sentence structure, just as it can to morpheme endings, such as singular-plural cases. The question is what it will produce.

REFERENCES

Baer, D. M., Peterson, R. F., and Sherman, J. A. The development of imitation by reinforcing behavioral similarity to a model. *J. Exp. Anal. Behavior,* 1967, *10,* 405–416.
Bricker, W. A., and Bricker, D. D. The use of programmed language training as a means for differential diagnosis and educational remediation among severely retarded children. In *Peabody papers in human development.* Nashville: George Peabody College, Division of Human Development, 1966.
Chomsky, N. *Syntactic structures.* The Hague: Mouton, 1957.
Guess, D., Sailor, W., Rutherford, G., and Baer, D. M. An experimental analysis of linguistic development: The productive use of the plural morpheme. *J. Appl. Behavior Anal.,* 1968, *1,* 297–306.
Lenneberg, E. H. On explaining language. *Science,* 1969, *164,* No. 3880, 635–643.
Lovaas, O. I. A behavior therapy approach to the treatment of childhood schizophrenia. In J. P. Hill (Ed.), *Minnesota symposium on child psychology.* Vol. I. Minneapolis: University of Minnesota Press, 1967. Pp. 108–159.
Risley, T. R., and Wolf, M. M. Establishing functional speech in echolalic children. *Behavior Res. Ther.,* 1967, *5,* 73–88.
Steinman, W. M. Generalized imitation and the discrimination hypothesis. *J. Exp. Child Psychol.,* 1970, *10,* 79–99.

OPERANT LANGUAGE DEVELOPMENT:
The Outline of a Therapeutic Technology

TODD RISLEY, BETTY HART and LARRY DOKE
University of Kansas

TODD RISLEY was graduated from San Diego State College, and received his M.S. and Ph.D. degrees in psychology from the University of Washington. Before joining the University of Kansas faculty, he taught psychology at Florida State University. He is presently an associate professor at the University of Kansas, and is also active professionally as Editor of Journal of Applied Behavior Analysis; *member of the Board of Editors of* Journal of Applied Behavior Analysis *and* Journal of Experimental Child Psychology; *and member of the Board of Directors, Society for the Experimental Analysis of Behavior and Center for Applied Behavior Analysis.*

Dr. Risley is currently engaged in the application of behavior analysis techniques to preschool aged culturally deprived children as part of a massive research project in an impoverished community.

This chapter summarizes operant language-modification research so as to emphasize that these many diverse studies in fact constitute a therapeutic technology. Two important points pervade this discussion:
1. The overwhelming importance of imitation in these studies, and the resulting casual treatment of the subtleties of linguistic categories.
2. The absolutely critical position of measurement in these efforts, that is, the necessity of finding reliable ways to measure what is important rather than merely studying what we can conveniently measure.

Behaviors necessary for adequate functioning in society are behaviors which other members of society exhibit. Significant behavior modification consists of producing a correspondence between the child's behaviors and those of other members of society. Such behaviors can often be produced by another person explicitly demonstrating the appropriate behavior to the child. When such demonstrations evoke similar but previously absent behavior from a child, the child is said to have acquired the behavior "through imitation." Many behaviors of "normal" children are undoubtedly acquired in this manner. Most behavior modification efforts are premised upon the effectiveness of the therapist's "modeling" of the desired behavior in producing similar behavior from children. When such demonstrations are not effective—that is, when the child does not imitate—there can be little hope for rapidly producing significant acquisition of new behavior. The alternative, shaping each new behavior by differentially reinforcing successively closer approximations of the desired behavior, while often necessary, requires a therapist (of considerable skill). Even then the shaping process is frequently slow and arduous. Consequently, the development of procedures to establish or to improve imitative responding has been a necessary part of operant behavior modification research.

Baer and Sherman (1964) found that the probability of normal preschool children imitating a model's behaviors could be increased by reinforcing such imitations. They also found that reinforcing the child's imitation of some of the model's behaviors produced an increased probability of the child's imitating other model behaviors without reinforcement. They further demonstrated that continued, intermittent reinforcement of some imitations was necessary to maintain a high probability of both the reinforced and nonreinforced imitative behaviors.

The implications of this study for behavior modification were subsequently demonstrated by Sherman (1965) while reinstating verbal behavior in mute psychotic adults. For one subject, differential reinforcement procedures were used to shape a single, one-word imitative response. Once this response could be reliably evoked whenever the therapist said the word, the patient began imitating other words also. This result was a demonstration that a class of topographically different imitative behaviors can be increased by reinforcing only some of them (in this case, only one). This was a replication, in a behavior modification context, of Baer and Sherman's findings.

The findings of the Baer and Sherman study were further extended by Sherman with another patient in the same study. When shaping proved ineffective in establishing an initial imitative verbalization, because of an almost total absence of any vocal noises to differentially reinforce, Sherman began reinforcing imitations of motor behaviors in order to "establish a functional class of imitative behavior, such that strengthening nonverbal responses would result in the strengthening of imitative vocal and verbal responses " (Sherman, 1965, p. 160). Once the patient was reliably imitating new motor behaviors, Sherman began extending the class of imitative behaviors by presenting successively closer approximations to vocalizations for the patient to imitate, such as mouth opening, coughing, blowing out a match, blowing (without a match), some unvoiced sounds, and finally a voiced sound. Once this initial repertoire of imitative vocal sounds was produced and consistently reinforced, the patient began imitating other sounds. Three such sounds were then chained into one imitative word using a procedure detailed by Risley (1966); whereupon the patient began imitating other words as well. Several conclusions may be drawn from these two studies: (1) the probability of imitation can be increased by reinforcement; (2) reinforcing some imitative behaviors will increase the probability that similar new behaviors will also be imitated; (3) reinforcing some imitative behaviors will maintain a high probability of other similar behaviors being imitated without reinforcement; and (4) the imitation of new, dissimilar behaviors can be established by reinforcing imitations of successively closer approximations of those behaviors. These findings have been replicated and extended in subsequent behavior modification research with children.

Procedures have been developed for children who exhibit no discernible imitation as a basis for establishing an elaborate imitative repertoire. Baer, Peterson, and Sherman (1967), Lovaas, Freitas, Nelson, and Whalen (1967), Metz (1965), and Risley (1968a) have established initial imitative motor behaviors by combining shaping and fading techniques with physical manipulations or "putting through" procedures (Konorski and Miller, 1937). For example, imitative clapping was established by: "The experimenter . . . holding [the child's] arms and bringing her hands together. Reinforcers were first delivered contingent upon not struggling and then contingent upon slight cooperative movements while the experimenter moved [the child's] hands. Successively greater force produced by [the child] was then reinforced while fading out the force supplied by the experimenter in bringing [the child's] hands together, until the experimenter would clap his hands and then just touch [the child's] arm and [the child] would clap her hands. The experimenter then faded out touching [the child's] arms, first to a gesture which was made smaller and finally eliminated until, . . . [the child] would respond to the model stimulus of the [experimenter's] clap alone" (Risley, 1968a, p. 30). Lovaas (1966) used similar procedures involving physical manipulation of the child's mouth and lips to establish initial imitation of speech.

Baer et al. (1967), Lovaas et al. (1967), and Metz (1965) established initial motor imitation and then extended the imitative repertoires of retarded and autistic children to encompass complex motor behaviors involving manipulations of physical objects. Baer et al. (1967) began imitation training of three retarded children with simple motor behaviors such as arm raising, touching various objects, standing up, etc., where the criterion of similarity between the model's and the child's behavior was primarily in the topography of the behaviors. They then proceeded to gradually more complex behaviors, until the children were imitating such behaviors as placing a hat on a hobby horse, putting a glove in the pocket of a coat, tapping pegs into a pegboard with a hammer, etc. All these behaviors involved manipulation of objects where the criterion of similarity was primarily in the function of the behavior in producing changes in the positions of objects. (For example, even though a child's movements in picking up the glove, walking to the coat, and moving the glove toward the pocket might be topographically similar to the model's movements, these similarities would not be recorded and reinforced as imitations unless they resulted in the glove being firmly in the coat pocket.) As imitation training progressed, certain responses were demonstrated which, if imitated on their first presentation, were deliberately not reinforced on the first or any future occasion. These nonreinforced imitations were of progressively more complex behaviors, similar to the imitative behaviors which were being reinforced. These demonstrations were consistently imitated (even though those imitations were never reinforced) so long as imitations of other demonstrations *were* reinforced. When reinforcement was no longer contingent upon any imitations, the probability of these nonreinforced imitative behaviors sharply decreased, as did the previously reinforced imitative behaviors. When reinforcement was again made contingent upon the previously reinforced imitative behaviors, the probability of the nonreinforced imitative behaviors quickly increased, together with the reinforced imitative behaviors. This study combined the conclusions drawn from the Baer and Sherman (1964) and the Sherman (1965) studies into a program for developing an extensive imitative repertoire with children; demonstrating that this development does not depend upon the reinforcement of every imitative behavior, but does require the reinforcement of some imitative behaviors.

RUDIMENTARY SPEECH

Whether or not imitation is crucial to the normal development of language, it is a crucial part of all procedures for remediating language deficits. Therefore, when vocal imitation is absent, language training begins with procedures for establishing vocal imitation. Kerr, Meyerson, and Michael (1965) established initial control over a mute retarded child's vocalizations. They first reinforced any vocal sounds produced by the child. Then, after fading in vocal "models" by the experimenter so as not to disrupt the child's rate of vocalizations, they began reinforcing only those vocalizations of the child which were emitted shortly after the experimenter's vocalizations. The child began to respond to the experimenter's "model" vocalizations by emitting a vocalization, usually within five seconds. Lovaas, Berberich, Perloff, and Schaeffer (1966), after using similar procedures to obtain temporal control over the vocalizations of mute schizophrenic children, proceeded to establish imitative vocalizations. They presented models for more "overt" vocalizations (i.e., vocalizations which could be physically prompted by manually moving the child's mouth and lips, and which produced visual as well as auditory stimuli), particularly vocalizations which the child already occasionally exhibited. Then, by a combination of exaggerating the visual components of the modeled vocalization and physical prompts, they produced approximations to a matching vocalization. These approximations were shaped to more precise matches and maintained by differential reinforcement while the physical prompts and exaggerated visual components were faded out.

Once some vocal imitation has been established or when some vocal imitation is already exhibited by a child, the vocal imitations are elaborated into words and phrases of increasing length and complexity by shaping—or by chaining short vocal imitations together. Lovaas (1966) and Lovaas et al. (1966) have apparently relied upon shaping to accomplish this elaboration with schizophrenic children, presenting sounds, words, and phrases of increasing length, and differentially reinforced successively closer matches.

In some cases shaping alone is not sufficient to accomplish this elaboration. With retarded and aphasic children who imitate only individual sounds or short syllables, Risley (1966) found that simply presenting longer words or phrases and differentially reinforcing closer approximations to exact imitations produced no improvement. The children's responses to these longer models were so stereotyped that no variations closer to the desired imitation occurred which could be differentially reinforced. In these cases, Risley (1966) and Sloane, Johnston, and Harris (1968) have employed chaining procedures to produce more elaborate imitations. With these procedures a word or phrase is divided into short units (e.g., 'potato' might be divided into 'po,' 'ta,' and 'to,' if the child can imitate short syllables). These units are then presented in sequence, and the child is reinforced for imitating each unit (e.g., 'po' [experimenter's model]-"PO" [child's response]-S^R [reinforcement], 'ta'-"TA"-S^R, 'to'-"TO"-S^R). Then reinforcement is omitted except for the final unit in each sequence (e.g., 'po'-"PO," 'ta'-"TA," 'to'-"TO"-S^R). The model for the final unit ('to') is faded until the child is saying the final unit after saying the previous unit without the model (e.g., 'po'-"PO," 'ta'-"TA"-"TO"-S^R). In effect, the child's own imitative response to the previous unit ("TA") becomes the discriminative stimulus for the final response in the sequence ("TO"). Then the next-to-last unit is faded out, and so on, until the child is producing the sequence of responses in the absence of all but the model for the initial unit in the sequence (e.g., 'po'-"PO,TATO"-S^R). Then the model of the complete word or phrase is faded in (e.g., 'potato,' 'po'-"PO TATO"-S^R), and the model for the intial unit faded out until the child is imitating the complete word or phrase (e.g., 'potato'-"POTATO"-S^R). This imitative word or phrase can then be chained together with other words or phrases by the same procedures to produce even longer and more elaborate vocal imitations.

Once a child is imitating words and phrases of a length sufficient for rudimentary functional speech, and when he imitates new words and phrases of such length with little additional training, the next step is to transform such imitative vocalizations into rudimentary language. This is accomplished by using imitation to establish appropriate labeling of objects, events, and relationships in the child's environment. Wolf, Risley, and Mees (1964), Hewett (1965), Risley (1966), Lovaas (1966), Risley and Wolf (1967) and Sloane, Johnston, and Harris (1968) all have used similar procedures to convert imitative speech into functional language. The autistic, retarded, and "brain damaged" children in these studies, although diagnostically disparate, were similar in that they imitated words and phrases from other person's speech, TV commercials, songs, etc. First they were simply reinforced for imitating words said by the experimenter until they were consistently and quickly imitating those words.

Once reinforcement for imitation had produced a high probability of successful imitation of the verbal prompt alone, a picture or object was presented together with the verbal prompt, and the child was reinforced for imitating the name of the object. The imitative prompt was then faded out, while the child continued to receive reinforcement for saying the object's name.

The experimenter holds up an object (if necessary holding the spoonful of food behind it) and says, "What is this?" When the child looks at it, the experimenter immediately prompts with the object's name. The child is reinforced for imitating the prompt. When the child is reliably looking at the object without the food being held behind it, the time between the question "What is this?" and the prompt is gradually lengthened to more than five seconds. If after several trials the child continues to wait for the presentation of the verbal prompt, a *partial prompt* is given, for example, "Trr" for train. If the correct response does not occur within about five seconds more, the complete prompt is then presented. A correct response is followed by a social consequence such as "right" or "good," and the partial prompt is immediately repeated. A correct response to the partial prompt results in a bite of food.

When the child begins saying the name when only the partial prompt is presented, the experimenter continues the above procedure but begins to say the partial prompt more softly. The loudness of the partial prompt is varied according to the child's behavior. When the child fails to respond to a partial prompt and the complete prompt is presented, the next partial prompt is given more loudly. When the child correctly responds to the partial prompt, the next partial prompt is given more softly.

This continues until the experimenter only "mouths" the partial prompt and then, finally, discontinues it altogether as the child responds to the object and the question "What is this?" with the name of the object.

Throughout this procedure, whenever the child inappropriately imitates the question "What is this?," a time-out is programmed, i.e. the object is withdrawn and the experimenter looks down at the table. After two or three seconds of silence by the child, the experimenter looks up and continues the procedure.

After the child has been taught to name several pictures or objects, naming any new picture or object can be quickly established. However, the child often will not correctly name an item at the beginning of the next daily session or subsequent to learning other new items in the same session. A new response cannot be considered to be added to a child's naming vocabulary until he can name an item when it is presented again after other items have been learned, and following a passage of time. This is accomplished by gradually changing the context in which the item is presented. After a child is consistently naming new items on repeated presentations, a previously learned item is presented. When the child names the old item he is reinforced and the new item is presented again. When the child is reliably naming a new item when it follows one presentation of any of several previously taught items, two, then three, then four old items are presented between each presentation of the new item. (The well-established naming of old items need be reinforced only intermittently with food to maintain accuracy and short latencies.) When the child is reliably naming a new item under these conditions, another new item is introduced. When an item is reliably named the first time it is presented in several subsequent sessions, it can be considered to be a member of the child's naming vocabulary. Only occasional reviews in subsequent sessions are needed to maintain it. Once naming is established, the response units can be expanded to phrases and sentences. In some cases this expansion occurs without explicit training. When multiple word units have to be taught, the procedure is the same as in teaching individual words; the phrase is chained together as described previously, and mimics of the phrases are reinforced until the phrases are consistently imitated. Then a question appropriate to the imitated phrase is introduced and followed by an imitative prompt. The imitative prompts are then gradually faded into partial prompts, which are then also faded out. In this case the partial prompts are the first word or words of the phrase.

At first, phrases such as "That's a ———," or "I want———" are taught, using the child's newly acquired naming vocabulary. Then more varied phrases are taught, such as answering the appropriate questions with "My name is ———," "I live at ———." "I am ——— years old," "My sisters' names are ——— and ———."

Food reinforcers coupled with mild food deprivation have generally been used in this rudimentary language training. Although formal training sessions with food reinforcers are generally continued to rapidly establish specific categories of speech such as more elaborate responses to complex questions (Risley and Wolf, 1967), prepositions, pronouns, and time relationships (Lovaas, 1966), and expanded narrations (Risley, 1968a), further elaboration of language is more conveniently established in "natural" settings.

Once the child has a naming vocabulary, a few phrases, and will readily imitate new words and phrases, this behavior can be readily maintained and is most efficiently elaborated by taking advantage of the naturally occurring events and reinforcers in the environment. To maximally utilize such events and reinforcers, the environment is arranged so that the child can obtain few reinforcers without the help of the attending adult. With motorically skilled children this often means that the adult physically impedes the activities of the child, preventing his direct attainment of the available environmental reinforcers. The child's language is then elaborated by prompting for requests, descriptions, and comments appropriate to each situation; and by reinforcing the appropriate verbal behavior by permitting access to the environmental reinforcers as well as praise and social interaction; and finally by fading out the prompts. In this way appropriate requests, descriptions, and comments may be established and maintained—using naturally occurring reinforcers in their natural context.

For example, Risley and Wolf (1967) reported that, for one child the comment, "Out (or in) the door," was maintained by opening the doors to and from the experimental room. The experimenter would say, "Out the door," and when the child would mimic this, the door would be opened. After several trials on succeeding days, the experimenter began introducing a partial prompt, saying only, "Out," and the child continued to say, "Out the door." The partial prompt was then gradually faded out until the experimenter put his hand on the door knob and looked at the child, and the child said, "Out the door." The experimenter gradually faded in the appropriate controlling stimulus—the question, "Where are you going?" This was presented by at first mumbling it softly as they approached the door and then increasing the volume on succeeding trials. Whenever the child inappropriately imitated the question "Where are you going?" the experimenter repeated the question at a lower volume and followed it with a loud partial prompt: "Where are you going? *OUT!*" On succeeding trials the partial prompt, "Out," was then decreased in volume until the child responded to the closed door and the question, "Where are you going?" with the response "Out the door." The same procedure was used to establish appropriate answers to the question, "Where are you going?", such as "Up the stairs," "Down the hall," or "In the car." In each case, the reinforcer which maintained appropriate answering was simply being allowed to proceed up the stairs, down the hall, and so on. In this manner the child came to make appropriate verbal comments about his environment.

This procedure has been labelled "generalization" (Risley and Wolf, 1967; Lovaas, 1968). This is somewhat misleading, as generalization usually refers to the *phenomenon* of the occurrence of appropriate behavior under other than the original training conditions, whereas, here, it refers to a *procedure* used to establish this occurrence. In fact, this procedure is more used to establish new language than to "generalize" previously taught speech.

Investigators who have developed speech in deviant children to this point, had observed that soon after language training in natural settings has begun, new language which has not been specifically trained begins to appear with increasing frequency (Wolf, Risley, and Mees, 1964; Salzinger and Feldman, 1964; Lovaas, 1967; Risley and Wolf, 1967; Hall, 1970). These observations are reported as anecdote, since the behavior involved had exceeded the capacities of our available measurement procedures. To capitalize upon the naturally occurring events and reinforces in the environment to establish new and more sophisticated language, it became necessary to devise a system to reliably record and quantify spontaneous speech.

SPONTANEOUS LANGUAGE

We have spent the past three years developing such a measurement system and extending our procedures for modifying the spontaneous speech of disadvantaged preschool children.

A daily 15-minute sample is taken of each child's verbalizations during free play. The sample is recorded by one of three observers who move with the child from one

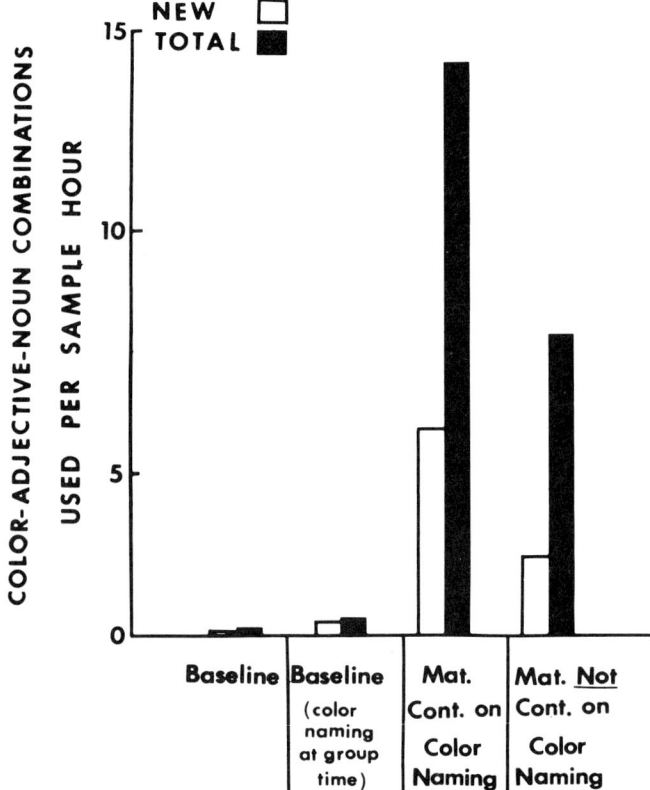

Fig. 1. Average new and all color-noun combinations used per sample hour for a group of 15 children. The sequence of experimental conditions was: baseline, color naming at group time, materials contingent on color naming, and materials no longer contingent on color naming.

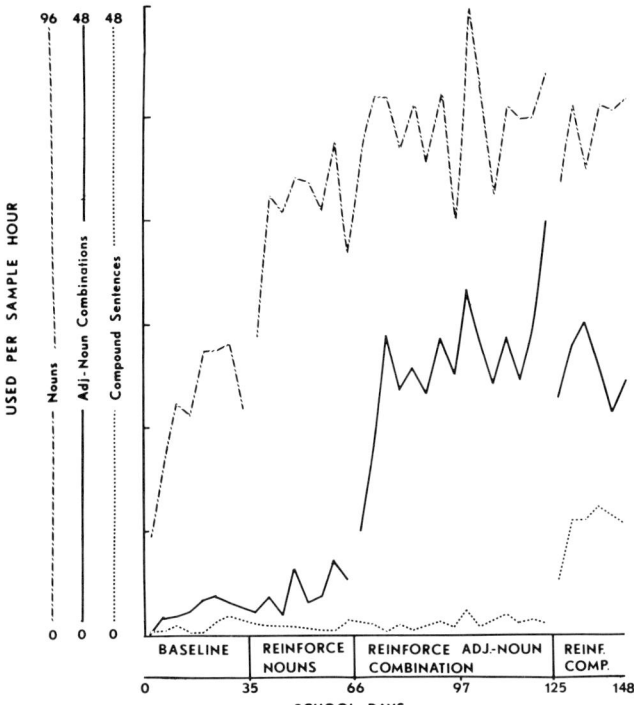

Fig. 2. Average use per 15-minute sample of nouns *(broken line)*, adjective-noun combinations *(solid line)*, and compound sentences *(dotted line)* by twelve children under these experimental conditions: baseline (days 1–34); access to preschool materials contingent on use of a noun (days 35–65); access to preschool materials contingent on use of an adjective-noun combination (days 66–124); and access to preschool materials contingent on a request in the form of a compound sentence (days 125–148). Note the different scale for nouns versus adjective-noun combinations and compound sentences.

activity to another. These observers write down in longhand "everything said" by the child. Each of the three observers focuses on the same four children every day throughout the year, rotating them systematically through four 15-minute daily blocks so that a regular sequence of early and late, indoor and outdoor, observations are obtained on each child. The resulting records are transcribed onto IBM cards and analyzed by computer.

Whenever a child is absent from school, the observer assigned to that child records a reliability sample with one of the other observers, both observers recording independently "everything said" during a given 15-minute period by the prime observer's child. Over the year, inter-observer reliability is calculated for the prime observer with each of the other two observers in terms of agreement on each child's use of specific words and language categories.

Over a three-year period, the spontaneous speech of four-and-one-half year old disadvantaged children has been studied in a typical preschool free-play situation. In the first year of study it was found that though a group of 15 children learned to name colors appropriately in a group-teaching situation, color naming did not increase in their spontaneous speech in a nonteaching situation until they were required to name by color the preschool materials they wanted to use. When access to preschool materials was thus made contingent on use of color-adjective-noun combinations, the rate of such usage increased markedly in the group (see Figure 1). This effect was replicated the following year with another group of children and other aspects of language. Marked increases were seen, successively, in children's usage of nouns, adjective-noun combinations, and compound sentences when access to preschool materials during free play was made contingent on the use of each of these aspects of lan-

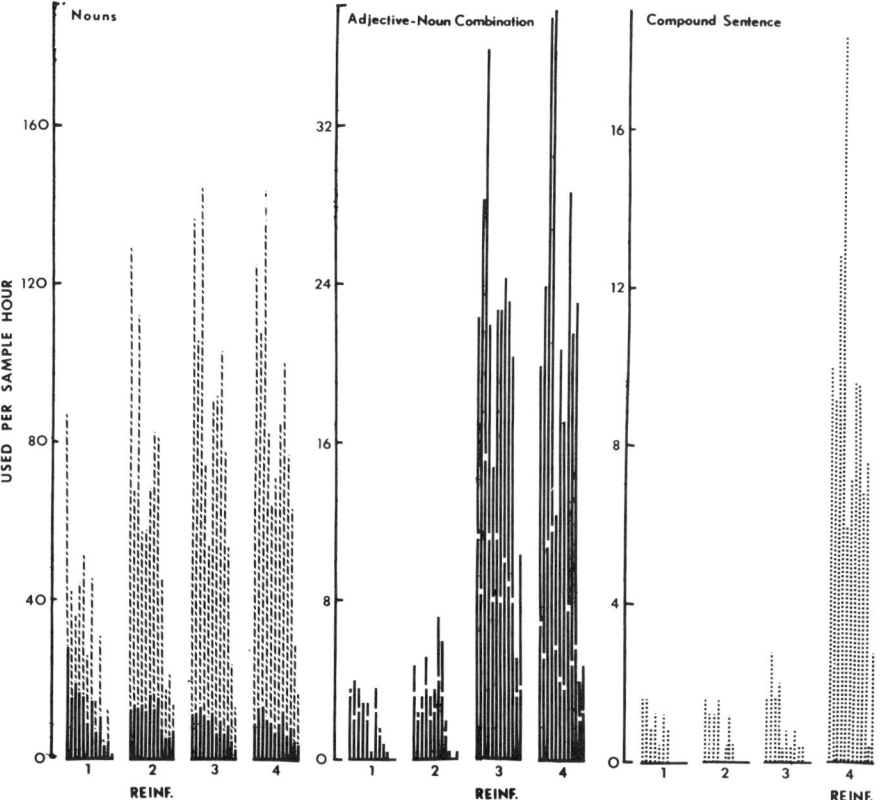

Fig. 3. Average use per 15-minute sample of nouns (*broken lines*), adjective-noun combinations (*solid lines*), and compound sentences (*dotted lines*) by each of the twelve children across school days comprising each experimental condition. The conditions were: baseline (days 1–34); access to preschool materials contingent on use of a noun (day 35–65); access to preschool materials contingent on use of an adjective-noun combination (days 66–124); and access to preschool materials contingent on use of a compound sentence (days 125–148). In each set of twelve bars the succession of children is the same, from the children who exhibited the most different words over the school year on the left (child 1) progressively to the child who exhibited the fewest different words over the school year on the right (child 12). Note the different scale on each ordinate.

OPERANT LANGUAGE DEVELOPMENT

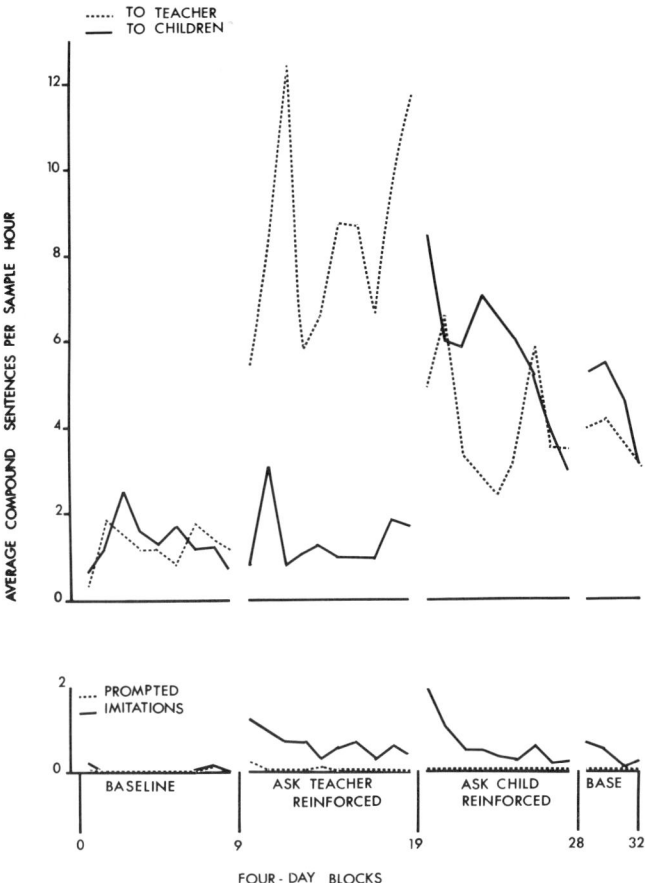

Fig. 4. (*top*) Average number of compound sentences directed to a teacher (*dashed line*) and to other children (*solid line*) per sample hour over four-day blocks comprising each experimental condition. (*bottom*) Average number of requests prompted in the form "You need to ask for ———" or "Why do you want?" (*solid line*) and in the form of a compound sentence which the child imitated (*dashed line*). The sequence of experimental conditions was: baseline—free access to materials (blocks 1-9); materials contingent on compound sentence request to teachers (blocks 10-19); materials contingent on compound sentence request to other children (blocks 20-28); and baseline—free access to materials again (blocks 29-32).

guage (see Figures 2 and 3). In the third year of study the dependence of the effect on teacher prompting was investigated. We also examined whether spontaneous speech to children as well as to adults could be modified. High rates of compound sentence usage in requests for preschool materials were established. These compound sentences were first directed to teachers, and then to children, in accordance with who was dispensing the preschool materials during free play. The children's rates of using compound sentences were found to depend only minimally on teacher prompting (see Figure 4). The conclusions at the end of the three years of investigation are that the materials available in the regular preschool environment can be used to effect important changes in children's behavior, and that significant and lasting modifications may be made in specific aspects of the spontaneous speech of disadvantaged children.

Although we rely heavily upon contingent social interaction to develop appropriate behaviors, we must not forget that social interaction may function as a reinforcer partially because it occasions the assistance of another person in obtaining other reinforcers, and that an important function of language is to guide the other person to efficient assistance. The essence of the use of "natural reinforcers" to elaborate language is to arrange the environment to maximally necessitate the child's obtaining the cooperation and assistance of other people to acquire those reinforcers.

SUMMARY OF DISCUSSION

QUESTION: Did you compare these children with the others not in the program?

RISLEY: Yes. We have, but we don't have it in all language categories. We have taken weekly samples in another Head Start program near our preschool project. We have taken daily samples in professors' children in the Lawrence preschools. And we have compared these with our children. Over the year we have a lot of different measures. On most of our measures of language complexity the university children are high and continue relatively unchanged throughout the year. The Head Start children are low and continue relatively unchanged throughout the year. Our children begin the school year comparable to the Head Start children and end the year comparable to the university professors' children. This is true for each of the aspects of language we have thus far analyzed: number of words spoken, size of vocabulary used, and number of complete sentences uttered. However, I can't attribute these effects to any one particular part of our program. We have many other procedures for modifying language also incorporated into our program.

QUESTION: At least you can say whatever it is you are doing would be beneficial if incorporated into the Head Start program.

RISLEY: Correct. Our children start off looking like the other Head Start children and end up looking like the professors' children along several dimensions of language.

QUESTION: Did you record anything else besides the nouns and the adjective-noun combinations?

RISLEY: We recorded everything.

QUESTION: In terms of your analysis I assume you coded these.

RISLEY: I'm reporting only on the aspects of speech which we manipulate. You can chop up language a million different ways, so the ones I am reporting on are the ones to which we specifically tried to apply this given procedure to test its power. Incidentally, we are now using this same procedure to work on reading. It doesn't have to be focused on speech. It provides a beautiful teaching situation. The other children are occupied with materials and a particular child walks up to the teacher and says, "I want something." Thus we have a reinforcer. He is telling you what it is. It is a microteaching situation. We can work with that one child at that moment to get any kind of behavior. So we work on narration, saying, "What do you want to do with it?" "Why do you want to use it?" "Tell me about it." We try to generate verbal narration about the object. Or we can work on reading, saying, "O.K., find it's name over there on the list. It's name looks like this. Now, find it over there." We can expand this procedure to almost any aspect of behavior.

QUESTION: Are you operating on the assumption that there is any different cultural language code issue there?

RISLEY: No, I'm not really operating on that assumption. I don't consider any particular code or grammatical constraint as very important. Children can say things one way one place and another way another place. The real question is getting general language facility. I don't think compound sentences are critical, and I have a hunch that trying to find the key and the most important kinds of speech is probably not a very fruitful quest. I think a better concentration is on general language facility —getting children to use language in a variety of ways.

QUESTION: Then you are interested in a social facility?

RISLEY: Right. The fact that children have facility with compound sentences isn't as important as that they have facility with another category of speech.

QUESTION: How did you determine from the 15-minute samples which things to code on the IBM cards?

RISLEY: Everything is coded on IBM cards. I mean everything is put on IBM cards.

QUESTION: The words?

RISLEY: Yes. The secretary types from the verbatim samples, and the words are punched on cards.

QUESTION: Your tactic is to promote language facility in a wide variety of ways, and you are assuming that for this Head Start population that will be useful. I can think of two logics you might be following. One is sort of a random sampling "law of large numbers" logic. You will surely incorporate within this grab bag some very useful things. But another would be sort of the generalized imitation logic. If you teach them to handle a half-dozen or a dozen categories in a row, will they be able to handle any new categories that come along?

RISLEY: Yes. I think that we might produce generalized skill in handling language categories. However, it is also likely that some particular language categories are more useful than others.

QUESTION: Do you know what these are?

RISLEY: I don't know what they are, but I can look for differences. We have extensive normative data on the spontaneous speech of our children and disadvantaged children and the middle-class professors' children. I can enumerate any number of differences. But I can't say whether those differences are important.

QUESTION: Can't you try to work out prerequisites?

RISLEY: Yes. I was thinking of a slightly different tactic. That would be to look at the categories of language that are present in the speech of the professors' children, present in the reading books they will be faced with in early elementary school, and absent in the language of our children. That would probably be the tactic I would use in determining which language categories to emphasize.

QUESTION: If you want new things to come out without explicit teaching, isn't this more likely to develop if they have the prerequisites for these new behaviors to start with.

RISLEY: Yes, by definition, a prerequisite *is* prerequisite. If only we knew what they were for language.

QUESTION: When your secretary is typing the observer's notes, is there ever a time when there is a question about which category to put a word in?

RISLEY: Yes.

QUESTION: Doesn't it require a certain amount of inference?

RISLEY: On the normative data we have tried to define categories so that our definitions become fairly clear, if somewhat arbitrary.

QUESTION: Don't you have particular problems in single-word utterances where one woud can function as a verb or as a noun?

RISLEY: Yes. We have gone through the literature to see what other people have used, and we have tried to devise our set of definitions to be compatible.

QUESTION: How would you handle "watcha" as in "Watcha going to do?"

RISLEY: We probably would categorize that as two words "what" and "ya," as that is the way the observers would spell it.

QUESTION: You wouldn't break it down into "what are you"?

RISLEY: No. We generally categorize it as our observers write it down. One of the interesting things about this measurement procedure is that it gives categories of speech as the man on the street sees it, not as the linguists see it. That is an advantage when we are trying to work with significant behavior. What is important to the child probably is more closely related to the way the man on the street sees it or writes it down. We are, by the way, comparing that with tape recordings of the children's speech so we can ask, "How does it differ as the man on the street sees it and as the linguist might see it?"

QUESTION: Whenever you have used models and prompts, etc., I'd be curious to know in what dialect or accent have these been given? I understand these children are mostly from the Head Start program in Kansas City.

RISLEY: Yes. It depends on who the teacher was.

QUESTION: What about the responses? Are they predominantly in their own dialect?

RISLEY: Our contingencies aren't on dialect.

QUESTION: In other words, you don't consider that important to investigate?

RISLEY: It would be interesting to investigate it, but we can't get reliability on that in our observations. Apparently, pronunciation and enunciation aspects are not terribly important to people. They don't even agree whether they are there or not.

QUESTION: Won't that turn out to be important when they get in public schools?

RISLEY: Maybe.

QUESTION: And to get jobs eventually?

RISLEY: Maybe, too. We also have a lot of imitation training going on, where we train children to be able to repeat things quickly with facility and easily, so they might shape up if they get to those contingencies.

QUESTION: You said you have analyzed the linguistic forms by a computer. If you have recorded everything, how have you handled the memory problem with your programming?

RISLEY: Memory problem?

QUESTION: Computers are so finite in terms of how much memory they have.

RISLEY: We usually do restrict our analysis to an aspect of speech where we can give it a vocabulary.

QUESTION: So you don't look at contingenices between words but you examine isolated forms, form classes?

RISLEY: We do that, too, but the problem is really devising the program to tell the computer what to count, what an "X" is, what a subordinate clause is, or something like that. Interpret any statement I made about analyzing language as analyzing a particular aspect of language. We have it all on tape. It's just a matter of finding the programs. But we just are not doing it "shotgun." We are deciding what are we interested in and taking a look at that particular aspect. If we get interested in something else later, we can go back and look at the data for that aspect.

QUESTION: Once these children leave your influence, won't a lot of this go down the drain for lack of adequate reinforcement in their own environments?

RISLEY: It depends on what you mean by "go down the drain."

QUESTION: Cease to be emitted.

RISLEY: I think that would be true. In other words, the rate of compound sentences certainly will drop. But these children will be more likely to be able to come up with a compound sentence when one is required. My rate of doing algebra is nearly zero right now. If somebody were to pay me enough, I could do algebra. But had I not been through some necessary training, no matter how much someone offered me to do algebra, I wouldn't be able to do it. My rate of algebra would still be zero. What I'm saying is that there is a difference between language facility and rate of a particular aspect of language.

QUESTION: Wouldn't that be typical? Reacquisition is fast and it can be managed without programming. Put a terminal contingency on it, and you have it.

RISLEY: Correct.

REFERENCES

Baer, D. M., Peterson, R. F. and Sherman, J. A. The development of imitation by reinforcing behavioral similarity to a model. *J. Exp. Anal. Behavior,* 1967, *10,* 405–416.

Baer, D. M., and Sherman, J. A. Reinforcement control of generalized imitation in young children. *J. Exp. Child Psychol.,* 1964, *1,* 37–49.

Birnbrauer, J. S., Bijou, S. W., Wolf, M. M., and Kidder, J. D. Programmed instruction in the classroom. In L. P. Ullman and L. Krasner (Eds.), *Case studies in behavior modification.* New York: Holt, Rinehart and Winston, 1965. Pp. 358–363.

Brigham, T. A., and Sherman, J. A. An experimental analysis of verbal imitation in preschool children. *J. Appl. Behavior Anal.,* 1968, *1,* 151–158.

Hall, R. V. Reinforcement procedures and the increase of functional speech by a brain-injured child. In F. L. Girardeau and J. E. Spradlin (Eds.), *A Functional Approach to Speech and Language, Monograph No. 14.* Washington, D.C.: American Speech and Hearing Association, 1970. Pp. 48–59.

Hart, B. M., and Risley, T. R. Establishing use of descriptive adjectives in the spontaneous speech of disadvantaged preschool children. *J. Appl. Behavior Anal.,* 1968, *1,* 109–120.

Hart, B. M., and Risley, T. R. The use of preschool materials for modifying the language of disadvantaged children, *J. Appl. Behavior Anal.* (in press).

Hewett, P. M. Teaching speech to an autistic child through operant conditioning. *Am. J. Orthopsychiat.,* 1965, *35,* 927, 936.

Kerr, N., Meyerson, L., and Michael, J. A procedure for shaping vocalizations in a mute child. In L. P. Ullman and L. Krasner (Eds.) *Case Studies in behavior modification.* New York: Holt, Rinehart and Winston, 1965. Pp. 366–370.

Konorski, J., and Miller, S. On two types of conditioned reflex. *J. Gen. Psychol.,* 1937, *16,* 264–72.

Lovaas, O. I. A program for the establishment of speech in psychotic children. In J. K. Wing (Ed.), *Childhood autism,* Oxford: Pergamon Press, 1966.

Lovaas, O. I. Some studies on the treatment of childhood schizophrenia. *Res. Psychother.,* 1968, *3,* 103–121.

Lovaas, O. I., Berberich, J. P., Perloff, B. F., and Schaeffer, B. Acquisition of imitative speech by schizophrenic children. *Science,* 1966, *151,* 705–707.

Lovaas, O. I., Freitas, L., Nelson, K., and Whalen, C. The establishment of imitation and its use for the development of complex behavior in schizophrenic children. *Behaviour Res. Ther.*, 1967, 5, 171–181.

Metz, J. R. Conditioning generalized imitation in autistic children. *J. Exp. Child Psychol.*, 1965, 2, 389–399.

Peterson, R. F. Some experiments on the organization of a class of imitative behaviors. *J. Appl. Behavior Anal.*, 1968, 1, 225–235.

Reynolds, N. J., and Risley, T. R. The role of social and material reinforcers in increasing the talking of a disadvantaged preschool child. *J. Appl. Behavior Anal.*, 1968, 1, 253–262.

Risley, T. R. The establishment of verbal behavior in deviant children. Unpublished dissertation. University of Washington, 1966.

Risley, T. R. The effects and side effects of punishing the autistic behaviors of a deviant child. *J. Appl. Behavior Anal.*, 1968a, 1, 21–34.

Risley, T. R. Learning and lollipops. *Psychology Today*, 1968b, 1, 28, 62–65.

Risley, T. R., and Wolf, M. M. Establishing functional speech in echolalic children. *Behavior Res. Ther.*, 1967, 5, 73–88.

Salzinger, K., Feldman, R. S., Cowan, J. E., and Salzinger, S. Operant conditioning of verbal behavior of two young speech-deficient boys. In L. Krasner and L. P. Ullman (Eds.), *Research in behavior modification*. New York: Holt, Rinehart and Winston, 1964, Pp. 82–105.

Sherman, J. A. Use of reinforcement and imitation to reinstate verbal behavior in mute psychotics. *J. Abnorm. Psychol.*, 1965, 70, 155–164.

Sloane, H. N., Jr., Johnston, M. K., and Harris, F. R., Remedial procedures for teaching verbal behavior to speech deficient or defective young children. In H. N. Sloane, Jr. and B. D. MacAulay (Eds.), *Operant procedures in remedial speech and language training*. Boston: Houghton Mifflin, 1968. Pp. 77–101.

Wolf, M. M., Risley, T. R. and Mees, H. Application of operant conditioning procedures to the behavior problems of an autistic child. *Behaviour Res. Ther.*, 1964, 1, 305–321.

Approaches to the Description and Delineation of Defective Speech

THREE APPROACHES TO SPEECH RETARDATION

GERALD M. SIEGEL
University of Minnesota

GERALD M. SIEGEL is a professor in the Department of Communication Disorders at the University of Minnesota. He is a fellow of the American Speech and Hearing Association, and is editor of ASHA Monographs.

From its inception as a profession, speech pathology has stood at the intersection of many basic and clinical disciplines. As a consequence, speech pathologists are sensitive to the intellectual reverberations in fields that touch generally on the human condition, and particularly on speech, language, and communication. There are three areas of active research that have special significance for speech pathologists concerned with delayed language: (1) learning theory, (2) interpersonal approaches, and (3) linguistics or psycholinguistics. This chapter will focus on the relevance of these areas to the language disorders of children.

Disciplines such as speech pathology can make a special contribution by placing the theoretical developments that emanate from the basic study of human behavior into the context of compelling human problems. In this respect, speech pathologists present a testing ground for various competing theories or orientations. For example, we ask of any theory of speech or language development what insights it generates about children who fail to demonstrate normal development. We are directly concerned with the extent to which language skills are learned rather than inherited as we attempt to understand the nature of disordered language. Similarly, the ways that various approaches categorize verbal behavior are significant to a therapist whose task it is to effect some modification in such behavior. These are the considerations pursued in this chapter. For purposes of discussion we will take considerable license with such terms as verbal behavior, speech, language, and communication. Though each of these has special connotations for particular fields of study, they will be used here as roughly equivalent. They will refer primarily to expressive verbal behavior rather than to such theoretical notions as the speaker's "linguistic competence."

Preparation of this paper was supported by Grant OE-09-332189-4533032 from the Bureau of Education of the Handicapped to the University of Minnesota Center for Research and Development in Education of the Handicapped.

SPEECH RETARDATION AND LEARNING THEORY

Maturation Sets the Pace

The notion that "maturation sets the pace" in speech development appears often in speech pathology textbooks. In its early days, speech pathology was strongly influenced by medical science. Theories of speech disorders hewed closely to the medical model. Speech is an extremely complex motor act, and it seems plausible that a defect in so finely tuned an instrument as the vocal system might result in a speech disorder. These considerations have led speech pathologists to be particularly preoccupied with physiological and maturational variables. Even when considering "functional" speech disorders, the tendency has been to search for causes within the child, rather than in his interaction with his environment.

It must be acknowledged, however, that the vocal system is extremely robust and is capable of sustaining considerable insult. Individuals have learned to speak effectively without a tongue or a larynx and to make compensations for a gaping hole in the palate, or for extreme deviations in dental structure. Even when an obvious structural deficiency is present, as in the case of a cleft palate, only very imprecise relationships can be drawn between the severity of the physical disorder and the extent of the speech difficulty.

This is not to suggest that physical parameters of maturation are unrelated to speech development. Speech development is obviously intricately related to motor and sensory development. It is not yet clear, however, what specific motor and sensory states are required for adequate speech, and how these interact with learning. We often note that speech is an "overlaid function." In order to talk, we temporarily divert various organs of the body from their primary functions to serve the speech act. Normal respiration is suspended to provide a flow of air through a highly modulated vocal tract. The tongue, lips, and palate are employed to shape the vocal configuration, rather than to serve the processes of ingestion. If a child can adequately perform these basic acts with the organs used in speech, does this insure that he has sufficient maturation and function to perform speech acts as well? At this time, we cannot specify such relationships. Explanations of speech disorder which rely primarily on descriptions of organic conditions must be embraced very cautiously.

This seems especially true when the organic problems are presumed or inferred rather than observed. Diagnostic categories such as congenital aphasia, minimal brain damage, and dyslexia all imply an organic lesion which is presumably too elusive to observe directly but powerful enough to interrupt speech development. It is crucial that we have interdisciplinary research programs to examine the development of normal and deviant speech in the context of the child's expanding physical capabilities. We must learn much more about the relationship between development in the physical and the behavorial spheres. All too frequently, the physical variables which are presumed to be the cause of the child's problem are inferred from behavorial information, rather than independently observed.

Speech is Learned

The statement that speech is learned behavior can be expressed in at least as many ways as there are theories of learning which deal with speech acquisition. The most common "learning" formulations are basically informal ones which acknowledge that speech is acquired in the context of a responsive environment. Contemporary formal theories of learning tend to describe behavioral episodes with respect to antecedent and reinforcing stimuli. Skinner has proposed that learned behavior be described in terms of the antecedent stimulus (S) which sets the occasion for a response (R) to occur which, in turn, evokes other stimulus consequences (S^R). The familiar configuration is expressed:

$$S\text{----------}R\text{----------}S^R$$

Opinions differ whether Skinner's approach to verbal behavior can account for the complexities of speech and language. Nonetheless, his system provides a useful way to sort out some significant variables operating in the development and retardation of speech in children. For example, we can schematize the early stages of speech development in terms of several "stages."

Stage 1. During the first month or two of life, children emit noncrying vocalizations in the absence of any obvious stimulation. We do not have precise descriptions of the child's vocal repertoire in these earliest months, but there are strong suggestions that the child comes into the world with, or soon acquires, an extensive vocal repertoire which subsequently contracts. In this first stage, the child's vocalizations do not appear to be systematically affected either by antecedent or subsequent stimuli. No systematic links can be drawn between vocal acts and the stimuli in the environment (see Figure 1).

Stage 2. Somewhat later, social reinforcement becomes linked with vocal behavior. Studies by Rheingold (1959), Weisberg (1963), and Todd and Palmer (1968) show that infant vocal patterns from about three months on are amenable to contingent social reinforcement. Routh (1969) has further shown that it is possible to differentially reinforce consonants versus vowel sounds. In this stage, however, the child's

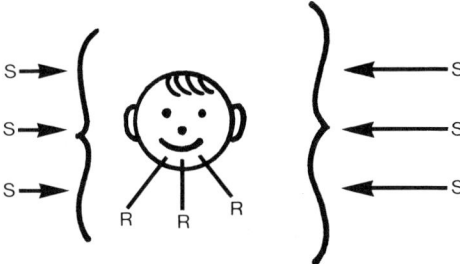

Fig. 1. The infant's vocalizations are not systematically related to specifiable internal or external stimuli.

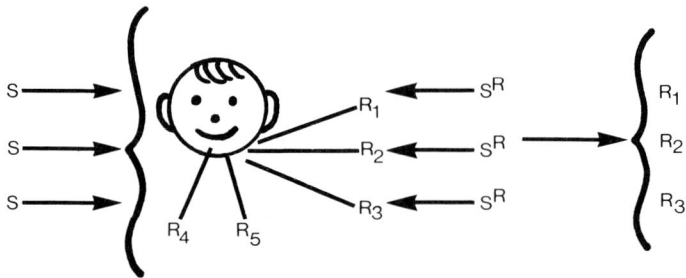

Fig. 2. The infant's vocalizations are differentially reinforced.

vocalizations do not appear to be under the control of antecedent stimuli. Weisberg found that neither the simple presence of an adult nor the presentation of noncontingent stimulation altered vocal rate. This should be more fully investigated. Figure 2 indicates that the responses are not yet under the control of antecedent stimuli, but that some selective or differential reinforcement is already possible. This selective conditioning is crucial for any theory that attempts to deal with how the child's repertoire is shaped to approximate the phonemic system of the adult community.

Stage 3. The configuration is completed when the child's responses are linked with antecedent as well as reinforcing stimuli. The antecedent stimuli assume increasing importance while reinforcement consequences become obscured in complicated patterns of conditioned reinforcement, stimulus-response chains, and self-reinforcement. This is diagrammed in Figure 3. It is at this point that the child's responses may be designated as "meaningful." That is, they occur in the presence of appropriate setting stimuli or cues.

Extensions to Abnormal Speech Development

Figure 3 is a rough representation of a learning model whose adequacy to account for speech acquisition is still undetermined. Still, the representation may have merit as a way of highlighting processes that can significantly retard speech. Within the model, the important sources of variation are (1) the child as an organism, (2) the

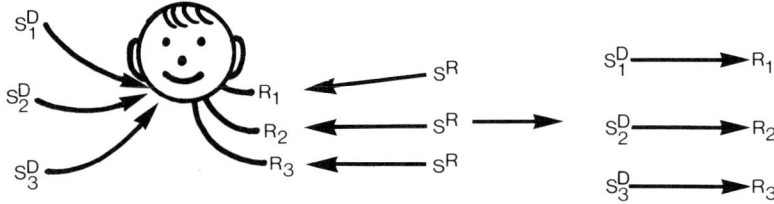

Fig. 3. The infant's vocal repertoire comes under the control of both antecedent and consequent stimuli.

initial setting or stimulation conditions, and (3) the reinforcement variables attendant on his behavior.

The organism. The first source implicates the child himself as a defective organism. There are numerous ways in which a major pathology or disability can impede speech acquisition. The child may have severe paralysis of the muscle systems required to make the necessary responses. He may have a profound hearing loss and be incapable of processing auditory stimuli. These are conditions in which the child either cannot make the crucial responses or cannot receive the crucial stimuli necessary for speech. Though these are obviously "organic" conditions, it is helpful to think of them as conditions which affect the child's capabilities for interacting with his environment, rather than as static attributes of the organism (Bijou, 1966). Because a child is deaf does not mean he cannot learn to speak. His hearing may be augmented through a hearing aid, or it may be possible to reach him through other sensory modalities. The significant fact is not that he does not hear, but rather that he does not receive auditory stimuli. These are two very different statements about the child. Similarly, the fact that an organism is not able to make vocal responses does not mean he cannot learn to use some variant of expressive language. For years attempts to teach speech to our cousin, the chimpanzee, failed dismally. These failures lent a great deal of credulity to the assertion that language is an inherently human function that could not possibly occur in other species. Recent work suggests that the problem may have been in the choice of response mode. Though chimpanzees apparently cannot master vocal behavior, the Gardeners (1969) have reported a successful attempt to teach language to a chimpanzee through the American Sign Language.

When a child with a behavioral disorder also has organic problems, there is always a strong temptation to ascribe the behavioral problems to the organic condition. But an organic condition can affect a child in very subtle ways. For example, the child with some marked physical disability, such as cerebral palsy, may simply not be allowed the same range of experiences as his normal peers. This may impede the development of skills that are within his physical capabilities. While it is true that one source of speech retardation is to be found in the child himself, the nature of these effects is likely to be extremely complex. We should avoid simplistically assigning causes of speech defects to an imperfect organism.

Improper reinforcement. The model suggests that proper reinforcement is necessary to strengthen and fashion appropriate speech skills. Unfortunately, there is little experimental evidence to indicate what factors lead to delayed language, and so we are bound to theoretical speculations and anecdotal evidence. In interviews with parents, the speech retarded child is often reported to have been very quiet during his early years and to have lacked a "need for speech." In motivational terms this suggests that the child produced little verbal behavior, and that verbalization was not differentially reinforced over other methods for manipulating the environment.

Not too long ago there was a story circulating among speech clinicians about a youngster who failed to utter a single word until his sixth year, when he exclaimed one day, "The damned toast is burned." When his amazed parents asked him why he had never spoken before, he explained, "everything was all right until just now."

The parameters that determine when reinforcement is appropriate for speech development are extremely complex. They go well beyond a simple statement of the amount of reinforcement. All of the factors that have been shown to determine the effectiveness of reinforcement of other behaviors should apply to the reinforcement of speech as well, in a much more complex fashion than is usually permitted in laboratory studies. It is possible that children come to the speech learning task with different requirements for the amount and the quality of reinforcement. It is possible that these differences must be made explicit if some cases of speech delay are to be avoided. Milisen (1954, p. 8) made a classic statement of this position in regard to the development of articulation disorders. He insisted that virtually any child, regardless of the cause of his problem, can learn adequate articulation skills if "the environment has been trained to begin early in creating a desire as well as a medium of communication." It is a frustrating experience for a speech correctionist to discover that a child's mother is actively punishing the new response the therapist is trying to teach the child ("It sounds strange when he talks that way"). Despite the complexities, the therapist must attempt to examine the reinforcement variables that are maintaining the child's current behavior, and perhaps suppressing the acquisition of new responses.

Improper stimulation. The child must learn not only to emit certain responses, he must also learn the contexts in which they are appropriate. Though the milkman, father, and cabbages share certain properties, the child must learn that "Daddy" is appropriate to only one of these. Discretion alone dictates this! As in the case of reinforcement, stimulation may be inappropriate for a number of reasons, in terms of quality and sufficiency. To a great extent, speech appears to be modeled after the significant adults in the child's environment. It is not unusual to find that a child with a severe articulation disorder has a parent with a similar problem. If the opportunities to model speech are scarce, or if the model is itself defective, disordered speech may develop. Or it may be that the kind of stimulation provided by the environment is somehow not properly matched to the child's behavioral propensities. Horowitz (1965) suggested that developmental retardation may in some instances be due to an overabundance rather than a paucity of stimulation, depending on the child's threshold of arousal. She assumes that children differ in these thresholds and that, if proper measurement devices can be developed, it may be possible to intervene early where the normal practices of a family are simply not properly matched to the child's requirements.

Therapy. The historical cause for some behavioral deficit may be entirely unrelated to the necessities for remediation. Whatever the original source of a child's failure to develop adequate speech, the clinician's task is to marshal the currently available resources to help the child modify his behavior. Our current knowledge strongly suggests that these forces are contained within the reinforcement and stimulation contingencies highlighted by the model under discussion. For the most part, speech therapy consists of the systematic application of reinforcement for responses that increasingly approximate some norm, and in the presence of appropriate cues. If the child has little or no verbal repertoire, the task is to develop the necessary prerequisite behaviors that will move the child toward at least minimal verbal expression. Initially, this will involve a concentrated effort to bring about any sort of reasonable vocal behavior through direct reinforcement, shaping, and perhaps the nurturing of an imitative repertoire along the lines described by Baer, Peterson, and Sherman (1967).

If a child has the necessary responses, but emits them in inappropriate contexts, the program may have to concentrate on the antecedent contol. A great deal of speech therapy is fundamentally concerned with stimulus shift—bringing a response pattern into the context of appropriate stimulus conditions. McLean (1970) discusses this at great length in relationship to articulation therapy.

Summary of learning variables. A basic learning scheme can be used to organize our understanding of the acquisition of speech and to direct attention to variables that may contribute to the failure for such development. The primary variables are the child, the stimulation he receives, and the reinforcement his behavior generates. Even if we cannot accurately describe the original source of the child's problem, these same variables can be implemented in a program of therapy.

INTERPERSONAL APPROACHES

The second major area of concern is the "interpersonal" nature of speech. For the most part, speech occurs in the context of other persons, and one important way to study it is as a flow of behavior between a speaker and a listener. This approach is not inconsistent with the learning model discussed earlier, since the source of all reinforcement for verbal behavior is ultimately a listener. This is explicitly acknowledged in Skinner's (1957) definition of verbal behavior as behavior whose reinforcement is mediated by another person.

The interpersonal approach was recently discussed by Siegel (1967, 112–113):
> Briefly, this framework suggests that whenever *A* and *B* are together in a social situation, the behavior of each is at least partially a function of the responses and characteristics of the other. This approach seems especially cogent in the study of communication disorders since speech events are almost always interpersonal, involving both a speaker and a listener. Even if *A* is a speech clinician and *B* a child coming for correction, not only does the clinician modify the behavior of the child, but the child also exerts some influence over the behavior of the clinician.

Siegel summarizes a series of experiments in which retarded children were assembled with each other and with normal adults in a variety of dyadic interactions. In the experiments involving adult-child interactions, the retarded children were first classified as either high or low in verbal ability according to their performance on the Parsons Language Sample (Spradlin, 1963). The adults consistently used more simple, redundant verbal constructions with low-level children than they used with high-level children. The verbal behavior of the adults in these experiments was strongly influenced by the verbal characteristics of the children. These results raise some important and unanswered questions. To what extent do the adjustments spontaneously made by adults with retarded children facilitate the child's verbal performance? How do experienced and untrained clinicians differ in their response to these children? Does extensive practice in clinical work make the clinician more amenable or less amenable to the cues provided by children with differing verbal characteristics?

Rosenberg, Spradlin, and Mabel (1961) arranged a series of dyadic assemblies with retarded children in which the dyad could consist of: (1) two high-level children; (2) two low-level children; (3) a heterogeneous grouping of one high and one low-level child. Verbal output was greatest when the two children were of comparable verbal level, regardless of whether that level was high or low. The finding suggests that even severely retarded children are to some extent "socially sensitive." This raises some important issues concerning the kinds of assembly variables that might enhance performance of these youngsters.

We do not know why speakers modify their behavior in accord with listener characteristics. Perhaps adults have previously been reinforced for changing their speech patterns with verbally advanced and retarded children. Perhaps the source of the reinforcement lies in the child's response to the adult. It is conceivable that these results are best discussed in some framework other than learning theory. In any case, they do appear relevant to the management of children with severe language difficulties.

The interpersonal approach also lends itself to characterizing communication disorder in a way amenable to laboratory investigation. Speech is disordered in terms of its effect on a listener. There are no speech pathologies in nature. In normal communication we think of a speaker who has some "intent"—some message to communicate to a listener. Communication occurs when the speaker successfully encodes his intent, and in some way modifies or influences the listener. Communication is disordered when there is some defect in the speaker, the listener, or in the link between them. In the case of a deaf child, communication is defective because he does not adequately receive messages. The aphasic's difficulty is in the formulation of the message to be sent. In many communication disorders, the failure is in the transmission system between the speaker and listener, as in the case of a severe articulation problem, stuttering, or a voice disorder.

Formulations of this sort have an intuitive appeal, but they fall short of providing an operational model for communication disorder. In most interpersonal situations, the speaker's intent is an elusive property of his behavior. There is often no immediate way of telling whether the listener has been affected by the speaker's efforts, so that it is not obvious whether or not communication has been accomplished.

Elsewhere in this volume, Rosenberg describes an interpersonal strategy which has seemed to us admirably suited to the study of disordered communication. It is a two-person communication paradigm that has been used by several investigators (e.g., Maclay and Newman, 1960; Krauss and Weinheimer, 1964; Rosenberg and Cohen, 1966). In this paradigm, one person is designated the speaker and the other is the listener. Both have a set of stimuli, and it is the task of the speaker to communicate to his partner across a visual barrier so the partner can correctly select which stimulus is being described at any time. In this arrangement, the speaker's intent is defined as the particular design he is to describe. The adequacy of his communication is measured in terms of the listener's accuracy in selecting the correct designs.

At the University of Minnesota, we have initiated research to study communication disorder experimentally with this paradigm. (Tom Longhurst is engaged in this project for his doctoral research.) Speakers were given the task of communicating to a listener which of several ambiguous line-drawings to select. Communication between the two was regulated through a microphone-to-earphone system. Communication disorder was defined as distortion in the transmission link between the speaker and listener.

Adult subjects were assigned to several conditions. In one, the speaker had a clear channel for communication. Data from previous experiments suggest that performance will be essentially errorless in this situation. In a second condition, the listener received undistorted messages, but the message in the speaker's own earphone was distorted. In a third condition, the speaker heard his messages as undistorted, but distortion was introduced in the listener's ears. Finally, both speaker and listener were presented distorted transmissions of the speaker's messages.

Data are still being analyzed. We are basically interested in the verbal strategies devised by the listener and speaker to cope with the distortion introduced into the line, and in the extent to which the speaker is influenced by his own feedback in contrast to the performance feedback he receives from his partner. Though this is speculative, one can conceive of the severely misarticulating child as constantly attempting to send messages through a distorting transmission system of the sort described here. Children with severe articulation difficulties often have extensive language deficits. The general language deficiencies may reflect the child's attempts to deal with the responses he gets from listeners because of his articulation. That is, the child may be shaped to use linguistically aberrant forms of expression in his attempts to communicate through a defective transmission system of the sort we are attempting to model in this experiment.

LINGUISTIC APPROACHES

Developments in learning, and particularly in behavior modification, have provided some extremely potent approaches for modifying deviant behavior. What behavior modification has not done, however, is to specify the response units that characterize either delayed or normal speech. What are the useful ways to describe speech delay? If responses are to be reinforced, what are these responses? How are they sequenced in normal development, and how should they be sequenced in the case of abnormal development?

Linguistic analysis offers the promise of a method for specifying linguistic units so they can be put in the service of a behavioral analysis. It is not enough to find a logically compelling system for segmenting the stream of language. What is needed is a way of talking about language in terms of approaches the behavior modifier has developed and the therapist must use. Ultimately, a linguistic analysis must touch base with behavior if it is to make much of a contribution to the management of children with serious language problems.

At the same time, the mere specification of units is not sufficient. The task for the speech pathologist is to go beyond the descriptive system, to the concept of a communication disorder. No description of the speech or language of a child, no matter how elegant, will automatically identify the features of the child's linguistic performance which render him a disordered speaker. This simply means that a variation is not the same as a disordered speaker. The task remains to identify those particular features of a child's performance which mark him as an abnormal vendor of the language. Despite our continual attempts to devise formal diagnostic tests, the same considerations apply to information gleaned from such instruments. No test can tell us when a child is or is not retarded. There must be some other validating criterion.

The first thing that linguistics will provide is a way of talking about language. Even a relatively modest specification of the morphological feature of pluralization has already led to some creative implementations within the sphere of behavior modification (Guess, Sailor, Rutherford, and Baer, 1968). The next task, and this is not necessarily the linguist's, involves sorting out those linguistic features which appear relevant to the designation of speech retardation. Some serious research efforts are required to discover the ways in which linguistic subsystems are locked together in the development of verbal adequacy. Even after better methods are devised to describe language, it will still be necessary to determine how various levels of adequacy set the stage and are prerequisite to more advanced levels.

A number of investigators have recently turned to the task of implementing descriptive linguistic systems for retarded language performance. Notable among these are efforts by Laura Lee (1966), Carrow (1968), and Menyuk (1964). Haas (1963) has made such an effort with specific regard to severe articulation disorders. Speech pathologists will await with a good deal of anticipation further developments in linguistics. It will be a great boon if more of these efforts are directed toward the child with delayed language.

SUMMARY

There are three areas of current activity that promise to enhance our understanding of children with delayed speech. *Learning theory* provides a way of categorizing the stimulus events that impinge on the child and are responsible for the development of a repertoire of verbal behavior. At the same time, this approach suggests ways of organizing therapy. The *interpersonal approach* more clearly highlights the speaker-listener interaction and suggests ways for modeling communication disorder. *Psycholinguistics* offers the promise of identifying the behavioral units with which to enter the first two areas.

Ultimately, understanding of the language problems of children with language delays will be greatly enhanced at the points where these various approaches intersect—where linguistics helps us to identify what is or is not learned, learning theory suggests how it is learned, and the interpersonal orientation concerns the circumstances in which the learning occurs and is manifested.

SUMMARY OF DISCUSSION

QUESTION: In your learning theory model you cite a study in which they have conditioned the consonant type of responses versus vowels. Would you care to speculate about the relevance of such consonant versus vowel conditioning on later phonological development? Specifically, do you feel that in this approach you can condition the child at this very early age to respond, say, in terms of a C-V-C type of utterance category?

SIEGEL: To produce that sort of utterance? No, I shouldn't say so.

QUESTION: By the time you have gone through your conditioning experiment, won't you really have a hard time sorting out how much he has gotten from the conditioning experiment itself and how much is brought about by his own developmental sequence?

SIEGEL: I don't think so.

QUESTION: Can you condition a child in an American English environment to reinforce something which is not an English phoneme or an English phonemic sequence?

SIEGEL: There are certain kinds of deficiencies which can be identified early. For example, a deaf child. It would be interesting to find ways to condition the vocal repertoires of deaf children. The anecdotal data that continually reappear in the literature say that deaf children babble for awhile and then they stop. I'm not at all sure whether it would be possible to modify that pattern and maintain the early vocal behavior of deaf children. If we could get to the child with stimuli other than auditory it would be possible to maintain that vocal behavior. I simply don't know what ultimate effect that would have on the child in terms of subsequent language development. There have been no longterm studies on that. Most of the studies are of the sort to demonstrate that it is indeed possible to make some modification. The study by Routh I mentioned, the selective reinforcement one, is crucial, because the problem in trying to understand the child's phonemic development or speech-sound development in terms of a learning theory is to account for the modifications in his behavior that occur over time. The child becomes increasingly like the native speakers of the language around him. And if learning theory has some relevance, there must be some stimulus events which are related to that. Routh's study shows that it is possible to do some selective reinforcement. That might be one mechanism. What the source of the reinforcement is I'm not sure. There have been speculations about secondary reinforcement, carried through the child's own utterances of his sounds, and things of that sort.

QUESTION: Is not that consonant-vowel distinction, in terms of distinctive features, one people distinguish very early?

SIEGEL: Yes. Some studies involving children as young as 21 days old, or within the first couple of months, attempt to tap the child's abilities to discriminate across phoneme boundaries. Moffitt, at the University of Minnesota, attached electrodes to a child and got what appeared to be distinctive patterns of heart rate in relationship to, say, /ba/ versus /ga/ consonants after satiating the child. My version is a simplistic one which seems to implicate environmental selection of some aspect of the child's behavior to reinforce. There must be some interaction between the child's perceptual capabilities and the power of some reinforcing program of that sort. I don't know what this has to do with ultimate language learning, or whether modifications in the child's early behavior will have any far-reaching effects.

QUESTION: In reference to your interpersonal studies, have you any idea how you are going to analyze the message or structural analysis?

SIEGEL: Yes. This is the criterion problem, and that is what we are wrestling with now. The data by Krauss give us some help. I'm not sure how they relate to communication adequacy. Krauss finds, for example, that one dimension that changes when you put two adults in this task is the direction or length of the utterance. If the adult says first, "An hourglass-shaped thing with a long tail at the end standing on its side," the next thing he says is, "An hourglass on its side." Finally he just says, "Hourglass." So he codes it in that way. That appears to be a relatively sensitive index of changes occurring as communication becomes more efficient. I don't know exactly where we go from there. I assume some output measure will constitute one way to measure it. Maybe some attempt to assess type-token ratio or some attempt to get at the redundancy of the speaker's message as he handles these stressful kinds of situations will come about. It may also turn out that important variables have to do with changes in pitch and rate and intonation or something of this sort. We're really not sure now.

QUESTION: Mothers who come to the clinic reveal a good deal of anxiety about the language problems of their children. They worry about what it might mean now, what it might mean in the future. We feel that one important part of a clinical program is to help the parents with their feelings and with their handling of the child. And as the parents calm down, we very often see the children beginning to talk a good deal more and a good deal better, even though obviously showing language difficulty. It seems as though there has been an inhibition which has been provoked by the mother's anxiety which begins to lift. It certainly doesn't put an end to the language disorder, but it helps a good deal in getting the process started. Have you found this to be true?

SIEGEL: Yes. That concern for setting conditions is a relevant concern for clinicians.

QUESTION: You mentioned something about what a child does when it appears to him that he is not communicating. Have you made any observation of that?

SIEGEL: No. I was suggesting that it is important to look at the effect of a communication failure on other aspects of behavior. In the speech pathology literature where people address the question of the relationship between articulatory deficiencies and "language deficiencies," they usually suggest that the child who has a severe language deficit will have articulatory problems as well, because that is an expression of the same basic deficit. A child who has essentially adequate language but a severe articulation problem may devise strategies to "communicate" in the presence of this failure in the transmission system. I have no data but I do hope to explore that.

QUESTION: Fluent aphasias are practically never seen in children with acquired brain disease. I don't know of any neurological reason to account for that. But does not the maintenance of a fluent aphasia in adults have something to do with a person's comprehension of whether or not he is talking silly?

SIEGEL: Yes. Regardless of what problems the child has, language serves a communication function in generating reactions from environment with which he must deal. He must deal with monitoring his own behavior. At the same time, he must monitor the listener's behavior. That is what defines the communication situation. Those forces somehow are brought to bear on the development or the maldevelopment the child demonstrates.

QUESTION: You mentioned that one way in which you plan to use the speaker-listener paradigm is to distort the transmission. Are there additional ways that situation can be exploited?

SIEGEL: One possibility would be to use disordered speakers or disordered listeners. The problem is knowing exactly what dimensions to introduce in order to have some experimental control over the source of the disorder. If I knew how to describe the nature of a disordered speaker, I could create a disordered speaker by imposing certain things between the speaker and the listener.

QUESTION: In the naturalistic setting where an individual with a communication disorder evokes a response from a listener, the nature of that response may often affect the way the individual sees himself. Could not what you are proposing lend itself to the introduction, a structured introduction, of affect?

SIEGEL: It could. The problem is that when I introduce a disordered speaker, I don't know what parameters I introduce. That is a complex phenomenon. In a way, what I want to know is what happens to a normal speaker when he is functioning as though he were a defective speaker.

QUESTION: But you have said you don't know the parameters of a defective speaker, so how can you study a normal speaker when he is subject to those parameters?

SIEGEL: Right. I don't know what dimensions are important. I am just going to have to start out with some intuition.

QUESTION: You might interrupt systematically, but how can random interruption be systematic? Are you interested in just any gross interruption of communication?

SIEGEL: There are many parameters. I have purposely devised this to be loose, rather than pinning either speaker or listener roles. I chose not to do that, because I think that reduces the experiment to a neat methodology, but I am afraid it "trivializes" the kinds of questions I want to ask. So a number of things are floating free— listener variation, speaker variation, and things in between. I would like to identify some source of distortion. I don't really care much what it is as long as it reduces the listener's capability of performing the task. I chose interruption rate because that is something my laboratory is equipped to deal with. I can introduce interruption rates across a number of parameters, and there are some data from audiometric literature, intelligibility literature, concerning effects of interruption rates upon listener's ability to select which of several sets he has heard through a set of earphones.

So what I would like to start to do is identify some interruption rates which cause the listener to perform poorly, at perhaps 50 per cent of his former performance. That is one way I can manage the variable of listener performance. Another way would be to have a computer there instead of a listener and tell the speaker, "Now your listener did well," "Now your listener did poorly," and observe the behavior of the speaker. I would rather not do that, because then there is no contingency between the speaker's actual behavior and the report he is getting from the computer. So I want to devise a way in which I could actually manipulate through some external means the likelihood the listener will or will not perform adequately. It doesn't matter to me whether it parallels or serves as an analog for any kind of specific disorder, because they are all different anyway. But it must constitute an analog for a situation where for some reason a listener's performance vis-a-vis a speaker is less than optimal. And then I want to study the strategies that the speaker will use or adopt to deal with that. The crucial question is what dimension those strategies will take.

QUESTION: Do you propose to start with specific instructions for a listener to perform with a prescribed interruption rate that guarantees he can only perform 50 per cent? Will you allow a speaker to make whatever modifications he wants to make to beat that interruption rate, like shorten words and go to monosyllables and stuff like that?

SIEGEL: Yes. And we hope to find what dimensions of speaker-listener interaction are responsible for it.

QUESTION: If you have a phonological disorder, won't that make pluralization difficult?

SIEGEL: Right. And that raises an incredibly complicated problem. The specific nature of the interruption may have an overbearing effect on the quality of the speaker's adaption.

REFERENCES

Baer, D., Peterson, R., and Sherman, J. The development of imitation by reinforcing behavioral similarity to a model. *J. Exp. Anal. Behavior,* 1967, *10,* 405–416.
Bijou, S. W. A functional analysis of retarded development. In N. R. Ellis (Ed.), *International review of research in mental retardation.* New York: Academic Press, 1966. Vol. 1. Pp. 1–19.
Carrow, Sister Mary Arthur. The development of auditory comprehension of language structure in children. *J. Speech Hearing Dis.,* 1968, *39,* 99–111.
Gardner, R. A., and Gardner, B. Teaching sign language to a chimpanzee. *Science,* 1969, *165,* 664–672.
Guess, D., Sailor, W., Rutherford, G., and Baer, D. An experimental analysis of linguistic development: The productive use of the plural morpheme. *J. Appl. Behavior Anal.,* 1968, *1,* 297–306.
Haas, W. Phonological analysis of a case of dyslalia. *J. Speech Hearing Dis.,* 1963, *28,* 239–246.
Horowitz, F. D. Theories of arousal and retardation potential. *Ment. Retard.,* 1965, *3,* 20–23.
Krauss, R. M., and Weinheimer, S. Changes in reference phrases as a function of frequency of usage in social interaction: A preliminary study. *Psychon. Science,* 1964, *1,* 113–114.
Lee, L. Developmental sentence types: A method for comparing normal and deviant syntactic development. *J. Speech Hearing Dis.,* 1966, *4,* 311–330.
Longhurst, T. Effects of communication disorder on speaker and listener behavior. Unpublished Ph.D. thesis, University of Minnesota, 1971.
Maclay, H., and Newman, S. Two variables affecting the message in communication. In D. Willner (Ed.), *Decisions, values and groups.* New York: Pergamon Press, 1960. Pp. 218–228.
McLean, J. Extending stimulus control of phoneme articulation by operant techniques. In F. Girardeu and J. Spradlin (Eds.), A functional analysis approach to speech and language. *ASHA Monographs,* 1970, *14,* 24–47.
Menyuk, P. Comparison of grammar of children with functionally deviant and normal speech. *J. Speech Hearing Res.,* 1964, *7,* 109–121.
Milisen, R. A rationale for articulation disorders. *J. Speech Hearing Dis.,* Monogr. Suppl. 4, 1954, 5–18.
Rheingold, H. L., Gewirtz, L., and Ross, H. W. Social conditioning of vocalizations in the infant. *J. Comp. Physiol. Psychol.,* 1959, *52,* 68–73.
Rosenberg, S., and Cohen, B. D. Referential processes of speakers and listeners. *Psychol. Rev.,* 1966, *73,* 208–231.
Rosenberg, S., Spradlin, J., and Mabel, S. Interaction among retarded children as a function of their relative language skills. *J. Abnor. Social Psychol.,* 1961, *63,* 402–410.
Routh. D. K. Conditioning of vocal response differentiation in infants. *Develop. Psychol.,* 1969, *1,* 219–226.
Siegel, G. M. Interpersonal approaches to the study of communication disorders. *J. Speech and Hearing Dis.,* 1967, *32,* 112–120.
Skinner, B. F. *Verbal behavior.* New York: Appleton-Century-Crofts, 1957.
Spradlin, J. Assessment of speech and language of retarded children: The Parsons Language Sample. *J. Speech Hearing Dis.,* Monogr. Suppl. 10, 1963, 8–31.
Todd, R. A., and Palmer, B. Social reinforcement of infant babbling. *Child Develop.,* 1968, *39,* 591–596.
Weisberg, P. Social and nonsocial conditioning of infant vocalization. *Child Develop.,* 1963, *34,* 377–388.

A BEHAVIORAL SYSTEM FOR ASSESSING LANGUAGE DEVELOPMENT

DONA L. HEDRICK and ELIZABETH M. PRATHER
University of Washington

DONA LEA HEDRICK is an assistant professor of speech and has been employed by the Child Development and Mental Retardation Center at the University of Washington since 1966. She is currently assistant director of the speech and hearing services within the CDMR Center. As such, she directs the clinical training program of the graduate students in speech pathology in the CDMR facility. In addition, she is a staff member of the Behavioral Research Unit at CDMRC where the current language research was conducted. As a member of the Speech Department, Miss Hedrick also teaches classes in the language area at the University of Washington. Prior to the present appointment, she was a speech and language therapist at the Pilot School, an experimental program for brain-injured children at the University of Washington.

Miss Herick's academic training includes B.A. and M.A. degrees from the University of Iowa and a Ph.D. degree from the University of Washington.

ELIZABETH M. PRATHER is an associate professor in the Department of Speech of the University of Washington. She received her B.A. degree in Speech at the University of Nebraska and her M.A. and Ph.D. degrees in Speech Pathology and Audiology at the University of Iowa. She has taught at the University of Washington since 1964 in the areas of speech diagnosis and research methods. In addition, part of her time is spent at the Child Development and Mental Retardation Center in language diagnosis and research. Mrs. Prather's early research, conducted as a research associate at the University of Iowa, was in the area of measurement of articulation and stuttering severity.

Speech and language clinicians are often asked to evaluate the speech and language maturity of children. The recent emphasis on language research has resulted in useful diagnostic tools (REP, D'Asaro and John, 1961; ITPA, Kirk et al., 1968) and in information about linguistic development (McNeill, 1966; Lee, 1966; and Menyuk, 1969). Interest in the child occasionally centers only on obtaining an adequate estimate of his age level of functioning. More often the purpose of the appraisal includes therapeutic recommendations. Such recommendations are useful when the clinician can identify the progressive steps needed for the training program.

In order to determine specific therapeutic needs, the clinician must know the sequence of steps prerequisite to normal language learning. Spradlin, in discussing language testing, has indicated: "A second problem with most of the tests is that even if we assume that adequate performance on the tasks sampled by the sub-tests are

---

The Sequenced Inventory of Language Development Test (SILD), which is an integral part of the language model presented in this chapter, was developed by the staff of the Child Development and Mental Retardation Center, University of Washington. LuVern H. Kunze, program administrator; Dona Lea Hedrick and Elizabeth M. Prather, principal investigators; Jane Rieke, Annette Rominger, and Francine King, Children's Bureau Staff at the University of Washington.

necessary, the test is not ordered in such a way as to indicate the point at which we should start training or therapy (Schiefelbusch et al., 1967)."

Although broad stages of language development (such as crying, cooing, babbling, first words, and word combinations) have been identified, there is no systematic definition of the small progressive steps of language learning. Such a system would involve basing a scale of language testing on a theoretical model of language development, and testing children longitudinally to determine developmental steps. We felt that if such a scale were constructed and validated, clinicians could eventually use it as a basis for determining specific remedial programming.

The first two steps in the development of such a tool are: (1) development of a theoretical model of the hierarchy of language behaviors; and (2) a preliminary study to test the hypothesized ordering of the behaviors that fit within the model or are generated from it. The purpose of our presentation is to discuss these two steps.

EXPERIMENTAL LANGUAGE MODEL

Receptive Language Model

The first of the two major sections of the model is the receptive portion. The receptive model contains three categories of behaviors. The first category is *awareness*. Items included under the category of awareness are those items that require observable response to sound or speech presented in the immediate environment. The items in this section are used only at the youngest age levels.

The next category is that of *discrimination*. The child's ability to respond differentially to sound or speech stimuli is evaluated from mother's reports of differential responses at home and by the child's demonstration of discrimination of noise makers and speech sounds within the testing situation.

The third category of receptive behaviors is *understanding*. The items in this category require the child to demonstrate that speech has become meaningful by having him perform directed tasks. The items progress from correct responses to speech under three conditions: (1) speech accompanied by gestures, (2) speech accompanied by situational cues, (3) speech alone. The directed tasks change in both vocabulary and in length and complexity.

Expressive Language Model

The second major section of the model is expressive language. This section is much more difficult to construct. The presumed progression occurs within many different kinds of expressive behaviors, among which could be included linguistic, quantitative, and psychological paradigms. Five classifications are included in this model. Three are expressive behaviors, two are types of expressive measurement. The three expressive behaviors include assumed levels of progression from motor to presymbolic vocalization to symbolic vocalization. The two expressive measurements are based entirely on symbolic utterances.

The major headings of the expressive language model may be outlined as follows:
   I. Expressive Behaviors
      A. Imitating
      B. Initiating
      C. Responsive
   II. Expressive Measurements
      A. Verbal Output
      B. Articulation

Under expressive behaviors, the first category is imitating behaviors. Items included in this subsection require the child to repeat an immediately previous motor or speech event. This event is initially produced by someone other than the child. No known intervening stimulus occurs. (Imitating behaviors are included in the model even though it is not known whether or not they are important precursors to development of normal language. Inclusion seems necessary to provide us with data to allow us to try to answer this question. Moreover, imitative items allow direct testing prior to an age when other expressive behaviors are readily obtained in the examination situation.)

The second category of expressive behaviors is initiating behaviors. The items under this category include motor and speech behaviors that occur without any apparent relationship to a previous *verbal* event. Antecedent events might be nonverbal environmental actions or objects or might represent some "drive state" of the the individual. The antecedent event may be known or unknown, but it is not a verbal event. It is difficult to elicit, systematically, initiating behaviors in a testing situation where the child is primarily responding to the examiner's instructions. The Parsons Language Scale (Spradlin, 1963) does attempt systematic sampling of initiating behaviors, but the author reports that such test items showed poor reliability of administration and scoring. For this reason, our initiating test items are, in the main, based on information obtained from the parents.

The last category of expressive behaviors is responsive behaviors. The behaviors under this category include only vocal responses that are appropriate to preceding vocal stimuli presented by the examiner. Items that require motor responses are not included in the expressive model. All such items are included under the understanding section of the receptive model.

The next major heading is expressive measurements. The two categories in this section include verbal output and articulation. For all children two years of age and older, a 50-response language sample is obtained as described in Chapter 7 of Johnson et al. (1963). From this language sample, quantitative and descriptive data are obtained. The second category, articulation, includes the data on the articulation skills of children two years of age and older. These articulation behaviors are assessed through the use of selected items from the Photo Articulation Test (Pendergast et al., 1969).

REPORT OF PRELIMINARY STUDY

Items which fit within the framework of the above language model were collected from sources such as the REP Scale (D'Asaro and John, 1961) and the Denver Developmental Screening Test (Frankenberg and Dodds, 1967). We wrote specific behavioral instructions for the stimulus presentation and the response requirements for these traditional language items. In addition, we formulated new items to test language behaviors needed for the hierarchy of the model. These items represented the experimental edition of the SILD Test.

SEQUENCED INVENTORY OF LANGUAGE DEVELOPMENT TEST CONSTRUCTION

The experimental edition of the scale included 148 receptive language items and 162 expressive items (310 items total) representing an expected performance level from birth through five years. The procedures for the administration of the items and the ordering of the items were the outgrowth of two previous studies, each of one year in duration. In addition to these items, all children over two years of age were given the Peabody Picture Vocabulary Test, portions of the ITPA and PAT, and a 50-response language sample was obtained.

SUBJECTS

The subjects consisted of 82 children selected from the Well Child Clinic at the University of Washington. Most were children of families in which at least one parent was obtaining a university degree. There was no attempt to make the sampling representative of the general population. Subjects ranged in age from three months to four years. They were divided into 15 age groups, each representing a three-month age interval. The number of children in each interval ranged from four to eight with a mean of 5.5.

EXAMINATION PROCEDURES

The examining teams were composed of a primary examiner and a recorder. The two original pilot studies had been used to isolate the specific items to be tested at a given age level; hence, only a portion of each scale was administered to any one child. All testing was administered on an individual basis with a parent present. Testing time varied from a minimum of 30 minutes for infants to a maximum of 75 minutes for children two years of age old and older.

RESULTS

A pilot or preliminary study never yields conclusive results. Many limitations imposed on the preliminary study need consideration in any cross-sectional or longitudinal work in the future. Only 82 children between the ages of three months and four years have been tested. This number is insufficient for basic normative data. In addition, these children were not representative of a general population. However, the preliminary data have been useful in determining which items among the original 310 showed a progression of "correct response" with age, and in establishing the sequence of items along an age continuum. Each test item was scored according to the percentage of correct responses obtained from the children tested at each age interval. Each item was placed sequentially within the framework of the language model according to the age level at which it was passed by at least 75 percent of the subjects.

The items retained include those that show a progression of correct performance with age. For example, in the receptive scale one item is that of asking the child to "give me" the only object that is on the table (asking without an accompanying gesture). Approximately half of the children aged 15 to 17 months completed this item. More than 75 percent completed it by the ages of 18 to 20 months. All children responded correctly at the 21 to 23 month level. In our sequencing of items, this item would be placed at the 18 to 20 month age level though it would be tested at earlier age levels.

It has been necessary, on the basis of the preliminary data, to eliminate or revise many of the original items for one or more reasons:

1. Elimination of items in which percentage of correct response did not increase with increasing age. (Example: Asking for first and last name. This item was responded to correctly by 75 percent at the age level of 30 to 32 months but was responded to with less consistency at older age levels.)
2. Elimination of items in which percentage of correct response remained low at all age levels. For example, imitation of rhythmic patterns did not show developmental progression.
3. Revision of items in which criteria for scoring the items were poorly defined and unreliable among examiners. (Example: Child's response to the question "when did you see Daddy?")
4. Revision of items that did not appear to test what they were designed to test. (Example: Our original speech sound discrimination items were probably testing receptive vocabulary more than speech sound discrimination per se.)
5. Revision of items in which the examiners reported difficulty in administering the items. (Example: Testing response to intonation with phrase, "don't touch.")

Table I shows the ordering of the receptive test items based on the preliminary study. Minimal instructions for each item are shown. Complete instructions for administering and scoring each item are available in the SILD Test Manual (Hedrick and Prather, 1970). At the end of Table I is the receptive profile where the numbers of the test items are placed within the age intervals at which they were passed by at least 75 per cent of the children. The profile also shows the distribution of the items according to the language model. Table II gives the equivalent information for the expressive test items.

TABLE 1

Language Reception Items and Profile.* The items are listed in developmental sequence.

1. Responses to verbalization. Speaker is approximately 3 feet in front of child. Stimulus "Hi there" is given at a time when the child is not looking at the examiner. Attempt a second time if there is no response the first time.

    Looks up or smiles: 1st trial   2nd trial

2. Turns to "Look here" spoken at approximately 3 feet, 90° angle from child. Test both ears.
    a) Left ear—turns to localize
    b) Right ear—turns to localize

3. Response to various sounds initiated at approximately 3 feet, 135° from child. Randomize presentations.
    a) cellophane—left ear—turns to localize
    b) rattle—left ear—turns to localize
    c) cellophane—right ear—turns to localize
    d) rattle—right ear—turns to localize

4-mr. Does the child respond to noises in the home? Ask mother "How does baby respond to doorbell, telephone, vacuum cleaner, door-slam, etc." Have mother describe ways in which child responds to different sounds. Score yes if mother can give two examples of response to sound.

5. Response to familiar and unfamiliar voices. Mother and examiner alternate in calling child's name while child is engrossed with a toy.
    a) Examiner's voice—turns to localize
    b) Mother's voice—turns to localize

6. a-mr) Ask mother if child responds with appropriate gesture to "come up" or "come here."
    b) Responds with appropriate gesture to verbalization "come up" or "come here" accompanied by gesture. Examiner moves around table to the child.

7. Responds appropriately to "don't touch." A *cup, spoon,* and a *shoe* are placed before the child and if the child spontaneously reaches for any of them, the examiner says "don't touch."

*Copyright ©, 1970 by D. L. Hedrick and E. M. Prather.

TABLE 1 *(continued)*

---

8. For all children 8 months or older ask "What kinds of words does the child understand?" List a representative sample or circle examples listed. Must have two examples from parent, not including examples given by examiner.

    a) Toys—doll, car, book, etc. _____

    b) Names of family members—daddy, baby, grandma, etc. _____

    _____

    c) Items of clothing—shoes, socks, shirts, etc. _____

    _____

    d) Verbs—see, want, cook, come, etc. _____

    _____

    e) Names of acquaintances _____

    f) Household tools—scissors, hammer _____

    _____

    g) Names of outdoor items—trees, flowers, etc. _____

    _____

    h) Descriptive words—fast, hard, old, etc. _____

    _____

    i) Pronouns—I, me, you, etc. _____

    j) Names of buildings _____

    k) Names of games _____

9. Gives toy on request when verbal request is accompanied by a gesture. A *ball, car,* and *doll* are set before child and examiner asks for whatever toy child puts his hand on by saying, "Give it to me, give it to me," and holding out his hand.

10-mr. Ask mother if child responds appropriately by going to or looking toward such sounds as doorbell and telephone. It is important that the examples illustrate differential responses for a yes score. _____

(Cont.)

TABLE 1 *(continued)*

11. Responds appropriately to four different direction commands. Toy car is placed at opposite end of table out of reach. Circle correct responses. These commands are *not* to be accompanied by gestures.
    a) Get the car
    b) Put it on the paper
    c) Give it to me
    d) Where's the light/point to the light

12. a) Child responds to a specific word. A *cup, spoon,* and *shoe* are placed before the child. The examiner says, "Show me the _____," naming an object the child is not touching.
    b-mr) If child does not show the object, ask mother if child responds to specific words at home.

13. Child responds by pointing or touching on command. Toy *bear, chair, key, tree, box* and *socks* are set on the table in that order. Circle correct response. Each command is given once.

a)	Show me the chair	yes	no	d)	Show me the box	yes	no
b)	Show me the socks	yes	no	e)	Show me the tree	yes	no
c)	Show me the key	yes	no	f)	Show me the bear	yes	no

14. Responds by looking or moving toward a familiar person when named. Examiner asks "Where's mama?"

15. Points to parts of body in response to command "Where is" or "Show me." Circle correct responses. If child does not respond, ask mother if child will do so at home.

    Examiner's Report   *Mother's Report*

a)	nose	yes	no	a-mr)	nose	yes	no
b)	eyes	yes	no	b-mr)	eyes	yes	no
c)	hair	yes	no	c-mr)	hair	yes	no
d)	mouth	yes	no	d-mr)	mouth	yes	no
e)	ears	yes	no	e-mr)	ears	yes	no

16. Responds to "sit down" and/or "stand up."
    (mr) If there is no response to the above, ask mother if child will sit down and/or stand up on request.

17. Responses to prepositional commands. The examiner puts two open boxes on the table, one facing up and the other inverted. The examiner hands the child a block and gives the following commands:
    a) Put the block on a box.
    b) Put the block in a box.
    c) Put the block beside a box.
    d) Put the block under a box.

18. Responds with gesture/vocalization to "bye-bye" when presented:
    a) Without accompanying gesture
    b) With accompanying gesture

TABLE 1 *(continued)*

19. Responses to number concepts of one or more than one. Place a box and six spoons on the table. Examiner then gives the following commands:
    a) Put one spoon in the box.
    b) Put in one more.
    c) Put in all of them, or put in the rest of them.

20. Child's response to directions involving plurals. Four plastic cars and a box are placed on the table.
    a) Put the car in the box.
    b) Put the cars in the box.
    Cars are removed—four plastic spoons are placed on the table.
    c) Put some spoons in the box.
    d) Put a spoon in the box.

21. Responses to commands involving direction plus modifier.
    a) Let me see you walk.
    b) Let me see you walk fast.
    c) Let me see you walk slowly.

22. Child's understanding of words. Pictures of *book, stove, shoe,* and *pipe* are placed on table in that order. Examiner says:
    a) Show me what mom cooks on.
    b) Show me what you wear on your feet.
    c) Show me what you read.

23. Responses to commands involving two objects. *Ball, spoon, show, cup,* and *dog* are placed on the table in that order. Examiner says:
    a) Give me the cup and the spoon.
    b) Give me the cup and the ball.
    c) Give me the shoe and the dog.

24. Gross sound discrimination of noisemakers. See manual for exact directions. A sound is presented and the child is asked to "find the noise" or "show me which one it was." Response demands that the child reach for correct sound maker.
    a) bell
    b) rattle
    c) cellophane

25-mr. Ask mother if child understands taking turns. _____

(Cont.)

26. Responses to commands involving two actions. The *spoon, cup, dog, ball,* and *shoe* are placed on the table in that order. Circle *yes* if child completes both actions, regardless of order.

   a) Put the cup in your lap and give me the ball.   yes   no
   b) Hold the spoon in your hand and turn the cup over.   yes   no
   c) Give me the dog and put the shoe on the floor.   yes   no

27. Responses to questions involving contrasts of big and little. One pair at a time is placed before the child. Examiner says, "Show me the _____." A *yes* response is indicated only if the child responds correctly on all three items.

   a) big car   yes   no
   b) little candle   yes   no
   c) little ball   yes   no

28. Responses to requests to show colors. Place the six colored blocks on the table, in a random group. Child is asked to show:

   a) orange   yes   no   d) yellow   yes   no
   b) purple   yes   no   e) green   yes   no
   c) blue   yes   no   f) red   yes   no

29. Responses to questions involving hard and soft. One pair of items at a time is placed before the child. The soft item is always placed on the examiner's left. Examiner says, "Show me the _____ one."

   a) (circles) hard
   b) (triangles) soft
   c) (squares) soft

30. Responses to questions involving rough and smooth. One pair of items at a time is placed before the child. The smooth items are always placed on the examiner's right. Examiner says, "Show me the _____ one."

   a) (circles) rough
   b) (triangles) smooth
   c) (squares) rough

31. Responses to requests to show coins. A *nickel, penny, dime,* and *quarter* are placed before the child and he is asked to show the following:

   a) penny
   b) dime
   c) nickel

32. Discrimination of three bells: Low, medium, and high tones. Same instructions as number 24.

   a) high
   b) low
   c) medium

BEHAVIORAL SYSTEM FOR ASSESSING DEVELOPMENT

TABLE 1 *(continued)*

33. Responses to commands involving three actions. The *cup, spoon, ball, shoe, dog,* and *book* are placed on the table in that order. Circle *yes* if child completes the three actions in a command regardless of order. Number order of responses.

    a) Put the cup in your lap, give me the ball, and open the book. yes no
    b) Hold the spoon in your hand, turn the cup over, and put the dog on the book. yes no
    c) Put the spoon on the book, put the dog on the floor, and give me the cup. yes no

34. Responses to "number" requests. Place *eleven spoons* on the table. Examiner says, "Give me _____ spoons."

    a) 3 spoons   yes no   d) 7 spoons   yes no
    b) 4 spoons   yes no   e) 10 spoons yes no
    c) 6 spoons   yes no

35. Speech discrimination. See manual for exact directions. Circle correct responses, underline incorrect responses. Record score as fraction (number correct over total number of items). The (*) signs indicate a suggested reinforcement schedule for the phrase "good listening." More frequent reinforcement may be given.

Training List #1	*Test List #1*	*Training List #2*	*Test List #2*
bus	bus*	soap	soap*
bus	bum	soap	soap*
bick	bus*	loap	sip
bus	suss	roap	choap*
corn	bees*	soap	soap
beb	bus	soad	soat
bus	buh*		soap
bus	bose*		soup
foss	bus		soa
bus	bus		soap*
bus	fuss		zoap
	base		soap
	bus		foap*
	bus*		oap
	tus*		soap*
	bus		soab

(Cont.)

TABLE 1 *(continued)*

RECEPTIVE PROFILE

Ages	Awareness		Discrimination		Understanding	
	Sound	Speech	Sound	Speech	Words +	Words
3–5 mo.	3 (a) (c)	1 2 (a) (b)				
6–8 mo.	3 (b) (d) 4 (mr)					
9–11 mo.				5 (a) (b)	6 (a-mr) 7	
12–14 mo.					6 (b) 9	8 (a-mr) (b-mr) (c-mr)
15–17 mo.			10 (mr)			15 (a-mr)
18–20 mo.				13 (c) (f)	11 (a) (c)	8 (d-mr) (e-mr) 12 (a) (b-mr) 15 (b-mr) (c-mr) (d-mr) (e-mr)
21–23 mo.				13 (a) (b) (d) (e)	11 (b) 14 18 (b)	8 (f-mr) (g-mr) 11 (d) 15 (a) 16 16 (mr) 17 (b)
24–26 mo.				35		8 (h-mr) 15 (b) (c) (d) (e) 18 (a) 19 (a) (b)

TABLE 1 *(continued)*

Ages	Awareness		Discrimination		Understanding	
	Sound	Speech	Sound	Speech	Words +	Words
27–29 mo.				35		8 (i-mr) 17 (a) 19 (c) 20 (a) (b) (c) (d) 21 (a)
30–32 mo.				35		8 (j-mr) 17 (c) 22 (a) (b) (c) 23 (a) (b) (c)
33–35 mo.			24 (a) (b) (c)	35		8 (k-mr) 21 (b) (c) 25 26 (a) (b) 27 28 (a) (b) 29 30 31 (a)
36–38 mo.			32 (a) (b) (c)	35	26 (c) 28 (e) 28 (c) 33 (a) (d)	
39–41 mo.				35		17 (d) 28 (f)
42–44 mo.				35		33 (b)
45–47 mo.				35		34 (a)
48+ mo.				35		31 (b) (c) 33 (c) 34 (b) (c) (d) (e)

TABLE 2

Language Expression Items and Profile. The items are listed in developmental sequence.

1-mr.	Does baby cry? _____
2-mr.	Can you tell the difference between cries? Ask mother to describe how he cries when he is: (Score yes if mother can describe the difference between cries.)
	hungry _____
	cross _____
	in pain _____
3-mr.	Does baby laugh aloud? _____
4-mr.	Does baby talk when you approach him talking? _____
5-mr.	Does baby talk to people? _____
6-mr.	Ask mother what kinds of sounds the baby makes other than laughing and crying. Examiner records examples and circles sounds heard during the evaluation.
	a) Vowels _____
	b) Consonant-vowel combinations _____
	(c) Consonants _____
	d) Consonant-vowel combinations that sound like words _____
7-mr.	Does baby make any kind of vocalizations when something he likes is taken away from him?
8-mr.	Does baby talk to toys or things that move, like a mobile or to things in the house? _____
9-mr.	Does baby rock and make accompanying noises? _____
10-mr.	Does baby talk more when you talk back to him? _____
11-mr.	If you imitate the sounds he makes, does he continue to vocalize? _____
12-mr.	Does he ever imitate sounds that you make? _____

TABLE 2 *(continued)*

13.	This item to be administered when examiner meets child in waiting room. Record exactly what child says or NR for no response.

Examiner says: Child's Response

    a) Hi (name of child)   _____

    b) How are you?   _____

    mr) If child does not respond, ask mother if child answers these questions.

    Record what mother says _____

14-mr. Does he use different inflectional patterns? _____

_____

15-mr. Does baby use a question inflection? _____

_____

16-mr. Imitation of motor acts. The examiner attempts to obtain the responses first. If not successful he then obtains the mother's report.

    Examiner's observation   Mother's report

a)	returns ball by rolling	yes	no	a-mr)	yes	no
b)	blocks in box	yes	no	b-mr)	yes	no
c)	stacking blocks	yes	no	c-mr)	yes	no
d)	claps hands	yes	no	d-mr)	yes	no
e)	peek-a-boo	yes	no	e-mr)	yes	no

17-mr. Imitation of non-speech sounds.

    Examiner's observation   Mother's report

a)	tongue click	yes	no	a-mr)	yes	no
b)	motor sound	yes	no	b-mr)	yes	no
c)	cough	yes	no	c-mr)	yes	no

18-mr. Ask mother what names (consistent sound combinations) baby uses for objects he wants.

    Record phonetically _____

_____

19-mr. Mother reports child uses intonational patterns that sound like he is talking in phrases or

    sentences. _____

_____

(Cont.)

TABLE 2 *(continued)*

20-mr. Does child ever point to pictures or objects and act like he wants mother to name them for him? _____

_____

21-mr. Mother reports child says "no" or "no-no" when you ask him a question or take something from him. _____

_____

22. Child's response to balloon: (record what child says)
    a) Child gestures and/or vocalizes about balloon _____

    _____

    b) Child names or makes statement about balloon _____

    _____

    c) Child indicates he wants balloon _____

    _____

    d) Child asks for balloon at end of session _____

    _____

23-mr. Does he imitate inflectional patterns that he hears you make, like scolding or talking on the telephone? If mother can describe, score yes. _____

24-mr. Does the child ask questions? Ask mother for two examples.

_____

_____

25. Imitation of speech sounds. Circle the correctly imitated sounds. If sound is incorrectly imitated, record the production phonetically. Test all five.
    a) 'i' ___; b) 'm' ___; c) 'p' ___; d) 'n' ___; e) 'g' ___

26. Imitation of two syllable combinations
    a) ma-ma
    b) pa-pa

TABLE 2 (continued)

27. Examiner places, one at a time, pictures of a *ball, shoe,* and *baby* on the table before the child. Examiner asks, "What's that?" Record child's answer.

    a) ball _____

    b) shoe _____

    c) baby _____

28. Did child spontaneously imitate words during the examination? Record examples. _____

29. Does child imitate words on request? The child is shown one picture at a time. Examiner attempts to elicit an imitation. Circle ones imitated. Child must attempt to imitate at least two to score yes.

    a) pipe   d) dog
    b) cake   e) monkey
    c) table

30-mr. Ask mother if child relates immediate experiences to another member of the family. _____

31. The examiner places *car, shoe,* and *spoon* in front but out of reach of the child. Examiner asks, "Which one do you want to play with?" A correct response requires verbal naming.

    Record response of child. _____

32. Response to a question. Does child reply "yes" or "no"? Examiner takes several cars from a box and says:

    a) I have lots of cars here on the table (Examiner points to his cars). Do you have any here? (points to table area in front of the child) (no)

    b) Do you want one? (either yes or no)

    mr) If child does not answer, ask mother if he uses "yes" and "no" appropriately at home.

33. Repetition of digits and words: (two per second)

    a) 1–2   yes   no   d) yes   no   ball-bike
    b) 4–2–1   yes   no   e) yes   no   sky-tree-dog
    c) 5–5–1–4   yes   no   f) yes   no   shoe-cow-bell-chair

    Repetition of sentences:

    g) I see those kittens. _____

    h) There is a big ball in the box. _____

(Cont.)

TABLE 2 *(continued)*

  i) Now I'll play with cars and trucks. _____

  j) I don't know why he's crying. _____

34. A *block* and a *cup* are placed on the table. Examiner says, "I'm going to do some things with the block. I'm going to put it *on* the cup; *under* the cup; *beside* the cup; and *in* the cup. Now you tell me where it is. Where's the block?" Circle correct response or record what child says. It's:

  a) in _____

  b) on _____

  c) under _____

  d) beside _____

35-mr. Ask mother if child uses "why" questions. Ask for two examples of situations in which child uses "why." _____

36. Examiner asks child, "What do you play at home?" Record what child says. _____

37. Use of plurals. Give to all children two years of age or older.

  a) Here is a car. Here are two _____

  b) Here is a cat. Here are two _____

  c) Here is a dog. Here are two _____

  d) Here is a box. Here are two _____

  e) Here is a leaf. Here are two _____

  f) Here is a knife. Here are two _____

38. Response to "what" question involving noun answer.

  What do you wear on your feet? _____

39. Response to "what" question involving verb answer.

  What do you do when you are hungry? _____

40. Response to "what" question involving more than a single word response. If the child gives only a single word response, examiner says, "tell me more."

  What toys do you have? _____

TABLE 2 *(continued)*

41.	Responses to questions asking function.	
	a)	What are books for? _____
	b)	What are keys for? _____
	c)	What is a stove for? _____
42.	Response to "when" question.	
	When you go to bed, what do you wear? _____	
43.	Responses to "if" questions.	
	a)	If you had a penny, what would you do? _____
	b)	If you fell down, what would you do? _____
44.	What says meow? _____	
45.	What animals do you see at the zoo? _____	
46.	How did you get here today? _____	
47-mr.	Ask mother if child uses "how" questions. Example. _____	
48.	When did you get up? _____	
49.	What do you drink from? _____	
50.	Verbal identification of "how many." Examiner puts a certain number of spoons in front of the child and asks, "How many spoons are on the table?"	
	a)	2 spoons
	b)	3 spoons
	c)	5 spoons
	d)	6 spoons
	e)	8 spoons
	f)	10 spoons

Measurements Taken from Language Sample

51. MLR = _____
52. SC = _____

(Cont.)

TABLE 2 *(continued)*

53. Two and three word combinations _____

54. Verb phrases _____
55. Use of regular plurals _____
56. At least 75% subject-verb agreement _____

57. Prepositional phrases _____
58. Adjectives _____
59. Quantitative _____
60. Verb "to be" used alone (3rd person singular) _____

61. Pronouns used as subjects _____
62. Interrogative _____
63. Third person pronouns _____
64. Conjunctions _____
65. Verb "to be" used as auxiliary (3rd person) _____

66. Adverbs _____
67. Pronouns used as objects _____
68. Future tense _____
69. Dependent clauses _____
70. Use of negatives _____
71. Use of possessive pronouns _____
72. Use of irregular plurals _____
73. Use of past tense _____

TABLE 2 (continued)

EXPRESSIVE PROFILE*

Ages	Expressive Behaviors Imitating			Expressive Behaviors Initiating			Responsive		Expressive Measurements Verb. Output		Articulation
	Motor	Pre-Sym. Vocal	Sym. Vocal	Motor	Pre-Sym. Vocal	Sym. Vocal	Pre-Sym. Vocal	Sym. Vocal	Quant.	De-scrip.	
3–5 mo.					1 (mr) 2 (mr) 5 (mr) 6 (a-mr) (b-mr)		3 (mr) 4 (mr)				
6–8 mo.					6 (c-mr) 7 (mr) 8 (mr)						
9–11 mo.	16 (a-mr)	12		9	6 (d-mr)		10 (mr)				
12–14 mo.	16 (b-mr) (d-mr) (e-mr)	17 (a-mr)			14 (mr) 15 (mr)		11 (mr)				
15–17 mo.	16 (c-mr)	17 (b-mr)		20 (mr)	19 (mr)	18 (mr)					
18–20 mo.	16 (d) (b) (c)	17 (c-mr) 23 (mr) 24 (mr)		22 (a)	22 (a)						
21–23 mo.	16 (a) (e)	17 (b)	25 (a) (b) 26 (a)	22 (b)	21 (mr)		27 32 (mr)				
24–26 mo.			25 (c) (d) (e) 26 (b) 28 29			30 (mr)			51 52	53 54	[m-] [t-] [n-] [-n] [p-] [b-] [k-] [g-] [h-] [w-] [j-] [r-] [l-] [ɔ I] [aU] [u] [æ] [ɛ] [a] [i] [e] [aI] [U] [o] [I]
27–29 mo.		17 (a) (c)	33 (a)				31		51 52	55 56	[-m] [s-] [-s] [f-] [-f] [-tʃ] [-p] [-t] [d-] [-k] [ʌ]
30–32 mo.			33 (d)			35 (mr)	32 (a) (b) 34 (a) (b) (c) 36		51 52	57 58 59 60 61	[-ŋ] [ʃ-] [-r] [-d] [-g] [ð]
33–35 mo.			33 (g)				37 (a) 38 39 40 41 (a) (b) (c) 42 43 (a) (b) (c)		51 52	62 63 64 65	[z-] [-ʃ] [dʒ-] [ɝ] [br-]
36–38 mo.			33 (h)				37 (b) 44 45		51 52	66 67	[st-] [sp-] [ju]
39–41 mo.			33 (b) (e)				34 (d)		51 52		[ð-] [θ-] [-θ] [-v] [tr-] [kl-] [bl-]
42–44 mo.			33 (i)				37 (c)		51 52	68	[-z] [-dʒ]
45–47 mo.							37 (d) 46 47 (mr)	50 (a) 50 (b)	51 52	69 70	[v-] [tʃ-] [-l]
48+ mo.			33 (c) 33 (f)				37 (e) 37 (f) 48 49	50 (c) 50 (d) 50 (e) 50 (f)	51 52	71 72 73	

*Copyright ©, 1970 by D. L. Hedrick and E. M. Prather

DIRECTIONS FOR FURTHER STUDY

We have reported on the first two steps of our study (the devising of the language model and the preliminary ordering of the test items). We plan further work in two directions. The first is to obtain additional cross-sectional data to provide normative information concerning the chronological ages at which specific items are passed. The second direction involves longitudinal data and seems of more importance to us. We want to attempt to determine whether children progress similarly through the steps of language development and whether a sequence of steps can be predicted. If a sequence is found, then the clinician could program remediation on the basis of the results.

SUMMARY OF DISCUSSION

QUESTION: Would you comment on the validity and reliability of your measurements?

HEDRICK: Whether or not we are getting valid mean length responses, we are getting reliable data. We train the observers until they achieve a certain level of reliability with observers who have been recording a fair length of time. So there is a high level of agreement among observers whether the recordings are valid or not.

QUESTION: Is the mean number of morphemes really a very useful measure of language growth?

HEDRICK: With some children it is very useful. With others it is very difficult to really find out what a sentence is. Some children run things together, like "And I went downtown and my father took me to the store and I'm buying, and I'm going to buy apples and I did that and I brought them home." It is not always easy to find the terminating part of all those utterances.

QUESTION: Do you ever go over the tapes with the parents?

HEDRICK: No, but we have played speech samples for parents and for training clinicians and college students. We found the fathers are no better than the trained listeners in figuring out what the child said. The mothers did statistically better than the fathers.

I might add a little more here about the child's development of some of these things we have called "descriptive." For instance, all of our two-year-olds were using two- to three-word combinations. They all used verb phrases. They were using pronouns. At 30 to 32 months, prepositional phrases came into the language samples. We are not saying that children didn't use these words before. We do know that we obtain them from 75 per cent of the children in this kind of sampling procedure at the age of 30 to 32 months. We have some cross-checks on the data; for example, we have the age level where the children comprehend prepositions. Such comprehension comes as early as 21 months. We also have an item in the expressive scale to find out whether the child can use prepositions in a structured situation. So we have a cross-check of information. When do they use prepositions in structured situations? When do they use prepositions in a language sampling situation? And when do they comprehend prepositions and perform accordingly?

QUESTION: How valuable is the structural complexity score you get?

HEDRICK: Structural complexity is something that has been used by speech pathologists for many years as an index of the child's ability to use sentence structure. We never use this clinically, but we are using it in this test situation. We give a certain number of points for complete sentences, such as "I saw the ball." If the child uses a sentence that has a clause in it, then we give more points. But this particular measurement doesn't show very much. Up to the point at which the child has complete sentences it doesn't tell much. They get zero points. So it's useless. The fact that we have included it doesn't mean that we think it's useful. We put some things in our test to study how useful they are.

QUESTION: Could you tell us a little more about your articulation data?

PRATHER: Yes. Those of you familiar with developmental information on articulation know that our children are developing better articulation earlier than children in previous studies.

The bracketed sounds in the profiles are put in at the age at which 75 per cent of the children produce them correctly. They were maintained from then on at the subsequent age levels. This means that there is no "m" included at the 24-month level if the child at the next age level was not able to make the sounds. These are all sounds that were produced correctly from then on.

What we were testing in the articulation of one-word utterances was the child in a very selected environment and the examiner's perception of the child's performance. We have to be aware of that. And we should also remember that perhaps examiners require less from the younger children in production. If a two-year-old says "urr" in some way or another when he says "ran," do we really know whether we put the same requirements on the "urr" sound as we would if the child were four years old?

QUESTION: How generalized is the information that you can get from this type of study?

HEDRICK: We are using our pilot study results to program for our language classrooms. What we do in therapy is to find out where the child is, and where we want him to go. Then we just plan the successive steps to get him from one place to the next. Usually it is up to the therapist to figure those steps out.

We are about to begin a study of sequential patterns of development in children. We believe that these patterns are constant and that children who eventually end up with normal language at four years of age all go through them in language development. We plan to follow 90 children of two races longitudinally from three months to four years of age. We hope to have some children who don't have normal language at four years so that we can look at their development relevant to the development of the children who do have normal language at that age.

QUESTION: You have several items, some of which may turn out and some of which won't. Why do you want to put them all together in one big thing called a language development scale? Is it useful clinically to know what a child's language development is or something global like that? Wouldn't it be much better to know more specific things?

HEDRICK: It's helpful to know about the child's level of functioning.

QUESTION: But don't you need something more specific to tell the parent or to tell the clinician than a general thing like language age? Why do you want to put them all together in one big scale?

HEDRICK: I guess I don't understand what you're getting at.

QUESTION: Maybe I just didn't understand what those numbers all meant. What is going to happen to them eventually? Are they going to be added together or circled and underlined?

PRATHER: When we test a child and he comes out at 24 to 26 months in the imitation areas and at 12 months in the initiating areas, and at 9 months in the responsive areas, then I think one has some awareness of strength and weaknesses and some direction for therapy.

QUESTION: I was just worried that you're going to add them all together.

HEDRICK: And get a score? Oh, no. We want to avoid that. We don't want to come out and say at two years of age children should be doing this, because who knows what a specific child should do at two years of age. But we would like to be able to say, "If the child is doing this, the next thing he will be doing is this or this." We don't want a quotient because we're basically clinicians and we're concerned only about where do we go, not about this little score that we can put down.

QUESTION: This is not the first attempt of this kind, is it? We go through this repeatedly. Every generation of clinicians does this. What's going wrong? Why do we have to do this over and over again?

HEDRICK: Because no one ever gets the money to do the longitudinal study. I think that's basic. Also, people get tired of doing research that takes a long time to publish. That's practical. There are few people who want to work on something they are not going to get anything out of for four years.

QUESTION: Don't we often start over again and again because we don't use things developed by others, because we prefer our own terminology, or our own perspective? Isn't it true that we rarely use the tools or expand and develop or rethink tools that we already have? We try to go for our own system or our own new bit of terminology.

PRATHER: I think this may be part of the problem. Everything that comes out has to be unique.

QUESTION: That's one of the discouraging things in the available tests such as Beecomb's test, ITPA, and Spradlin's language sample. If we set aside the designative terms presumably applied to the items and look in the tests, we find that all are stolen from the Stanford-Binet, the Wechsler. They are sampling very much the same universe of items. I'm wondering why we have to readdress that so often.

HEDRICK: I think many of the scales are based on either a maturational theory or an operant theory, and behaviors that do not fit within those theoretical models are not put into the scale. We have tried to make an eclectic model that will use available knowledge. Say the child understands words. How are we supposed to present the stimulus? In our test we have definite, specific instructions about how the stimulus is presented.

QUESTION: Would it be possible as you go through your test to say, "Here are some things we have data on, we have some interpretations that were generated out of this model. Now, here are some things that weren't included in that, but there are data, there's experience, there's ordering, there's some kind of scaling in other experience"? I'm concerned that every time we start we throw away everything that may have been provided for us in some other context.

HEDRICK: We try not to ignore that sort of information. We try to take the things that do differentiate behavior. We have thrown out items that received ambiguous responses or that the recorders didn't agree on.

QUESTION: Don't you think it is a mistake if we continually ignore and do not exploit our past experience with some of the things we are putting together in more eclectic, more clinically directed kinds of evaluations?

HEDRICK: Yes. I should mention that many of the tests you were talking about were designed to yield a language age. I think the steps are too gross. For example, many changes in language behavior occur between the ages of three and four years. Most of the available scales (Baley, Denver Developmental Scale, etc.) look at behaviors at age three and behaviors at age four. I think these gross steps ignore too many of the changes that are going on.

QUESTION: A question from a slightly different angle. You say you're not developing an age scale but you're using a chronological age as a criterion for selecting the item. Why is that?

HEDRICK: For placement of items for testing. There is no reason to test a certain item at three months of age that requires the child to give a verbal response. And so we have used those age limits simply to find where we put the items in the testing protocol.

QUESTION: Is your primary interest here the development of sequences within individuals or across cases?

HEDRICK: We have used cross-sectional data for initial placement of items. But, primarily, we want to follow individual children over time and see whether large numbers of children go through some steps sequentially. Do most children have some sorts of language behaviors that develop sequentially?

QUESTION: I think ultimately the test of this kind is to use the longitudinal analysis, but you still start with this problem of somehow converging the information from the individual progression and across the cases. And even if you take this longitudinal analysis, if you group the individuals based upon the age gained and then apply let's say 75 per cent criterion at this point, arent't you sort of getting back to across-the-case analysis?

PRATHER: No. We are going to rank-order the items passed. The longitudinal study will follow children from the ages of three months to four years. We will have the items in the order at which those children pass them, and we will compare the rank ordering of the individual children.

REFERENCES

D'Asaro, M. J., and John, V. A rating scale for evaluation of receptive, expressive and phonetic language development of the young child. *Cerebral Palsy Rev.,* 1961, *22*(5), 3-4.

Dunn, L. M. *Peabody picture vocabulary test.* Circle Pines, Minnesota: American Guidance Service, Inc., 1959.

Frankenberg, W. K., and Dodds, J. B. *Denver developmental screening test.* University of Colorado Medical Center, 1967.

Hedrick, D. L., and Prather, E. M. (Eds.), *The sequenced inventory of language development.* Seattle, Washington: Child Development and Mental Retardation Center, 1970.

Johnson, W., Darley, L., and Spriestersbach, D. C. *Diagnostic methods in speech pathology.* New York: Harper and Row, 1963.

Karnes, M., et al. *Activities for developing psycholinguistic skills with preschool culturally disadvantaged children.* Urbana, Illinois: University of Illinois, 1966.

Kirk, S. A., McCarthy, J. J., and Kirk, W. D. *Illinois test of psycholinguistic abilities.* (Rev. ed.) Urbana, Illinois: University of Illinois Board of Trustees, 1968.

Lee, L. L. Developmental sentence types: A method for comparing normal and deviant syntactic development. *J. Speech Hearing Dis.,* 1966, *31* (4).

Lillywhite, H. *Manual for evaluation of speech, language and hearing development in children.* Portland, University of Oregon Medical School, 1956.

McNeill, D. Developmental psycholinguistics. In F. Smith and G. A. Miller (Eds.), *The genesis of language: A psycholinguistic approach.* Cambridge: MIT Press, 1966. Pp. 15-84.

Menyuk, P. *Sentences children use.* Cambridge: MIT Press, 1969.

Osgood, C. E., and Miron, M. S. *Approaches to the study of aphasia.* Urbana, Illinois: University of Illinois Press, 1963.

Pendergast, K., Dickey, S., Selmar, G., and Soder, A. *Photo articulation test.* Danville, Ill., The Interstate Printers and Publishers, Inc., 1969.

Spradlin, J. E. Parsons' language scale. *J. Speech Hearing Dis.,* January, 1963, *10*(Monogr. Suppl.).

A PROGRAM OF DEVELOPMENTAL RESEARCH IN AUDIOLOGIC PROCEDURES

ROBERT T. FULTON
Bureau of Child Research
Parsons State Hospital and Training Center

ROBERT T. FULTON, Ph.D., is research director for the Parsons component of the Kansas Center for Research in Mental Retardation and Related Aspects of Human Development.

". . . only through a proficient combination of instrumentation and human engineering can audiologists meet their true potential" (Fulton and Lloyd, 1969, p. xii). This is particularly true in the audiologic assessment of the mentally retarded or other difficult-to-test populations, such as preschool children and the behaviorally handicapped.

The audiometric assessment of such persons requires the audiologist to assemble and use the best instrumentation available to him. The difficult-to-test often challenge the examiner's skill with their disruptive or distracting behaviors. The occurrence of such behavior, however, need not preclude the application of effective procedures to identify and quantify audiologic pathologies.

The handicaps imposed by audiologic and otologic pathologies warrant the application of effective assessment procedures in any population. There is ample evidence (Fulton and Giffin, 1967; Fulton and Lloyd, 1968; Nudo, 1965; and Pantelakos, 1963) indicating that the retarded manifest an incidence of pathology greater than that found in intellectually normal populations. This high incidence, coupled with the obvious need for more effective procedures for training communicative, educational, and social skills, makes it imperative that the retarded be assessed with the most effective instrumentation and the most efficient procedures we can devise. Otherwise, such persons will not develop to the maximum allowed by their intellectual handicap.

Such populations must not become recipients of "gross" or "quick" measurements. Unfortunately, the use of inadequate assessment procedures currently prevails in the facilities available to many such populations. This condition is sometimes perpetuated because the examinees fail to perform appropriately in standard assessment programs. Many examiners are either unwilling or unable to take the time required to develop appropriate assessment procedures. Some examiners are unaware of existing procedures they could use in the assessment of retarded children.

A portion of audiologic research has been directed toward the development of new techniques. Unfortunately, however, much of this work has been in isolated, noncontinuing projects. Such efforts tend not to identify underlying principles or goals, and they generally do not develop into functional procedures.

This paper is an attempt to describe a program of developmental applied research in the audiometric assessment of the retarded and other difficult-to-test populations.

Inherent in any such program of research is a commitment to a philosophy, a goal, and a viable, objective procedural strategy. The goal of this program is to develop an audiometric test battery which is based upon a compatible and universal response system. Such a battery would be efficient, yet it would permit an examiner to obtain all the audiologic information necessary to delineate possible underlying pathologies.

It is our contention that all individuals should receive the benefit of a comprehensive diagnosis. We feel that physical, emotional, mental, and behavioral problems are not sufficient justification to preclude such service. It is clear, however, that with current techniques and procedures, the chance of attaining optimal assessment is limited. Such circumstances require, then, programmatic research and clinical efforts in which current procedures are carried to their fullest capabilities while intensive efforts are made to enhance the effectiveness, efficiency, and scope of new audiometric procedures.

The audiologic investigators at Parsons, cosponsored by the University of Kansas Bureau of Child Research and the Parsons State Hospital and Training Center, are committed to the task of providing better assessment for the retarded. Although healthy experimental diversification has been maintained, one central schema has prevailed and has been expanded during the past three and one-half years. It is to this schema that this chapter directs itself. Thus, this chapter does not describe a single investigation but a broad research and development plan and the investigations and events that have evolved from this plan.

The ultimate goal of the plan is the development of an audiologic test battery for retarded and difficult-to-test children. The test battery is illustrated in Figure 1. (Lattices should be read up and to the right.)

We are not particularly concerned about whether the examiner or experimenter assumes a physiological or behavioral approach to assessment. We are more interested in the appropriateness and adequacy of the methods used to determine the true condition of the auditory system.

The work described here is based on a behavioral approach using an operant conditioning paradigm. This paradigm is an excellent model for audiologic research:

$$S^D \longrightarrow R \longrightarrow S^R \pm$$
(Discriminative Stimulus)   (Response)   (Reinforcement)

In the operant paradigm, behavior (response) is controlled by its consequences (reinforcement). If a response (selective) occurs in the presence of a specified stimulus and a desirable event occurs, it is probable that the response will reoccur in the presence of similar subsequent stimuli. This series of events is called positive reinforcement. If, in the same chain of events, the response terminates or avoids an undesirable event, it is also probable that the response will reoccur. This latter contingency relationship is referred to as negative reinforcement. Positive reinforcement is usually the preferred of the two.

The operant model has been employed in audiologic research for some time. An

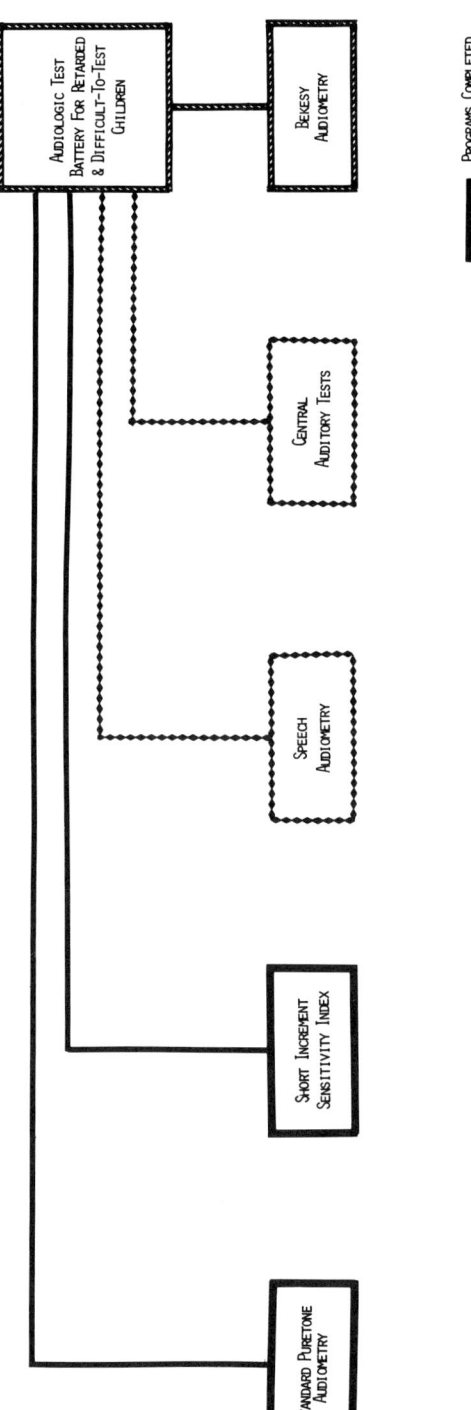

Fig. 1. Lattice of test components of audiologic test battery for retarded and difficult-to-test children.

auditory signal is presented, the subject responds and is reinforced. Most work with this model, however, has concentrated on the manipulation of the reinforcing event; hence the peep-show test, the toy-train test, the block-dropping procedure, and others. These tests and similar research projects have demonstrated the power of the reinforcement principle. However, these tests have not developed the paradigm to its maximum. If one accepts the power of the reinforcement principle and uses those events which have been predetermined to be reinforcing, and if one accepts a constant or specified response, as is usually the case in audiology, the stimulus environment is the only event which requires arrangement. Such a model contributes to the development of an audiologic test battery which employs a universal response mechanism. This is fundamental since audiology is a science in which the nature of the stimulus and its arrangements are basic.

Operant audiology at Parsons was initiated in 1964 by Lloyd and Spradlin. Their early work (Lloyd, Spradlin, and Reid, 1968; Spradlin, Lloyd, Hom, and Reid, 1968) drew upon Skinner (1953) and Meyerson and Michael (1960). Since that time other investigators (Bricker and Bricker, 1969a, 1969b, and LaCrosse and Bidlake, 1964) have made contributions to the advancement of operant principles in audiometric assessment. However, other than at Parsons, no known sustained program of developmental research has been conducted in operant audiometry.

Since 1966, Spradlin and myself, with the assistance of other colleagues, have investigated and expanded the basic operant audiologic paradigm. Many changes have been mechanical and/or technical but they are nevertheless important steps in the overall development. The research plan has been one of small-subject-sample systematic replications manipulating single or small clusters of related variables. This plan has been more effective and conducive to developmental research than one which calls for a series of group studies. Often a single subject indicates the failure of a single variable manipulation.

Standard puretone measurements are basic to audiologic assessment. It was therefore necessary for us to develop tests with standard puretone procedures. Figure 2 indicates the program components required to obtain standard measurements.

These measurements include air-conduction and bone-conduction threshold programs, with masking when appropriate. The administration of these programs depends upon the establishment of auditory stimulus control, the sytematic procedures for which have been reported by Fulton, Spradlin, and Lloyd (1968), and Spradlin, Locke, and Fulton (1969) and are schematically presented in Figure 3.

In the basic control program, the subject is trained to press a button in the presence of an auditory stimulus, usually a puretone. An appropriate response is immediately reinforced with the delivery of a predetermined reinforcing agent, usually edible (i.e., candy, cereal, etc.). Inappropriate responses, or responses outside the stimulus interval, are not reinforced. They cause a time out or delay in program continuation. The delay precludes the opportunity for the subject to rapidly receive reinforcing events. These contingencies are effective in establishing stimulus control or the systematic power of the stimulus to evoke a response.

Program development changed the procedures required to establish auditory stim-

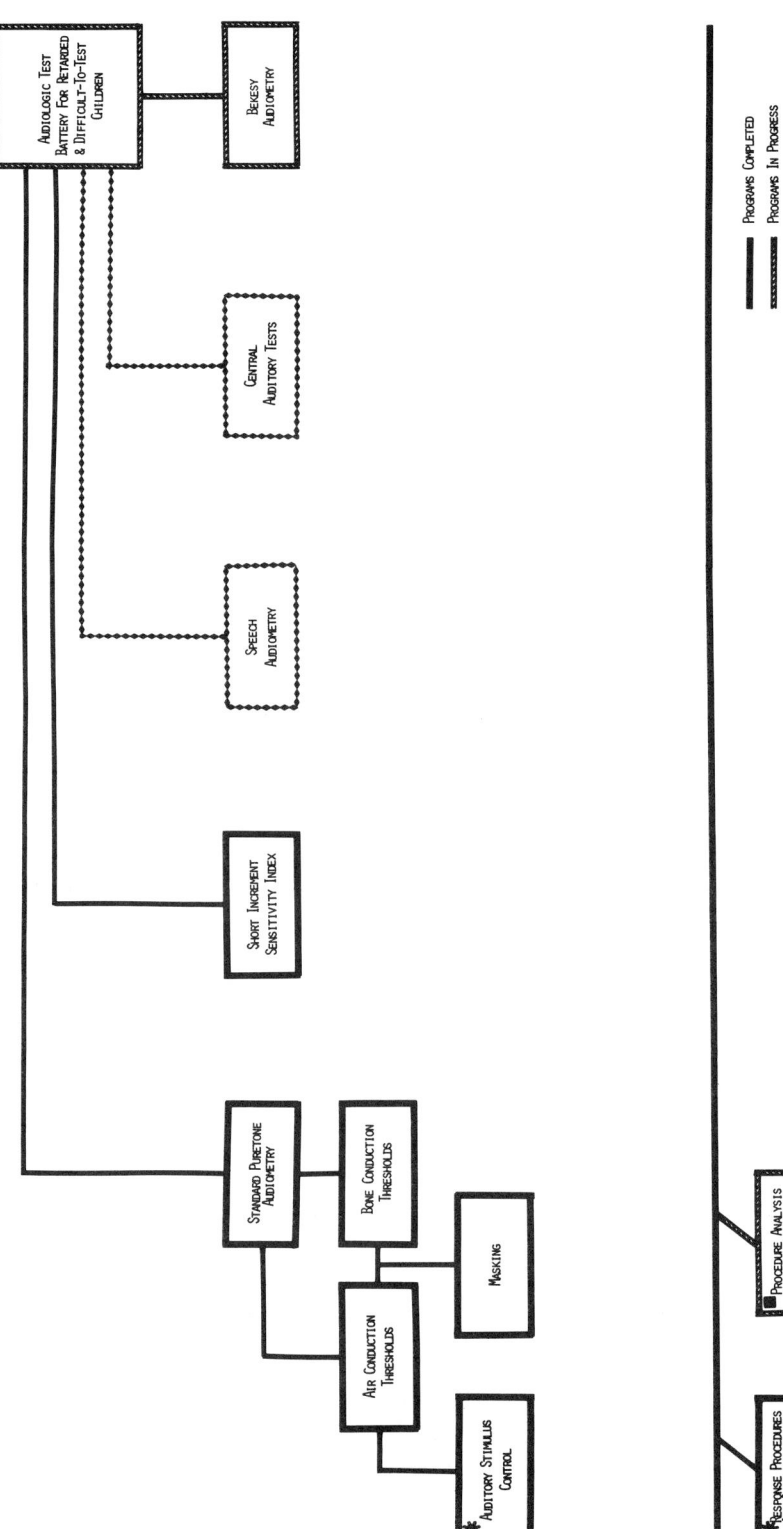

Fig. 2. Lattice of subprograms used to obtain standard puretone audiometric results.

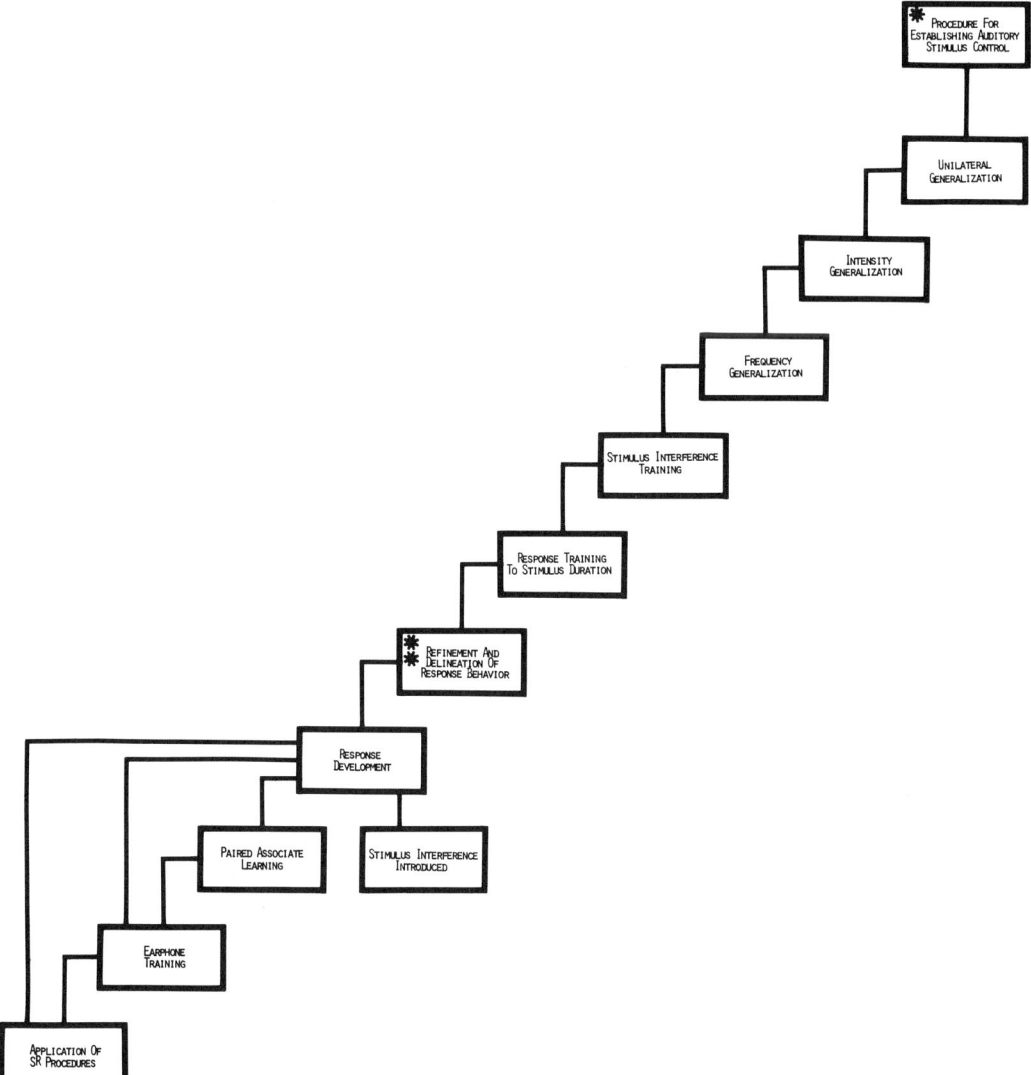

Fig. 3. Lattice of procedural steps used to establish auditory stimulus control.

ulus control. Orginally, the pairing of a stimulus light with the auditory signal facilitated the acquisition of stimulus control. However, empirical data indicate that such pairing is not usually required. Bricker and Bricker's (1969a) independent investigation of this question supported our finding and in fact indicated that paired-associate learning delayed the training time. Also, stimulus-interference training was originally a separate program designed to permit masking procedures which sequentially followed air-conduction thresholds. Currently, this procedure is an early and integral part of establishing auditory stimulus control. Early stimulus-interference training automatically prepares subjects for subsequent test procedures.

In our original programs, earphone placement training, when necessary, was not attempted until after auditory stimulus control had been established for sound-field speakers. This was found to be inefficient, so the earphone placement program was arranged to preclude all other programs; hence all training is subsequent to and contingent upon the subject wearing earphones. As previously arranged, the wearing of earphones remains a discriminative stimulus for the delivery of reinforcement.

A study (Reid, 1969) was directed toward the investigation of maintaining stimulus control and assessing thresholds under continuous and fixed rates of reinforcement. It was found that fixed rates of reinforcement were not sufficient to maintain stimulus control with some subjects. This finding is significant to the S^R procedure of establishing auditory stimulus control.

The development and arrangement of response consequences presented in Figure 4 has been the most complex and significant investigation thus far completed. The inclusion of response pre-delays and post-delays and intertrial probe control periods have been three of the most significant developments. The pre-delay controls the nondiscriminative responses occurring simultaneously with the onset of the stimulus. The post-delay controls discriminate responses occurring at the stimulus termination. The post-delay principle has significance in later test procedures such as the Short Increment Sensitivity Index (SISI) and speech audiometry (now under development). The establishment of control periods with conjunctive criterion has permitted the determination of validation measures (discussed later). Other contingencies have also contributed to the establishment of stimulus control. These contingencies are reported by Fulton and Spradlin (1971).

Stimulus-interference training, the seventh step in establishing stimulus control, is one of the most far-reaching principles in the entire program. This procedure establishes a new concept in discriminative audiometric procedures with difficult populations. Prior to the development of this procedure, subjects were trained to respond to a stimulus present/stimulus absent concept. In the current procedure, the subject is trained to respond to changes in his auditory environment. For example, he is trained to respond to changes: (1) in a minimally audible environment (ambient noise) as found in threshold assessment; (2) in a noticeably audible environment as used in masked threshold procedures; and (3) in an auditory environment in which the environment stimulus contains the same properties as the stimulus change itself, such as the SISI.

As previously noted, many programs and procedures developed for standard pure-tone have relevance to other audiometric test procedures. This is most evident in the SISI.

The SISI is a diagnostic test for assessing the probable presence or absence of cochlear pathology. This test is essentially an extension of standard puretone procedures and its administration is dependent upon the establishment of stimulus control. The program contingencies (previously discussed) of response post-delay and stimulus duration play an important role in the SISI. The post-delay is systemati-

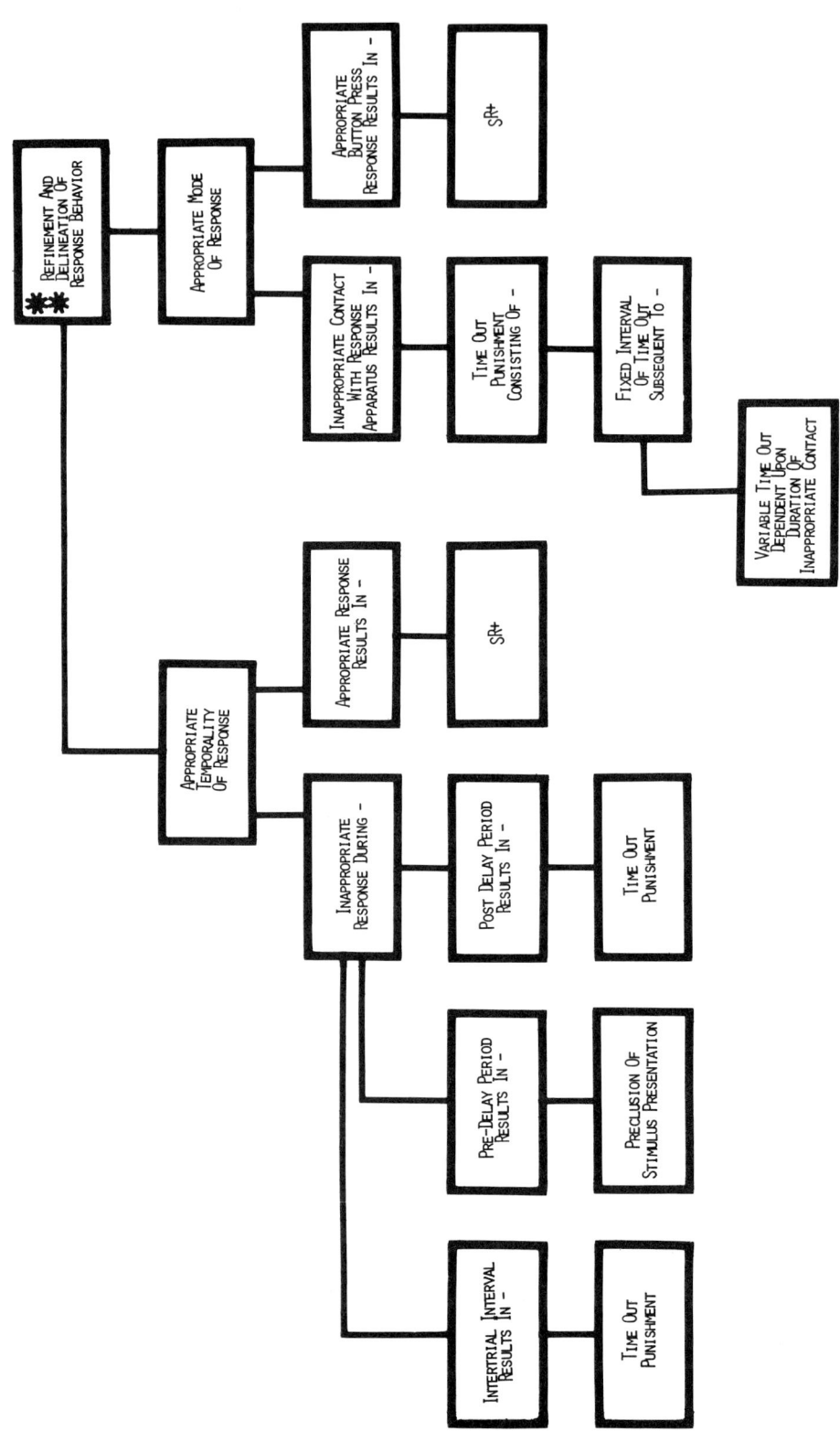

Fig. 4. Lattice of response contingencies used to refine and delineate response behavior.

cally increased as the stimulus duration is decreased, until such time as the stimulus duration is 200 milliseconds and the response circuit is available for two seconds. The stimulus-interference training in the puretone program is fundamental to the identification of intensity differences in the constantly present stimulus environment of the SISI.

The development of SISI procedures for the severely retarded, and an investigation of the effects of independent variables on test results, have been reported by Fulton and Spradlin (1969 and in press). Two significant conclusions were drawn from these studies: (1) it is possible to train severely retarded children to discriminate 200 millisecond stimuli at intensity differences of one dB; and (2) repeated SISI scores are subject to discriminative learning functions by both normal-hearing, severely retarded children and normal-hearing adults with normal intelligence.

Speech audiometry is an assessment procedure which relates auditory acuity (intensity) to complex verbal discriminations and perceptual processes. These relationships are often indicative of auditory pathologies. Results are also indicative of expectancies for performance with verbal auditory stimuli. Such information is critical to rehabilitative and social performance programs. Thus far, little experimentation has been directed to this area, largely because the test is dependent upon verbal or written responses. The response requirement has therefore made speech audiometry relatively unattainable with nonverbal children. However, there have been attempts to use a "point-to-the-picture" response mode with nonverbal children. Although this response mechanism is acceptable, current "point-to-the-picture" procedures do not provide a systematic method for assuring stimulus-picture associations.

Speech audiometry is the area where the next major investigation will take place. Investigations will examine some of the same response control problems, but the main effort will be centered around related symbolic associations, i.e., pictures, words, etc. Figure 5 illustrates the projected programs. Before assessment procedures can be established, a word-picture association training program will be developed. This program will provide impetus for other activities such as language development and auditory habilitation for the auditory impaired. Before word-picture association training can begin, however, a program of word stimulus discrimination must be developed. This program will require only auditory discrimination; therefore responses will not be contingent upon associations other than those which serve as an auditory stimulus. Because of the complexities of the stimuli in this area, two avenues of investigation will be taken. These two avenues will provide basic information on verbal auditory acquisition.

One avenue will be consonantal discrimination (see Figure 6). In this approach the subject's task will be to discriminate by acoustic properties only the *target* consonantal stimulus (actually a nonsense syllable comprised of the target consonant plus a constant vowel) from other consonantal stimuli. That is, the subject will not be required to identify the stimuli by label or name, but to discriminate its presence within a stimulus confusion battery. Choice of S^Δ confusion stimuli will be based on the Miller-Nicely (1955) confusion matrices.

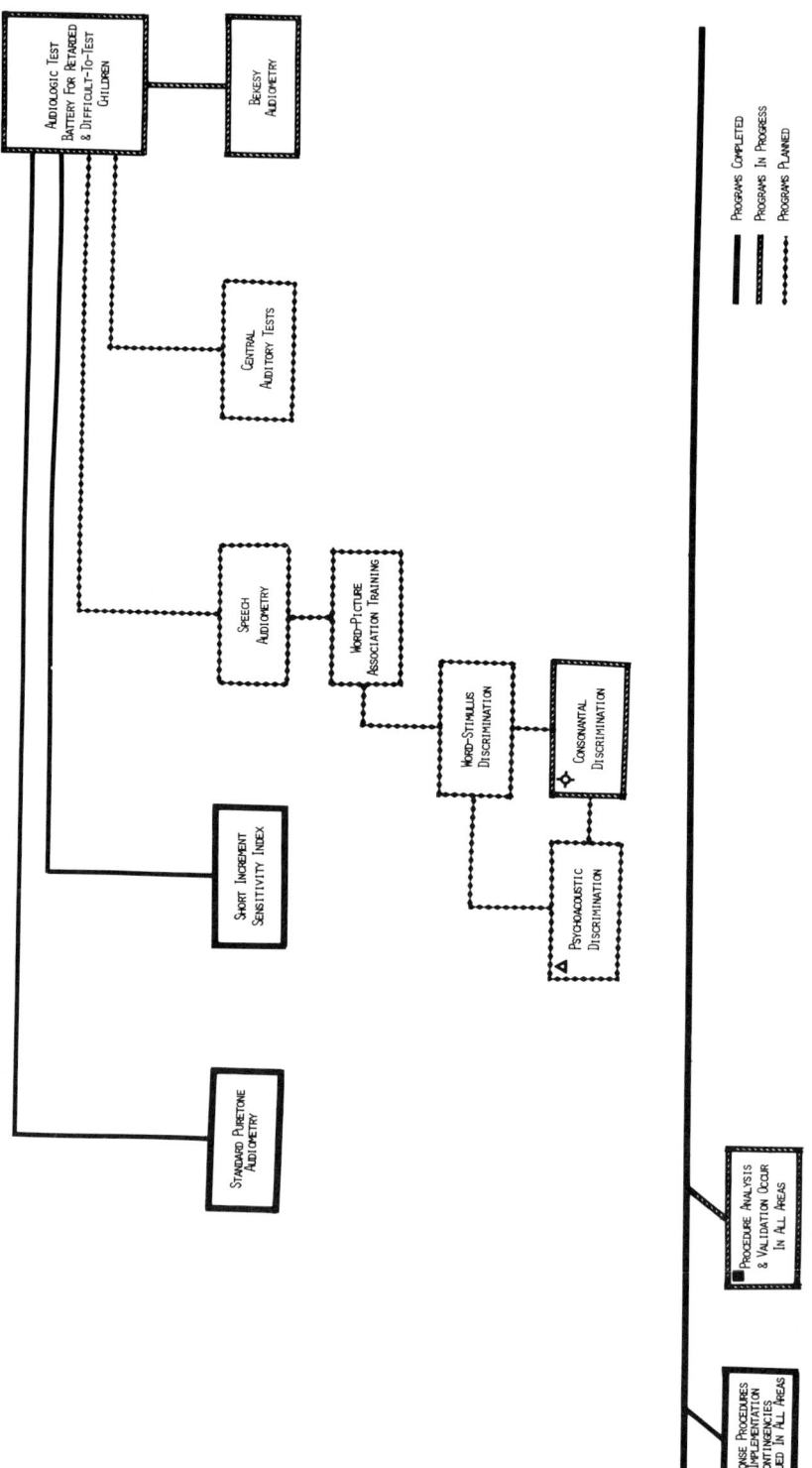

Fig. 5. Lattice of subprograms planned to obtain speech audiometry test program.

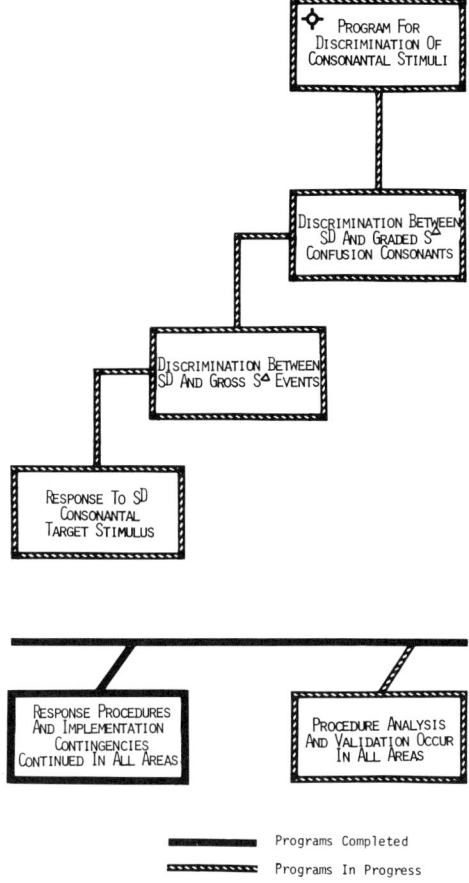

Fig. 6. Lattice of procedures used to train auditory discrimination of consonantol stimuli.

The subject will be trained to respond to the presence of the target stimulus (S^D). Auditory stimuli will then be shifted to include both the S^D and the gross confusion stimuli (S^Δ). The subject will be reinforced for appropriate discriminations and penalized for nondiscriminative responses. The S^Δ conditions will then be shifted to require more discriminative discriminations per confusion matrix assignment, until the subject is able to discriminate the S^D from the most confusing S^Δ condition (i.e., /s/ from /ʃ/).

The other approach, which may be less functional as far as verbalizations are concerned, is a program of psychoacoustic discrimination (see Figure 7). The primary purpose of this program is to establish indices and referents of basic auditory discrimination ability among low-level, retarded children. In conjunction with the assessment of discriminative indices, subjects will undergo training programs to determine the extent to which discriminative training can be applied.

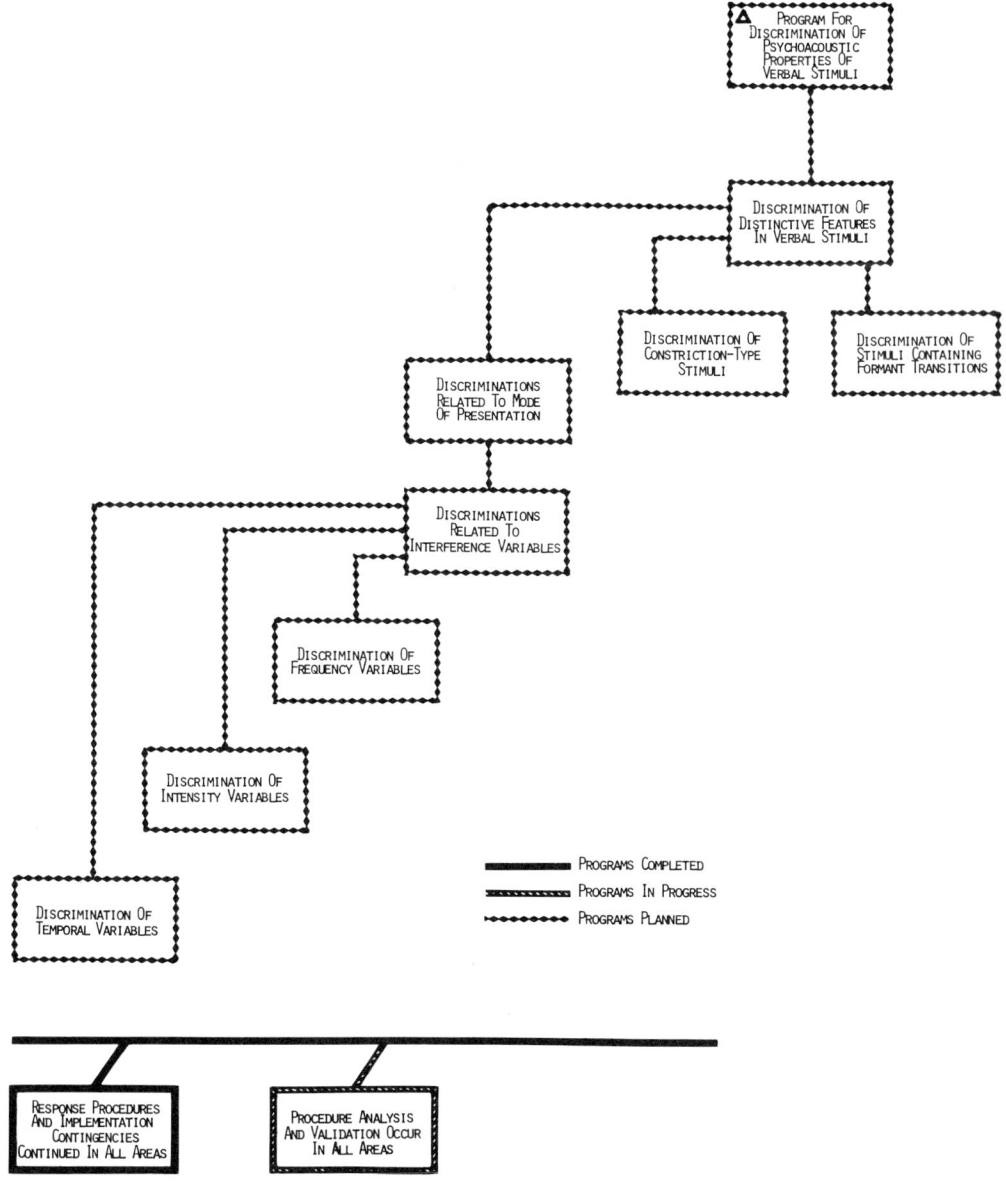

Fig. 7. Lattice of research areas to be investigated in the development of a program for the discrimination of psychoacoustic properties of verbal stimuli.

Initial discriminations in this program will be based on temporal, intensity, and frequency parameters. In the latter phases the stimulus will be shifted to include stimuli with more complex properties. These phases will include discrimination of artificially produced speech-type sounds such as constriction-type sounds (i.e., /s, θ, f/) and second formant vowel transitions (Liberman, 1957). Information from these basic discriminations will provide referents for more functional discriminations and speech production programs.

Much of the information gained from investigations in speech audiometry will have relevance to central auditory tests. However, it will be some time before the model can contribute to the procedural development of central auditory tests.

A few basic pilot investigations have been conducted in Bekesy audiometry, another area of the research model. Hollis and Fulton (1968) devised instrumentation modifications to convert the standard Grason-Stadler E800 Bekesy audiometer from the standard response mechanism to a two-button Blough (1958) procedure. The changes were validated with normal adult subjects. The Blough reinforcement training procedures have not been attempted with low-level, retarded children. The Blough reinforcement procedures (developed for assessing visual thresholds with pigeons) are too complex and cumbersome to employ with efficiency.

Frisina and Johnson (1966) developed a single-response Bekesy procedure for the deaf. The procedure requires the subject to make a single button-pressing response to an audible stimulus. Subsequently, a pre-set timer attenuates the stimulus for a predetermined period. The stimulus is then presented again and the intensity automatically increases until another response recycles the procedure. This apparatus arrangement can be quickly adapted to the same stimulus control and reinforcement procedures used in the standard puretone program. Pilot investigations indicate that a severely retarded subject under standard puretone stimulus control can be transferred to the Frisina-Johnson Bekesy procedure with little or no difficulty and that thresholds are reasonably compatible. The Frisina-Johnson procedure, however, violates the basic tenets of Bekesy audiometry, specifically the tracing envelope parameters, by instrumentally controlling the extent of attenuation. More work in the area of Bekesy audiometry is anticipated.

As an illustration of the overall goal, auditory test battery programs, and the programs leading to the establishment of the test battery are illustrated in Figure 8. There are certain relations which directly or indirectly connect test procedures.

As noted on Figures 2, 3, 5, 6, 7, and 8, a program of procedural evaluation and validation occurs in all areas. A more explicit lattice of these procedures is found in Figure 9. These procedures concentrate on four major analyses: validity, reliability, efficiency, and applicability. Analysis procedures vary from informal empirical clinical evidence to formalized group analysis.

If procedural changes are proposed, it is common to base changes on small sample experimentation; then, when the changes have been adopted, to expose the final modifications to a more rigorous and larger sample analysis. This should not be construed to indicate that procedures are refined to a point no longer subject to revision.

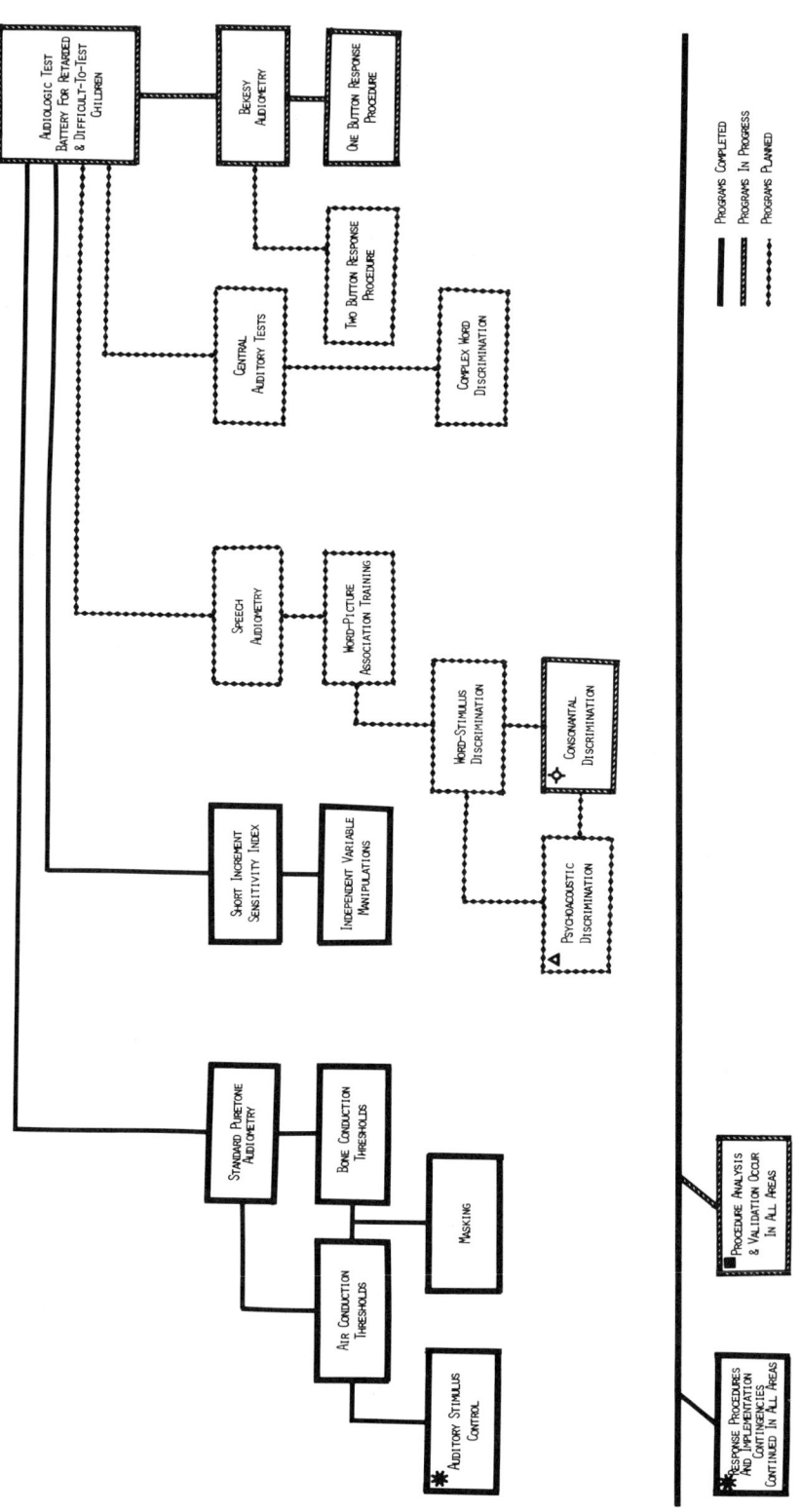

Fig. 8. Lattice of the audiologic test battery with major test components and subprograms.

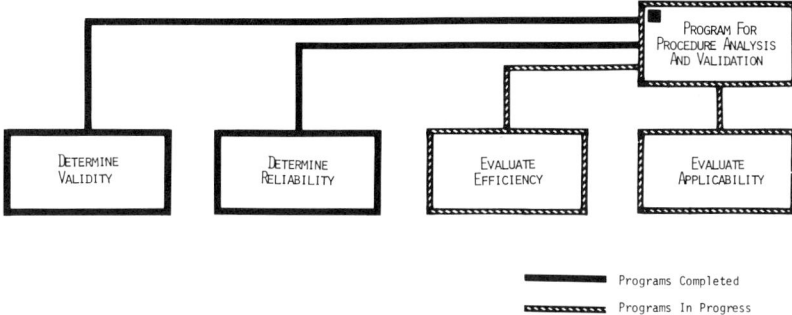

Fig. 9. Lattice of procedures used to analyze and validate programatic research.

Standard puretone threshold procedures have been refined to a point of relative efficiency but currently an item (procedural phase) analysis is being conducted in an "in-the-field" situation. It will indicate if further refinements are warranted. This analysis consists of determining the number of trials required to meet criteria for each procedural phase, determining the response relationships to the number of trials, and determining the time expended for each phase.

Intrasubject puretone validity measures have also been investigated by evaluating subjects with possible unilateral losses and subjects requiring masking procedures, and by comparing correlative standard puretone and speech audiometric procedures.

Intrasubject puretone threshold reliability studies (Spradlin, Locke, and Fulton, 1969; and unpublished data, Fulton) indicate that low-level, retarded children can consistently provide test-retest thresholds within ± 5 dB variability. Studies of the effects of maintaining stimulus control on test-retest threshold reliability (Fulton and Spradlin, 1971) indicate that reliability is contingent upon stimulus control criteria.

Currently, "in-the-field" investigations are being conducted to assess the applicability of puretone threshold procedures to other populations, such as young preschool children. Thus far, the data suggest that the procedure is applicable for all behaviorally difficult populations, contingent upon the ability of a subject to press the response button (children under 18 months of age tend not to have this skill), and upon selection of an appropriate reinforcer.

The appropriate selection of a reinforcer appears to be the greatest determiner of the success of this procedure. Thus far reliable results have been obtained for approximately 85 per cent of the subjects assessed. All subjects have been behaviorally difficult and untestable with standard tests. On occasion it has been necessary to limit food consumption prior to test sessions in order to enhance the reinforcing properties of edible reinforcers.

The adoption of the operant paradigm and the development of a systematic and compatible research plan have been efficient and productive in the drive to attain a comprehensive audiologic test battery for the retarded and other difficult-to-test persons. We have not yet attained our ultimate goal; however, our work has been sufficiently productive to suggest that developmental research could benefit from such a model, whatever its approach, behavioral or physiological.

Such an organizational schema permits the investigator to establish his ultimate goal to identify the programs necessary to achieve that goal and to describe the procedures necessary to arrive at any given point in the program.

It is recommended that similar models or approaches be established for research. Only through continued and sequential planning and development can research and application reach its maximal potential.

SUMMARY OF DISCUSSION

QUESTION: I didn't understand exactly what you meant by instrumentally controlling the extent of attenuation with Bekesy.

FULTON: Johnson and Frisina worked on a one-button type procedure with Bekesy with deaf children. When a stimulus was present and the subject pushed the button a timer attenuated the audiometer for a fixed interval. When the timer shut off the audiometer automatically increased itself until the next response was made. The problem is that this procedure takes away the envelope analysis function of Bekesy audiometry. In Frisina and Johnson's procedure there is no control over excursion. The timer is the determinant. Our procedure is similar.

QUESTION: I don't understand. You say the trouble with the procedure is that you have no control over the excursion?

FULTON Right. With standard Bekesy, you push the button to attenuate. When you release it, it automatically becomes louder. In the modified procedure we set the time, depending upon the subject, to control the excursion. With the timer you hit the button once and it automatically attenuates for as long as you have set the timer, whether the subject likes it or not. Thus envelope size is directly related to the timer setting.

QUESTION: Do you feel this basic operant procedure is really an efficient procedure? It seems very time consuming.

FULTON: We are concerned about that. Every three months the procedure is different. We try to eliminate things, save time, make changes without losing effectiveness. We are constantly working on that. We are evaluating all new children admitted to the institution, testing them the day after they arrive. Every test procedure or every step is identified by a phase number. We are keeping track of the number of trials, the amount of time, the number of responses, and we will do an item analysis and I think really be able to go to work on the efficiency aspect.

QUESTION: When you use auditory stimuli to establish stimulus control how do you deal with the completely deaf child?

FULTON: We have some deaf children. Most of them have some hearing at 250 or 500 Hz. That is one of the reasons we picked 500 Hz. They may be down to 80 or 90 dB but we can present a signal at that level. We have sometimes used bone conduction first. Whether it was tactile or whether it was truly a bone conduction response I don't know. But they picked the procedure up very quickly, and we immediately transferred it over to air conduction. It happened that they only heard 250 and 500 Hz, and 500 right at the maximum limit of the audiometer. And that's why we couldn't train them on 500 Hz.

QUESTION: Why did you say you would only use this for low-functioning children? Why couldn't this become a standard for the field? Anybody who is going to deal with audiometry for anyone could use this kind of technique.

FULTON: Because of time. To me time is not an important variable. I feel that if it is important to test a child's hearing, it really doesn't matter what the time element is. We test and test until we get the information we want. Unfortunatley, most clinicians tell me that's not the rule under which they work. They have to obtain information quickly. That is their biggest objection. They need a procedure that takes no more than an hour.

QUESTION: Aren't there certain classes of clients that come to a treatment center or to a large hospital audiology clinic that require some systematic shaping or conditioning procedure before you can use the various tests? Don't you have some fair predictions in audiology that we might use to classify subjects as candidates for a system like this?

FULTON: Yes. We have used block dropping and play audiometry and a lot of other behavioral procedures. At the present time we go in and ask the child to raise his hand when the tone is presented. And if we can't get good responses in 15 minutes, the research assistant puts him on this program. The program is automated. If the research assistant runs into complex problems he doesn't understand, I go back and work with the subject. The two of us can handle a pretty heavy load. A child who can work pretty well on block dropping can pick this up in about three minutes. Four and five-year-olds who can learn block dropping can be screened by this procedure in about 15 minutes. We cut corners with an outpatient when we have only an hour.

QUESTION: Doesn't your program fit into other kinds of training? Where you use alternative testing procedures aren't you really setting the repertoire or controlling the repertoire in ways that could be used by more language-related activities?

FULTON: Correct. The consonantal discrimination program we are getting into is not going to be an audiology test; it is sound discrimination training. Once we have established stimulus control, then all we have to do is change and manipulate the program. It has a much broader application than just language. We could go into reading, any type of thing.

QUESTION: What have you been able to do with preschoolers?

FULTON: We have not worked with them a great deal other than with staff children. The two limitations are finding an effective reinforcer and a child who has motor skill enough to push the button. Dr. Lloyd has worked with 18-month-old children and one seven-month-old.

QUESTION: Seven-months?

FULTON: A normal seven-month-old. He also used this procedure on an outpatient basis at Gallaudet and again with preschool deaf children.

QUESTION: Do you have enough sound discrimination information to comment on how it will lead you into your central battery?

FULTON: No. As a matter of fact, all we have done is pilot enough people by hand to give us an indication that we want to set up instrumentation. I don't know what we are going to come up with. We started on this once before on the two-choice type situation where we paired same and different. I am not an advocate of two-choice. I wanted to get away from it. We are setting it up now where each event will be by itself with a single-button response. It will be a one-event presentation, like "sa" or the discriminative stimulus one time, then six or seven seconds later a random presentation of another S^D or S^Δ. If he responds to S^Δ, he will be negatively reinforced. We are setting up a language of lights so each correct response will light up a light. When the child accumulates ten lights a window will light up and show the prize he will receive at the end. Every incorrect response will reduce the number of lights, and so on. So at the end of the session he may have 30 lights and three windows lighted up. Or it may be tokens which he can exchange for something.

QUESTION: What do you mean by "central auditory tests?"

FULTON: An example would be a test in which part of a word is presented to one ear, part to another ear, and the composite gives indications of central assimilation functions.

QUESTION: You appear to be modifying the speech signal, making it more difficult, or making it a different form of input. Once you establish your method of getting appropriate responses in speech audiometry, could then you evaluate various levels of central auditory testing depending on how you manipulate the stimuli?

FULTON: Yes. This system is pretty much directed to nonverbal subjects. I am interested in learning a little more about the acoustic properties than in just saying I can get a paired association like current speech discrimination procedures and letting it go at that. I think a lot of times we don't pay enough attention to auditory and acoustic properties. We make too many assumptions that people can hear and discriminate small parameters. I want to find out how this population functions. Do they make these kinds of discriminations? Audiologists perpetually develop new speech audiometry discrimination lists to solve problems of working with difficult children. I'm not convinced that I want to generate new word items until I know more about how children react to the acoustic properties of some of the words.

QUESTION: But haven't we seen a progression in speech audiometry from the word lists that were arbitrarily selected to test communication systems, to the point now where we are analyzing errors? Aren't we now dealing with closed message sets and analyzing type of error rather than just the score number?

FULTON: Yes. But again closed message sets and verbal reproduction are dependent upon verbal subjects.

QUESTION: Have you tried using condition-orienting responses with the very young children?

FULTON: Yes. That was my dissertation. I think we can get a lot better information in better ways.

QUESTION: Yes, but on the other hand, isn't a major aspect of auditory assessment in mental retardation a problem of early assessment? You may be able to obtain only very gross information at these very early ages, but I think that if you have some indication of hearing loss at very early ages you have a better opportunity to work on it.

FULTON: Yes, I don't deny that. My point is I have chosen to not make time a critical variable. What I want to do is get all the results I need. I think there is a place for gross information. I just choose not to adopt a philosophy of time and expediency control.

REFERENCES

Blough, D. S. A method for obtaining psychophysical thresholds from the pigeon. *J. Exp. Anal. Behavior,* 1958, *1,* 31–43.

Bricker, D., and Bricker, W. A. A programmed approach to operant audiometry for low-functioning children. *J. Speech Hearing Dis.,* 1969, *34*(4), 312–320. (a)

Bricker, D., and Bricker, W. A. Four operant procedures for establishing auditory stimulus control with low-functioning children. *Am. J. Ment. Deficiency,* 1969, *73*(6), 981–987. (b)

Frisina, D. R., and Johnson D. D. A non-verbal hearing test for children with deafness, Cooperative Research Project, No. OE5-0962-4-11-3, United States Office of Education Publication, Gallaudet College, Washington, D. C., 1966

Fulton, R. T., and Giffin, C. S. Audiological-otological considerations with the mentally retarded. *Ment. Retard.,* 1967, *5,* 26–31.

Fulton, R. T., and Lloyd, L. L. Hearing impairment in a population of children with Down's syndrome. *Am. J. Ment. Deficiency,* 1968, *73*(2), 298–302.

Fulton, R. T., and Lloyd, L. L. (Eds.), *Audiometry for the retarded: With implications for the difficult-to-test.* Baltimore: Williams and Wilkins, 1969. Pp. xii.

Fulton, R. T., and Spradlin, J. E. Operant audiometry with severely retarded children. Paper presented at the IX International Congress of Audiology, London, September, 1968. *Audiology,* 1971, *10,* 203–211.

Fulton, R. T., and Spradlin, J. E. SISI procedures with the severely retarded. *Parsons Demonstration Project Report* No. 92, 1969.

Fulton, R. T., and Spradlin, J. E. Effects of practice on SISI scores with normal hearing subjects. *J. Speech Hearing Res.,* in press.

Fulton, R. T., Spradlin, J. E., and Lloyd, L. L. Operant audiometery with the severely retarded: Positive reinforcement discrimination. Bureau of Child Research, University of Kansas and Parsons State Hospital and Training Center, 16mm film, 1968.

Hollis, J. H., and Fulton, R. T. Bekesy audiometer modification for Blough threshold techniques. *Parsons demonstration project report No. 84,* Parsons State Hospital and Training Center, 1968.

LaCrosse, E. L., and Bidlake, H. A method to test the hearing of mentally retarded children. *Volta Rev.,* 1964, *66,* 27–30.

Liberman, A. M. Some results of research on speech perception. *J. Acoust. Soc. Amer.,* 1957, *29,* 117–123.

Lloyd, L. L., Spradlin, J. E., and Reid, M. J. An operant audiometer procedure for difficult-to-test patients. *J. Speech Hearing Dis.,* 1968, *33,* 236–245.

Meyerson, L., and Michael, J. L. The measurement of sensory thresholds in exceptional children: An experimental approach to some problems of differential diagnosis and education with special reference to hearing. Cooperative Research Project No. 418, U.S. Office of Education, Department of Health, Education and Welfare, University of Houston, Texas, May 31, 1960.

Miller, G. A., and Nicely, P. E. An analysis of perceptual confusions among some English consonants. *J. Acoust. Soc. Amer.,* 1955, *27,* 338–352.

Nudo, L. A. Comparison by age of audiological and otological findings in a state residential institution for the mentally retarded: A preliminary report. In L. L. Lloyd, and D. R. Frisina (Eds.), *The audiological assessment of the mentally retarded: Proceedings of a national conference.* Parsons State Hospital and Training Center, 1965. Pp. 137–154.

Patelakos, C. G. Audiometric and otolaryngologic survey of retarded students. *North Carolina Med. J.,* 1963, *24,* 238–242.

Reid, M. J. Effects of reinforcement on auditory stimulus control and threshold assessment with retarded children. Unpublished Master's thesis, Kansas State University, Manhattan, August, 1969.

Skinner, B. F. *Science and human behavior.* New York: Appleton-Century-Crofts, 1953.

Spradlin, J. E., Locke, B. J., and Fulton, R. T. Conditioning and audiologic assessment. In R. T. Fulton, & L. L. Lloyd (Eds.), *Audiometry for the retarded: With implications for the difficult-to-test.* Baltimore: Williams & Wilkins, 1969, Pp. 125–163.

Spradlin, J. E., Lloyd, L. L., Hom, G. L., and Reid, M. J. Establishing tone control and evaluating the hearing of severely retarded children. In G. A. Jervis (Ed.), *Expanding concepts in mental retardation.* Springfield, Ill.: Charles C Thomas, 1968. Pp. 170–180.

THE LANGUAGE-RELATED BEHAVIOR OF DYSPHASIC CHILDREN

PAUL S. WEINER
University of Chicago

PAUL S. WEINER is an associate professor of pediatrics and psychiatry at the University of Chicago. He received his Ph.D. from the Committee on Human Development of the University of Chicago in 1952. After a year of clinical training at the Illinois Neuropsychiatric Institute and as a Fellow in Child Development at the Western Psychiatric Institute of the University of Pittsburgh, he worked as a clinical psychologist in various mental health facilities. In 1960 he returned to the University of Chicago as lecturer in the Department of Psychology and as Assistant Director of the Speech and Language Clinic. In 1965 he assumed his present post where he functions as Director of Psychological Services for the Pediatrics Department and Associate Director of the Mental Development Clinic.

Difficulties in learning language arise from many sources and take many forms. Deafness, neurological dysfunction, emotional problems, environmental deprivation, and intellectual dullness have all been linked to language difficulties. The specific focus of this volume is the language problems found in mentally retarded children. Little is known of the forms these problems take, of their relationship to the intellectual defects of the affected children, or of their relationship to other aspects of psychological functioning. In the search for understanding it may be helpful to turn to a related group of children whose linguistic inadequacies have been the major source of concern. These are the children who are usually designated as "congenitally aphasic." They too tend to suffer from intellectual impairment, though they differ from the mentally retarded in having at least one substantial area of adequacy or near adequacy, the nonverbal. The methods employed in studies of their language and language related behavior and the knowledge gained from these studies may be of use in considering the problems of the mentally retarded.

BACKGROUND

Language disorders have been discussed since the time of the ancients. As far back as the fifth century B.C. references to aphasia and aphasia-like disorders appeared in the Hippocratic Corpus (Benton and Joynt, 1960). The continuing interest over the centuries is evidenced by Benton and Joynt's (1960) conclusion that by the year 1800 almost all clinical forms of aphasia had been described. Modern study of language disorders tends to be dated from the publication of Broca's paper in 1861 on the localization of a center for speech in the brain. Since then, of course, there has been an ever-increasing flood of studies of the phenomena of aphasia and related disorders.

The literature on children's oral language difficulties, at least those not involving deafness or obvious mental retardation, seems to have a much shorter history. Gall is generally credited with the first reference, in 1835, to children "who know not how to speak, although they are not idiots, and understand nearly as well as other children, who speak" (Gall, 1835, p. 24). However, Luchsinger (1959) reports that Delius described the condition in 1757 in his work "De Alalia et Aphonia." Study of such children did slowly begin and the problem received its most common, though continually debated, designation of "congenital aphasia" in 1866 (Vaïsse, 1866). For many years virtually all studies of this disorder were made by physicians. This, of course, was true of a number of other children's disorders which have since become largely the province of other disciplines. Itard, whose study of the "wild boy of Aveyron" was the first description of an attempt to educate an apparently retarded child, was a medical man. So was Morgan whose description of a case of "congenital word blindness" (1896) may be considered as the beginning of the study of difficulties in learning to read. It is not surprising then that publications were, in major part, case studies of individual children who had been brought to a physician's office for help. The form of these studies followed what is perhaps an inevitable course. The first reports tended to be anecdotal in nature, at times consisting of a brief recounting of someone else's observations (Wilde, 1853). But this situation did not continue for long. The reports began to contain increasingly adequate descriptions, not only of the child's physical status but also his functioning in relevant areas of behavior. For the most part the reports continued to retain an impressionistic flavor and the exact methods of examination were not described. Only one full description of an appropriate diagnostic examination was published in this early period. This was presented by Liebmann in 1898. He provided not only examples of the kinds of information needed to establish a clear diagnosis and a basis for therapy but also detailed examples of his method of therapy. He seems to have been thorough in his examinations, delightful in his approach to children, and able to express his thoughts in remarkably simple language.

Despite any progress that occurred, some curious reports are to be found. One author (Town, 1911) described a child who had the unusual ability to speak far more words than he could understand. He was, it must be admitted, quite limited in both.

What must surely be the most thorough case studies were published in 1929. Ley provided a beautifully written description of "idiopathic audimutism in monozygotic twins." Worster-Drought and Allen in two articles presented a full study of a case of "congenital auditory imperception." These studies are worthy of note. They may well be the first instances in which standardized tests were used. To obtain some measure of his subjects' intellectual level Ley used two scales: that prepared by Herderschêe for use with deaf children, and that devised by Binet and Simon. In their work Worster-Drought and Allen used the "methods employed and described by Henry Head in the investigation of aphasia and associated speech defects" (1929, p. 289). While all the tests mentioned had clearly described directions for their administration, apparently only the Binet-Simon had norms based on a standardization group. Head's tests were not even intended for use with children. The theoretical models of functioning used in the two studies are also worth noting. Very understandably the notions which had been found appropriate to the study of adult aphasia were transferred to the examination of the children. Beyond the determination of physical status the investigators sought evidence on gnosic and praxic functioning and on the adequacy of various language functions: comprehension, repetition, spontaneous expression, reading, and writing. Because of the particular nature of their respective cases, Ley emphasized motoric functioning while Worster-Drought and Allen stressed auditory functioning. Only Ley sought to establish the level of intellectual functioning of his patient. The omission by the English researchers of any attempt to do this was apparently based on a recognition of the inappropriateness of the intelligence tests available to them. Finally, the Worster-Drought and Allen study seems to represent what may be termed a historical accident which leads to a cultural style. These authors' three publications on auditory imperception apparently set a trend for the study of congenital aphasia in the English-speaking world. While the use of Head's tests did not continue for long in this context, English and American publications have centered on children with problems in auditory comprehension. In contrast, continental publications have included a wider range of cases. If anything they have tended to concentrate on children, like those studied by Ley, whose major problem was in the realm of the production of language.

It is interesting to note Worster-Drought and Allen's assimiliation of other kinds of cases to their own schema. In their final theoretical article on congenital auditory imperception (Worster-Drought and Allen, 1930) they present a rather thorough discussion of the previous literature. However they tend to consider statements by other authors that some aphasic children understand spoken language, as simply an indication of an inadequate examination of auditory functioning. Apparently it did not seem possible to them that their findings in their own absorbing experience with the one child were not universal. (Perhaps it should be added that published accounts were such that they could not be sure of what many other investigators had done.)

The first formal investigation involving a number of children apparently was Ewing's (1930) study of youngsters with auditory problems. However, additional investigations that were not individual case studies appeared only after another 20 years had passed.

In a fairly exhaustive search of the literature four such studies were found to have been published in the 1950's (Goldenberg, 1950; Ajuriaguerra, Borel-Maisonny, Diatkine, Narlian, and Stambak, 1958; Goldstein, Landau, and Kleffner, 1958; Mark and Hardy, 1958). In the literature of the past decade 26 studies were located (Doehring, 1960; Goldstein, Landau, and Kleffner, 1958; Landau, Goldstein, and Kleffner, 1960; Rosenbluet, Goldstein, and Landau, 1960; Wilson, Doehring, and Hirsch, 1960, Olson, 1961; Ajuriaguerra et al., 1963; Crookes and Greene, 1963; Inhelder, 1963; Furth, 1964; Menyuk, 1964; Reichstein, 1964; Ajuriaguerra et al., 1965; Lowe and Campbell, 1965; Furth and Pufall, 1966; McReynolds, 1966; Stark, 1966, 1967a, 1967b; Stark, Poppen, and May, 1967; Lovell, Hoyle, and Siddall, 1968; Monsees, 1968; Stark, Cohen, and Eisenson, 1968; Poppen, Stark, Eisenson, Forrest, and Wertheim, 1969; Weiner, 1969a, 1969b). The topics covered ranged widely, from visual spatial memory and auditory discrimination, through sequence learning and structural characteristics of language productions to behavioral aberrations and play behavior. A number of interesting but not surprising changes took place as part of this turn to group investigations. The case studies had generally consisted of descriptions upon which hypotheses might be based. While some of the group investigations were in the nature of "informed fishing expeditions" (Ajuriaguerra et al., 1958), most provided tests of specific hypotheses. In seeking answers to specific questions, the authors have generally used standardized procedures. Whether these procedures consisted of tasks devised by the investigators for the specific study (Wilson, Doehring, and Hirsch, 1960; Monsees, 1968) or previously published tests (Stark, 1966, 1967a), they were carefully enough described to allow replication of the study. Of course, when a new and rather ill-defined area is approached, investigators are likely to have recourse again to a case study approach using rather impressionistic methods (Stark, 1967b).

During this same period an expansion in the kinds of children studied took place. Prior to the past decade, investigations had been limited to the problems of children with extreme deficiencies in language. After that children with more minor problems began to be included (Ajuriaguerra et al., 1963, 1965; Crookes and Greene, 1963; Inhelder, 1963; Lovell, Hoyle, and Siddall, 1968; Monsees, 1968; Weiner, 1969a; Weiner, 1969b). In two of the eight studies of such children the subjects were originally chosen because of severe dyslalia but were then found to make grammatical errors also (Crookes and Greene, 1963; Monsees, 1968).

Throughout this century of investigation the major thrust in both case and group studies has been the search for deficiencies in underlying psychological processes. The assumption has been that inadequacies in "language related behavior" would explain the disordered language. Attention has concentrated on various aspects of perceptual processing, memory functioning, motor responses, and general intellectual level. The bases for the specific choices of behaviors to be studied have varied. Particularly for the earliest case studies it would be difficult to say that any organized theoretical model was used in selecting the "language-related" behaviors to be observed. But the organization of all but the earliest brief accounts reveals at least some debt to the conceptual schemas derived from the study of adult aphasia by neurologists. More recently other models have come into use. One, devised by Wepman et al. (1960), is also based on the study of adult aphasics but is more akin to the theoretical conceptions of neobehaviorism than to the earlier neurological models. The other, avowedly neobehavioristic, is the analysis of normal language presented by Osgood (1957).

The methods used in obtaining the desired information on the language related behavior tended to be informal at first and were devised by the examiner as the case seemed to require. Even Liebmann's detailed description of an examination consisted of suggestions of the kinds of things an examiner might do, along with some examples. Standardized measures did not come into use until the late 1920's. It was particularly intelligence tests which came into general use in these studies, as they did in other areas of investigation during this period. Formalized measures of other aspects of behavior were not as common. The full use of standardized tests with aphasic children came with group investigations. In this context the term "standardized" is used to designate set procedures which may be repeated exactly by other investigators or examiners. The use of tests having published norms, aside from intelligence tests, began very recently, largely with the advent of The Illinois Test of Psycholinguistic Abilities.

In contrast to this concentration on language-related behavior, surprisingly little attention has been given to the disordered language itself. In the case studies attempts were made to provide a description of the children's language. Some of these descriptions were fairly extensive (Ley, 1929). Others consisted of a sentence or two on the child's apparent comprehension and on the language he produced. Since the language productions of the children were minimal, at least a reasonable impression could be given in a brief description. In the group studies not even this has been done. The diagnosis of "congenital aphasia" or "sensory aphasia" has been considered sufficient. The source of this essential neglect is undoubtedly the lack of appropriate conceptual tools for language description. It is only in the last few years, with the more recent developments in linguistics, that the first attempts at a structural analysis of aphasic children's language have been made. The major effort to date was by Menyuk (1964), with children with relatively mild dysfunction.

An attempt to summarize the substantive findings of this literature is difficult. Because of the variable adequacy of the published accounts it is probably wisest not to speak of "established facts." Even "generally accepted descriptions" may go beyond the actual state of affairs. Virtually every important factual or theoretical point has been called into question. It is nonetheless worthwhile to attempt to give an overview of those aspects of the findings which are relevant to this discussion.

The affected children, most often boys, are usually divided into two groups, those who have severe comprehension difficulties and those who seem to understand well but are able to speak very little if at all. These two groups are obviously the analogues of the "receptive" and "expressive" forms of adult aphasia-categories which are themselves the subject of much controversy. In seeking the underlying behavioral disabilities, those who have studied children with severe comprehension problems have emphasized their patients' (or subjects') difficulty in obtaining meaning from sound that they can hear. Worster-Drought and Allen termed the difficulty "congenital auditory imperception" because their subject (and others like him) found not only speech sounds but also many nonspeech sounds meaningless. They linked the problem to the agnosias, the "inability to interpret sensory impressions" (English and English, 1958, p. 20). However, they and others found evidence of a difficulty in dealing with verbal symbols also and therefore linked the affliction to the aphasias as well, but only secondarily. Uncertainty and even controversy have surrounded the problem of the children's auditory acuity. It is not uncommon for a partial hearing loss to be found or at least for the suspicion of such a loss to be present. Exact determinations of acuity tend to be difficult with these children, in part because of their inconsistent responses to sound (Reichstein, 1964). At least one author has even insisted that the problem is always one of partial hearing loss (De

Sanctis, 1925). The most recent investigations of "sensory aphasics" have been formal group studies done almost entirely in this country. The major hypothesis investigated has been that suggested by Orton (1937), namely that the basic difficulty of these children is an inadequacy in processing temporally ordered stimuli (Furth, 1964; Lowe and Campbell, 1965; Furth and Pufall, 1966; Stark, 1966, 1967; Stark, Poppen, and May, 1967; Poppen et al., 1969). The findings have generally been interpreted by the authors as supporting the hypothesis. Other aspects of auditory processing have been implicated (Hardy, 1956; Eisenson, 1968) but little work has been done in these directions.

Investigators describing children whose comprehension is apparently intact, have tended to emphasize the dyspraxic quality of their subjects. Their motor functioning has been said to be characterized by a general clumsiness which increases as the complexity of the act increases. However, there has been much controversy over this form of the disorder. Worster-Drought and Allen doubted its existence. More recently Eisenson (1968) presented the view that expressive difficulties unaccompanied by deficiencies in comprehension related to "an oral apraxia or dysarthric impairment" rather than to aphasia. Launay and Soulé (1952), while accepting the existence of this form of congenital aphasia, presented cases which pointed to a diversity of underlying defects. Ajuriaguerra and his coworkers (1958) also did not accept dyspraxia as the only possible source. They divided their subjects into two groups: a dyspraxic group whose members demonstrated a "profound incapacity to organize movements in space and in time" (p. 58) and a group with "prevailing difficulties in temporal organization" (p. 23). These same authors presented a challenge to the neatness of a receptive-expressive dichotomy with their finding of comprehension difficulties in many of their "audimutes with praxic difficulties."

The adequacy of a simple dichotomy was made even more questionable by the expansion of the study of congenitally aphasic children to include youngsters with relatively mild oral language disorders. To date the most extensive study of these "dysphasic" children has been done by a team of researchers headed by Ajuriaguerra (Ajuriaguerra et al., 1963). In the area of most immediate relevance, that of perceptual and motor problems, the major deficit they found was in what they termed "audioverbal perception." Operationally this involved a difficulty with tasks requiring the repetition of nonsense syllables. This was true even when the children, who had severe articulatory problems also, could pronounce the sounds correctly. Another important deficit was in verbal comprehension which was affected in almost all the children. On re-examining some of the same children, two years later on the average, they (Ajuriaguerra et al., 1965) found that the children had improved in a majority of the areas considered. Least changed, and with an implication of increased retardation, was "audioverbal perception." Inadequate performances in this function and in articulation were said to have retained "their pathognomonic significance" (p. 399).

The level and quality of the affected children's intelligence has frequently been commented on but rarely studied with any great care or exactness (Inhelder, 1963). It has been assumed that the children were of normal intellectual endowment. However, it is not rare for children with "mild" intellectual impairments, i.e., ones who are borderline defective or mildly retarded, to be included in a study. Indications of difficulties with abstractions have sometimes been attributed to the children's lack of language, in analogy with the problems of the deaf (Worster-Drought and Allen, 1930; Ley, 1930). Eisenson (1968) linked this frequently mentioned deficiency to the neurological dysfunction to which he attributes the condition.

While it is the extremes of the disorder which have been most often studied, it is the milder form which is most frequently encountered in speech clinics. Studies of this form have only recently begun to appear. Because of the vagueness of the descriptions of the children's language, it is difficult to establish the degree of correspondence of the samples included in the few existing studies. Of course, if Eisenson's view (1968) of the common auditory perceptual origin of all such problems is accepted, differentiations may be unimportant. However, this is as yet an unverified hypothesis.

CURRENT RESEARCH

The present report concerns an ongoing longitudinal study of children whose language disorders are mild. The youngsters selected for study probably are similar to Ajuriaguerra's dysphasic subjects in their linguistic problems. As will be seen, they are much like his children in certain other aspects of their functioning. The study continues the major direction of past research in that it concerns language-related behavior.

The subjects were eight dysphasic boys, who were five and six years of age at the start of the investigation. They had been selected because they gave indications in conversation of having difficulties with language structure beyond that expected of their age. Two of the children evidenced some difficulties in comprehension of language. However neither these difficulties nor those in expression were as severe as the ones usually described in children with "receptive aphasia" or "expressive aphasia." All of the children had been found to be within normal limits on audiological screening and on the Arthur Adaptation of the Leiter International Performance Scale, a nonverbal test of intelligence (i.e., IQ $>$ 80). The most severe motor problem was the mild clumsiness of one child. None was emotionally disturbed.

The measures of language-related behavior consisted of tests of perceptual and perceptual-motor functioning, e.g., a measure of the ability to discriminate between speech sounds and a measure of oral dyspraxia. These tests were intended to explore what is termed the "preceptual level" in Wepman's model of language functioning. This is considered to be the level at which stimuli are received, stored, and acted upon but are not given meaning. It is only at a higher level, the conceptual level, that meaning becomes involved. Perceptual level functioning which is considered to be modality-bound is regarded as basic to conceptual activity.

The tests chosen or devised for the study emphasized auditory and oral-motor functioning. Visual-motor tests were included but an equally thorough exploration of visual modality functioning was not attempted. Of the eleven measures included in the test battery six were constructed especially for the study. This was done less for the pleasure of devising new and uncertain measures than for the lack of fully described or published tests that might serve the purpose of the research design.

The responses of the eight dysphasic children on these tests were compared with those of eight individually matched normal control subjects. The normal children were matched on age and Leiter IQ and were also without sensory, motor, or severe emotional problems. Their mothers' descriptions indicated normal language development. None of them had a severe articulation problem. The socioeconomic status of the families of the two groups were much the same, with any differences being in favor of the experimental group. All the children were Caucasian and both natives and residents of the same general geographical area. Their parents were also native speakers of English.

The major findings were that the dysphasic children were deficient in auditory-vocal functioning and in the learning of linguistic rules. The sharpest difference between the two groups occurred on the measures requiring the reproduction of unstructured or structured strings of sound. The difficulty of the dysphasic children was great enough to prevent any overlap of the two groups in performance on the tasks involved. (While a simlar difference occurred on the test of speech sound articulation, this was in part a reflection of the rejection of any potential control subject who had a substantial difficulty in this area.) They were also inferior to the normal children in executing various oral-motor acts, with their inadequacy becoming greater as the complexity of the acts increased. Inadequacy, although not extreme, was also evident in their responses to two measures of the comprehension of oral language, one tapping comprehension of vocabulary and the other bearing on the understanding of grammatical constructions. There were only two kinds of tasks involving the auditory-vocal system on which they were not inferior to their controls: the ability to discriminate speech sounds and the speed of repetition of various sound combinations. In contrast, they were the equal of the normal children on the two visual-motor tasks.

A year later seven of the dysphasic children and their controls were retested. Four visual-perceptual tests (i.e., ones not involving a significant motor response) were added to the battery and a new auditory discrimination test was substituted for the one used in the first year. Again an auditory-vocal deficit appeared. The only test in the auditory-vocal series which did not show a statistically significant difference was that tapping the ability to distinguish between closely related speech sounds. Once more the adequacy of the dysphasics' visual modality functioning stood in sharp contrast to their auditory-vocal deficiencies. The dysphasics were the peers of the control group in every one of the visual-perceptual and visual-motor tests.

The third year of testing is only partially completed but the preliminary indications are that much the same pattern of inadequacies and adequacies will appear.

Despite this consistency in pattern an attempt to predict second year results from those of the first year were disappointing. A statistically significant rank correlation was found on only two tests: one portion of the test of diadochokinetic rate and the test of grammar comprehension. Individual variation in rate of change during the year was obviously considerable.

Before turning to a consideration of the tests used, I might add that language protocols were also gathered from the children. The stimuli used were the pictures of the Thematic Apperception Test. The differences between the language productions of the two groups were considerable. But that is another story.

It may be instructive to consider both the specific tests included in the battery and the children's responses to them. As noted already, the tests were chosen to accord with Wepman's language model. Instruments which would be appropriate for the children and would tap input, storage, and output processes were sought. For the auditory and oral-motor modalities the tests included were: a measure of auditory discrimination, two tests traditionally thought to measure memory for sequential material, two tests of ability to execute oral-motor acts, and a measure of speed of repetitive movements of the oral musculature. For the exploration of visual-motor functioning a test of the ability to copy geometric designs and one of ability to draw human figures were used. The visual-perceptual tests added in the second year explored the ability to distinguish figure from ground, the ability to remember geometric designs, the ability to discriminate the same designs, and the ability to recall visual sequences.

The inclusion of a test of auditory discrimination in the battery seemed necessary. First, it filled a slot in the language model. Also it provided a measure of an ability which has been found to be related to severe speech difficulties in young children (Weiner, 1967). However, the most used tests of this ability require the child to make a judgment concerning the identity of two words or nonsense syllables. This format is often difficult for normal kindergarten children and quickly proved to be impossible for at least some of the dysphasic children. A simpler form of the test presents the child with two pictures, e.g., of peas and of keys, and requires him to point to the one named, let us say, "keys." Templin (1957) had found a virtual identity between her preschool subjects' scores on a test of this sort and a test of vocabulary knowledge. This problem was readily solved in the present study by teaching the children the meanings of the words they did not know. The cost of this improvement was a reduction in the number of words that could be used, beyond that inherent in the picture form of the test. Since the dysphasic children particularly tended to be distractible and the test battery was already rather substantial, an increase in the number of words might have gone beyond their endurance. As a result, when no difference was found between the two groups in their responses to the test, it was difficult to know whether the children did not differ in this ability or the test was too gross. The only reasonable conclusion seemed to be that a severe problem in auditory discrimination did not exist in the dysphasic group. Another problem concerning the picture format might be mentioned. The dysphasics' ability to make auditory discriminations may be enhanced by the visual support offered by the pictures. A real difference may be masked in this fashion also.

Changing in the second year to the Wepman Auditory Discrimination Test,

(Wepman, 1958), which presents only pairs of words as the stimuli, solved the possible problems of number of differentiations and of visual support. However, many of the children seemed to find the format of the test difficult and several children in each group made so many errors that it was likely that they were responding at random. The question of the dysphasics' ability to discriminate speech sounds remains open.

Orton (1937), as already noted, hypothesized that the basic problem in congenital aphasia is an inability to deal with the sequential aspects of language. Menyuk (1969) has suggested that a short-term memory difficulty underlies the problems of children with mildly deviant language. Ajuriaguerra and his coworkers (1963) found a deficit in the ability of their dysphasics to handle such tasks as the reproduction of nonsense words. In all, it seemed appropriate to explore memory functioning with some thoroughness. Two tasks which are usually regarded as measures of this function were included in the test battery. One consisted of series of vowels, increasing in length at each step. Vowels rather than numbers or consonant-vowel combinations were used because of the fairly severe articulatory problems of the dysphasics. In fact, one of them could not even pronounce the vowels accurately. It also seemed worthwhile to see if the children reacted differently to meaningful strings of sound; therefore, sentences were also used, again increasing in length at each step. Since it was hoped to make length the major variable, an attempt was made to keep transformations to a minimum. Again, to avoid articulatory difficulties as much as possible, only the consonants acquired earliest in normal speech development were used (Templin, 1957). Sentences which met all the criteria were, to understate the matter, difficult to compose. The resulting test proved to be even more effective than had been hoped. Both tests, vowels and sentences, demonstrated an almost startling difference between the two groups in their ability to reproduce strings of sound. But beyond this the sentence test provided a demonstration of the dysphasics' difficulties with linguistic rules. There was a number of sentences which contained irregular past tense verbs, e.g., "Daddy bought a new tie today." This resulted from the decision not to use the /s/ phoneme and the awkwardness of a constant use of first or second person. During the first year seven of the eight dysphasic children made errors of morphology or syntax. Five of them substituted present tense forms for irregular past tense forms, e.g., "buy" for "bought" and "take" for "took." Only two of the control children made such errors, and then on much longer and more complex sentences. In the second year six of the seven remaining dysphasic children made such errors while none of the control subjects did. So far in the third year three of the six dysphasic children who have been tested have made such errors.

Certainly as important as the findings is their interpretation. Particularly vital is the question of the nature of the deficit revealed by the difficulty in repeating the vowels and sentences. The traditional interpretations of inadequacies on measures of this type are a general deficiency in auditory memory or a more specific problem in memory for sequences. An analysis of the kinds of errors made by the dysphasic children did not support the notion of a difficulty with sequential ordering. When the children, experimental or control, could retain and reproduce the vowels or the words, they seldom confused their order. The errors they did make were far more apt to be ones of "reproduction span," i.e., the omission of correct elements or the substitution of incorrect ones. With some variation this tended to be true in both the first and the second years of testing.

The reproduction of structured or unstructured strings of sound can probably be safely interpreted as a measure of memory functioning when normal subjects are being tested. There is some doubt whether this is necessarily so when language disordered children are involved. The act of repeating series of vowels or sentences is surprisingly complex. The child must attend carefully enough and long enough to perceive the stimuli accurately, must briefly store the material, be able to retrieve each element exactly when it is needed, and finally translate the auditory pattern into an organized motor response. When structured strings are used, a grasp of the necessary linguistic rules and of meaning may also come into play. There is thus a sizeable number of processes which may be at fault. Memory is but one possibility.

Perhaps the major question to be derived from this research is that of the relationship between the dysphasics' difficulty in auditory-vocal functioning and their language problems. This is a puzzle with many aspects. Neither the structure of imitation nor its role in language learning are well understood. A number of disparate observations beg understanding and integration. The dysphasic group's deficiency in imitation, i.e., in repeating strings of sound, seems to contrast, at times sharply, with the echolalic behavior of many young normal children and with that seen in some mentally retarded, emotionally disturbed, or even receptive aphasic youngsters (Fay, 1966, 1967a, 1967b, 1969; Fay and Butler, 1968). Also there are the observations made by Fraser, Bellugi, and Brown (1963) on the "control of grammar in imitation, comprehension, and production" of language. They found that normal children show an order of adequacy decreasing from imitation to comprehension to production. A disruption in this order seems probable in the dysphasic children, and indeed was found in a study of apparently similar children by three English investigators (Lovell, Hoyle, and Siddall, 1968). Comprehension was found to exceed imitation, which in turn was more adequate than spontaneous production of language. Fay and Butler (1968), in discussing echolalia by older children, postulate "the developmental nonconvergence of two independent systems; an audio-motor system and a deficient syntactic-semantic system" (p. 370). Similarly Fraser, Bellugi, and Brown conclude that the imitation performance of their normal children "did not work through the meaning system" (1953, p. 133). In contrast the dysphasic child's auditory-vocal difficulties and grammatical difficulties do seem to be interrelated. Futher exploration is certainly in order.

Many other questions present themselves: the course and ultimate fate of the dysphasics' language development, involving the question of whether the language is simply lagging behind or is deviant from the normal; the presence of symbolic and/or transmissive problems in their language functioning; the nature of their intellectual development and its relationship to their language learning; and finally the relationship between their difficulties and those of children who are considered to be mentally retarded. There is no dearth of researchable questions.

Before attention is turned to a final topic, it might be well to spend a moment on the relationship of the results of this study to those of previously published work on dysphasics. The findings have been quite consistent. A difficulty in auditory-vocal functioning has been found by each investigator who has touched on this area. The deficiency takes its clearest form in the imitative behavior involved in the repetition of strings of sound. A difficulty in the ability to effect voluntary movements of the oral musculature has also been evident. Each sample has shown severe articulatory problems. At least to this point auditory perceptual problems have not been demonstrated. However, auditory comprehension seems to have been at least mildly affected in most of the children studied. The available data link the dysphasic children more with the expressive end of what may be a kind of continuum than with the receptive end. However, this remains quite uncertain as does the whole matter of how to categorize most meaningfully the oral language disorders of children.

At this juncture it is appropriate to consider, at least briefly, the potential relevance of this material on congenital aphasia to the study of the language problems of the mentally retarded.

Perhaps most simply and directly there is the relevance which arises from the existence of overlapping membership in the two groups. Some children included in the studies of aphasic or dysphasic children clearly fell within the usual definition of mental retardation (Ley, 1929; Ajuriaguerra et al., 1958; Ajuriaguerra et al., 1965). They were accepted as subjects in the studies with the explicit or implicit explanation that the low level of their language development could not be explained by their mild intellectual impairment. This, of course, poses the problem of the nature of the relationship between the development of intelligence and of language structure—a much too complex problem to dispose of meaningfully in a few sentences. However, it is clear that the implicit working hypothesis both in clinical and theoretical definitions of congenital aphasia is that the two aspects of development should be closely linked. A child with a significant lag in language structure is considered to be aphasic or at least aphasoid (assuming of course the absence of certain other deficiencies). There seems to be no general agreement about the precise point along the scale of intellectual deficits at which a child is no longer considered aphasic. At any rate, to the degree that this kind of overlap does occur between the two groups the knowledge gained from the study of childhood aphasia is likely to be directed relevant.

But the broader question then presents itself: to what extent is the search for the basic deficiencies underlying language disorders, as exemplified in the study of language related behavior, a meaningful enterprise? To misapply some useful psychometric concepts, the approach seems to have face validity and perhaps even concurrent validity. More evidence of construct validity is needed before we can be certain that we are not dealing with epiphenomena rather than with basic processes. If this direction of investigation does prove to be valid in the study of aphasic phenomena, it should also be appropriate to the wide range of language problems that must certainly exist among the retarded.

The clinical relevance of the study of language-related behavior depends upon several factors. If it is assumed that the enterprise is meaningful, a number of clinically relevant consequences ensue. Diagnostic testing, similar to that done in the study described, would be the first step in devising a remedial program. Remedial measures might include attempts to help the child overcome the specific deficits found in the diagnostic examination, either as part of direct instruction in language or independently. On the other hand, means of minimizing the effects of a child's deficits might be sought, e.g., using a visual approach as much as possible when auditory functioning is poor. Remedial reading is a quite analogous effort. Diagnostic testing of related behaviors, e.g., visual discrimination and auditory discrimination, is a very much accepted part of the preparation of an individual remedial program. While there is controversy over whether and how the resulting information should be used (Cohen, 1969; Frostig, 1969; Silver, Hagin, and Hersh, 1967), remedial programs do generally take various basic skills into account. The diagnosis or remediation of oral language disorders would have to take into account the likelihood that the affected children are apt to be younger or duller than those involved in remedial reading programs. But this, as is true of the other more basic problems, can only be handled effectively if appropriate and well-designed studies are carried out.

SUMMARY OF DISCUSSION

QUESTION: There is some information about the neurology of verbal reproduction. The conduction aphasia described by Wernicke and Kleist seems to knock out that ability specifically and leaves comprehension and verbal production relatively intact except that the patient simply can't repeat what he hears. On the other hand, the transcortical sensory aphasia of Henschen and what Geschwind called the syndrome of the isolated speech area, seems to knock out everything but that. Comprehension is severely affected. Speech is very underproductive. And yet the person can repeat what he hears very well.

WEINER: Of course the problem in children is whether the findings on adult aphasia are completely relevant.

QUESTION: They definitely are not completely relevant. But don't they have something to do with what is going on?

WEINER: I suspect they do have something to do with it. The one autopsy on an aphasic child described in the literature does support the notion that we're dealing with a brain-injured population. The results made the authors wonder not why the child had so much difficulty but why he learned as much as he did. The primary auditory pathways were completely knocked out. The problem in relation to adult findings is really to determine the nature of the relevance to these children.

QUESTION: You made your decision to test discrimination in not a sound-free but in a controlled sound environment. Did you think about using some of the things like competing messages?

WEINER: I think it will be necessary to get to things like that. I was starting off to do a clinical study, one in which I could use tests that could be employed easily in the clinic. But I think to understand these children better, we must get into much more controlled procedures.

QUESTION: Little has been done in just plain discrimination testing with noise background. Isn't this a clinically available, feasible kind of thing that anyone with a tape recorder could do?

WEINER: Yes. I think this has to be done with the children to get some notion of their auditory functioning. There are at least a couple of simple things that can be done, but once beyond that, it really becomes complicated.

QUESTION: Isn't the dichotic stimulation notion very good? That is one of the few tests that has anything to do with hemispheric dominance that can be done in intact organisms without injecting barbiturates.

WEINER: Yes. The problem is why do these children who function rather well in all kinds of areas have difficulty in this area? So often the assumption is that it is a bihemispheric problem. Information on that would be very helpful.

QUESTION: Your results on dysphasic children on the imitation of structured strings are very interesting. I think that they are very much in line with some of the work that Dan Slobin and Lenneberg have done. Imitations of strings or sentences that exceed immediate memory span are dependent upon the grammatical structure in order to be able to repeat that sentence. This seems to conflict with the work of Fraser, Brown, and Bellugi. However, if you look at their sentences, you find that the order varies from four morphemes, I believe, up to only eight morphemes, and this may be one of the reasons that their results came out as they did. And I think that the point of whether a child needs to rely on the grammar if the sentence exceeds immediate memory span or not has not been studied sufficiently. Aren't your results very much in line with what happens in normal children?

WEINER: Yes. My most relevant results are from one child, one who functions best in everything else and worst in language. And this was based on what he did in the third year. He was still using "me" in his spontaneous production. He copied "I" sentences very nicely up to a certain point, and then the whole thing just broke down, and he reverted to the "me" and began to use the present tense.

QUESTION: What happens to the youngsters in the intervening years between the times that you test them?

WEINER: The children were in a clinic program that really did very little directly with language. They were much more involved in a general stimulation program and also in dealing with the parents and the behavior of the children. Only now are they beginning to try to think through how they can deal directly with the language of the children. I can't say that they received any kind of tuition that might affect their functioning directly. These children are now in public school, and this certainly may make a difference because they are being educated with variable results. The child I just mentioned still has really abominable articulation. When he begins to read aloud, his articulation straightens out. He does it quite well. As soon as he puts the book down, he reverts to his normal articulation patterns, which are miserable. He is the only one who apparently shows this kind of help from visual support.

QUESTION: You mentioned in a sense you were disappointed that the correlations were poor. Shouldn't you perhaps be encouraged if that is the case?

WEINER: In what sense?

QUESTION: If the correlations were very high, might not you assume that experiences that intervene during the year have no impact on these children, that the entire process is carried somehow with the neurological substrate?

WEINER: There might be variations there, too.

QUESTION: But wouldn't it be unfortunate if the correlations remained very high, given the probability that kids have varied kinds of experiences in the intervening period?

WEINER: And that they did. As you suggest, they apparently did respond in varying ways to their different experiences. Of course, as so often is true in children with any kind of pathology, the variation is tremendous. It is only in very general ways that these children are alike. In their language patterns and in almost everything else they vary.

QUESTION: You have indicated that such children have been studied for perhaps hundreds of years now. What happens to children who are congenital aphasics?

WEINER: This has been argued endlessly, and there is very little information. Since nobody had ever seen an adult with this kind of problem, who had had the problem as a child, it was originally assumed that it must straighten out. And then slowly reports appeared of young adults who were found to have the problem. That is, they still had language difficulties. It appears that some of them straighten out and some of them do not. The question is how to predict which ones will or which ones won't, assuming that there is no intervention.

QUESTION: Where a diagnosis has been made, are these children followed on into adulthood? And is there ever any powerful neurological evidence to suggest there was indeed some neurological problem?

WEINER: No one has followed any children up to adulthood. And neurological evidence is too variable to be significant. We occasionally find a child with classical signs or soft signs. Some have abnormal electronecephalograms. In one study there were significantly more abnormal electroencephalograms than in normal populations. But they vary in that, too.

QUESTION: Isn't this problem that you are mentioning—of following these people up over the years—isn't this one of the advantages provided by the Mental Retardation Research Center Program, in that by law they are committed for the next 20 years at least to study problems related to mental retardation? There are some precedents in other areas involving something like a rare case registry with collaborative efforts between centers on different kinds of problems. Might there be sufficient interest among the people here representing the centers, and even those outside of the centers, in developing collaborative efforts of this kind? Certainly there should be mechanisms available to record data on these children and to follow them up over a period of time.

WEINER: It is possible, but there are many problems in doing that.

QUESTION: But they are not insurmountable, are they?

WEINER: No, I'm sure they are not. I consider myself extremely fortunate to be able to keep this small group of children together for three years. Americans tend to be so transient that they just sort of drift away and you haven't the slightest idea where they have gone. And also the parents aren't always willing to continue with what may be rather time-comsuming procedures. What I have done—and so far it has proved successful—is to be as much help to the parents and the children as I possibly can, which means that an enormous amount of time is devoted just to talking to the parents, talking to the school personnel, visiting the school, and so on. But I think this is the only way that I can possibly hang onto these kids.

QUESTION: Isn't this exactly the kind of effort that can compensate in part for problems of attrition? If you have centers all collaborating and all having information on a group of people, even if they do move around there is a good possibility of being able to pick them up at a later date.

SIDMAN: You're suggesting that perhaps an interesting patient could be brought to several centers to be worked up by their particular techniques and perhaps a joint report put out on it, this kind of thing? This could be very useful. Miller and Taeuber did this recently with their well-known patient who had undergone a bilateral temporal lobectomy, and on whom many people had worked. They published a volume devoted to this one patient, a very, very useful thing. This would help in other areas too. For instance in studying further the crucial role of grammar in repetition, at least in adult aphasics. We have all heard of the person with repetition difficulty who can repeat "superheterogenous transsubstantiation" but can't repeat "no," "and," "but." It would be interesting to know what these children can and can't repeat.

QUESTION: People are now using imitation paradigms to assess comprehension. Just what is the role of imitation here? Before we make presumptions about what the nature of the difficulty is, a lot of variables have to be controlled. For example, if there is an error on an irregular verb, we might attribute that to some failure to appreciate an underlying rule, and it might be a function of something else, the frequency with which that irregular form appears in the child's normal language patterns, and so on.

WEINER: In our studies these were very common words.

QUESTION: They may be common words, but differ in the degree of their commonness. Couldn't there be many other variables?

WEINER: I would agree.

QUESTION: Isn't there a strong tendency to jump immediately into inferential statements about underlying patterns? That's sort of a jargon now. I think it has to be carefully explored.

WEINER: Yes. And there is also the danger of accepting traditional explanations, such as the repetition of strings necessarily means something specific. This is common.

QUESTION: Did stressing words help?

WEINER: I tried it with a number of the children. I virtually shouted at them, stressing the irregular form as much as I could. It didn't make any difference.

QUESTION: To get back to the hearing aspect, once you start playing around with inflections and stresses, and so forth, you have the problem of what is going in the ear. If it is not handled well, if he is getting weaker components or different components of the message, he may be unable to perform because you are taxing his system. I think this is something that we overlook quite frequently. Take something like the endings of a word which may in our environment be a very low-intensity kind of thing. It gets sloughed off, basically. And so we have a person who either has a very mild deviation in sensitivity or a mild deviation in some other auditory processing. In that case we are building a grammatical structure where the problem really is that he's not getting the input stimulations. Although in the environment it's there, it's just not getting through the ear and up the chain.

WEINER: Yes, that is a consideration. Certainly it's been clearly demonstrated in some brain-injured adults. They appear to be aphasic but turn out to have transmissive problems. That is, they can't get the input up to where it can be utilized.

REFERENCES

Ajuriaguerra, J. de, Borel-Maisonny, S., Diatkine, R., Narlian, S., and Stambak, M. Le groupe des audimutités. *Psych. Enfant.*, 1958, *1*, 7–62.

Ajuriaguerra, J. de, Guignard, F., Jaeggi, A., Kocher, F., Maquard, M., Paunier, A., Quinodoz, D., and Siotis, E. Organisation psychologique et troubles du développement du langage: Étude d'un groupe d'enfants dysphasiques. In J. de Ajuriaguerra, F. Bresson, et al. (Eds.), *Problèmes de psycho-linquistique*. Paris: Presses Universitaires de France, 1963. Pp. 109–142.

Ajuriaguerra, J. de, Jaeggi, A., Guignard, F., Kocher, F., Maquard, M., Roth, S., and Schmid, E. Évolution et pronostic de la dysphasie chez l'enfant. *Psych. Enfant.*, 1965, *8*, 391–452.

Benton, A. L., and Joynt, R. J. Early descriptions of aphasia. *Arch. Neurol.*, 1960, *3*, 205–222.

Broca, P. Remarques sur le siege de la faculte du language articule, suivies d'une observation d'aphemie (perte de la parole). *Bull. Soc. Anat. Paris*, 1861, *6*, 330–357.

Cohen, S. A. Studies in visual perception and reading in disadvantaged children. *J. Learn. Disabil.*, 1969, *2*, 498–503.

Crookes, T. G., and Greene, M.C. L. Some characteristics of children with two types of speech disorder. *Brit. J. Educ. Psychol.*, 1963, *33*, 31–40.

De Sanctis, S. *Neuropsichiatria infantile*. Rome: Stock, 1925.

Doehring, D. G. Visual spatial memory in aphasic children. *J. Speech Hearing Res.*, 1960, *3*, 138–149.

Eisenson, J. Developmental aphasia (dyslogia): A postulation of a unitary concept of the disorder. *Cortex*, 1968, *4*, 184–200.

English, H. B., and English, A. C. *A comprehensive dictionary of psychological and psychoanalytic terms*. New York: David McKay Co., 1958.

Ewing, A. W. G. *Aphasia in children*. London: Oxford University Press, 1930.

Fay, W. H. Childhood echolalia in delayed, psychotic and neuropathologic speech patterns. *Folia Phoniat.*, 1966, *18*. 68–71.

Fay, W. H. Childhood echolalia: A group study of late abatement. *Folia Phoniat.*, 1967, *19*, 297–306. (a)

Fay, W. H. Mitigated echolalia of children. *J. Speech Hearing Res.*, 1967, *10*, 305–310. (b)

Fay, W. H. On the basis of autistic echolalia. *J. Comm. Dis.*, 1969, *2*, 38–47.

Fay, W. H., and Butler, B. V. Echolalia, IQ, and the developmental dichotomy of speech and language systems. *J. Speech Hearing Res.*, 1968, *11*, 365–371.

Fraser, C., Bellugi, U., and Brown, R. Control of grammar in imitation, comprehension, and production. *J. Verb. Learning Verb. Behavior*, 1963, *2*, 121–135.

Frostig, M. Reading, developmental abilities, and the problem of the match. *J. Learn. Disabil.*, 1969, *2*, 571–574.

Furth, H. G. Sequence learning in aphasic and deaf children. *J. Speech Hearing Dis.*, 1964, *29*, 171–177.

Furth, H. G., and Pufall, P. B. Visual and auditory sequence learning in hearing-impaired children. *J. Speech Hearing Res.*, 1966, *9*, 441–449.

Gall, F. J. *Organology*. Translated from the French by Winslow Lewis, Jr. Vol. 5. Boston: Marsh, Capen and Lyon, 1835.

Goldenberg, S. An exploratory study of some aspects of idiopathic language retardation. *J. Speech Hearing Dis.*, 1950, *15*, 221–233.

Goldstein, R., Landau, W. M., and Kleffner, F. R. Neurologic assessment of some deaf and aphasic children. *Ann. Otol. Rhinol. Laryng.*, 1958, *67*, 468–479.

Goldstein, R., Landau, W. M., & Kleffner, F. R. Neurologic observations on a population of deaf and aphasic children. *Ann. Otol. Rhinol. Laryng.*, 1969, *69*, 756–767.

Hardy, W. G. Problems of audition, perception and understanding. *Volta Rev.*, 1956, *58*, 289–309.

Inhelder, B. Observations sur les aspects opératifs de la pensée chez des enfants dysphasiques. In J. de Ajuriaguerra, F. Bresson, et al. (Eds.), *Problèmes de psycho-linguistique*. Paris: Presses Universitaires de France, 1963, Pp. 143–153.

Itard, J. M. *The wild boy of Aveyron*. Translated by George and Muriel Humphrey. New York: The Century Co., 1932.

Landau, W. M., Goldstein, R., and Kleffner, F. R. Congenital aphasia: A clinicopathologic study. *Neurol.*, 1960, *10*, 915–921.

Launay, C., & Soulé, M. Trois cas d'audimutité. *Arch. Franc. Ped.*, 1952, *9*, 754–759.

Ley, J. Un cas d'audi-mutité idiopathique (aphasie congénitale) chez des jumeaux monozygotiques. *Encéph.*, 1929, *24*, 121–165.

Ley, J. Les troubles de développement du langage. *J. Belge Neur. Psych.*, 1930, *30*, 415–457.

Liebmann, A. *Vorlesungen ueber Sprachstoerungen*. Vol. 3: *Hoerstummheit*. Berlin: Oscar Coblentz, 1898.

Lovell, K., Hoyle, H. W., and Siddall, M. Q. A study of some aspects of the play and language of young children with delayed speech. *J. Child Psychol. Psychiat.*, 1968, *9*, 41–50.

Lowe, A. D., and Cambell, R. A. Temporal discrimination in aphasoid and normal children. *J. Speech Hearing Res.*, 1965, *8*, 313–314.

Luchsinger, R. Die Vererbung von Sprach-und Stimmstoerungen. *Folia Phoniat.*, 1959, *11*, 7–64.

Mark, H. J., and Hardy, W. G. Orienting reflex disturbances in central auditory or language handicapped children. *J. Speech Hearing Dis.*, 1958, *23*, 237–242.

McCarthy, J. J., and Kirk, S. A. *Illinois test of psycholinguistic abilities: Experimental edition*. Urbana, Ill.: Institute for Research on Exceptional Children, 1961.

McReynolds, L. V. Operant conditioning for investigating speech sound discrimination in aphasic children. *J. Speech. Hearing Res.*, 1966, *9*, 519–528.

Menyuk, P. Comparison of grammar of children with functionally deviant and normal speech. *J. Speech. Hearing Res.*, 1964, *7*, 109–121.

Menyuk, P. *Sentences children use*. Cambridge: MIT Press, 1969.

Monsees, E. K. Temporal sequence and expressive language disorders. *Except. Child,* 1968, *35,* 141-147.
Morgan, W. P. A case of congenital word blindness. *Brit. Med. J.,* 1896, *2,* 1378.
Olson, J. L. Deaf and sensory aphasic children. *Except. Child,* 1961, *27,* 422-424.
Orton, S. T. *Reading, writing and speech problems in children.* New York: W. W. Norton, 1937.
Osgood, C. E. A behavioristic analysis of perception and language as cognitive phenomena. In J. S. Bruner (Ed.), *Contemporary approaches to cognition.* Cambridge: Harvard University Press, 1957. Pp. 75-118.
Poppen, R., Stark, J., Eisenson, J., Forrest, T., and Wertheim, G. Visual sequencing performance of aphasic children. *J. Speech Hearing Res.,* 1969, *12,* 288-300.
Reichstein, J. Auditory threshold consistency in differential diagnosis of aphasia in children. *J. Speech Hearing Dis.,* 1964, *29,* 147-155.
Rosenbluet, B., Goldstein, R., and Landau, W. M. Vestibular responses of some deaf and aphasic children. *Ann. Otol. Rhin. Laryng.,* 1960, *69,* 747-755.
Silver, A. A., Hagin, R. A., & Hersh, M. F. Reading Disability: teaching through stimulation of deficit perceptual areas. *Am. J. Orthopsychiat.,* 1967, *37,* 744-752.
Stark, J. Performance of aphasic children on the ITPA. *Except. Child.,* 1966, *33,* 153-158.
Stark, J. A comparison of the performance of aphasic children on three sequencing tests. *J. Comm. Dis.,* 1967, *1,* 31-34. (a)
Stark, J. Atypical development and behavior in some non-verbal children. *Brit. J. Dis. Comm.,* 1967, *2,* 146-151. (b)
Stark, J., Cohen, S., and Eisenson, J. Performances of aphasic children on the PPVT and auditory decoding tests. *J. Spec. Educ.,* 1968, *2,* 435-437.
Stark, J., Poppen, R., and May, M. Z. Effects of alterations of prosodic features on the sequencing performance of aphasic children. *J. Speech Hearing Res.,* 1967, *10,* 849-855.
Templin, M. C. *Certain language skills in children.* Minneapolis: University of Minnesota Press, 1957.
Town, C. H. Congenital aphasia. *Psychol. Clin.,* 1911, *5,* 167-179.
Vaïsse, L. Des sourds-muets et de certains cas d'aphasie congénitale. *Bull. Soc. Anthrop. Paris,* 1866, *1,* 146-150.
Weiner, P. S. Auditory discrimination and articulation. *J. Speech Hearing Dis.,* 1967, *32,* 19-28.
Weiner, P. S. Mother's reactions to delayed language development in their children. *Except. Child.,* 1969, *36,* 277-279. (a)
Weiner, P. S. The perceptual level functioning of dysphasic children. *Cortex,* 1969, *5,* 440-457. (b)
Wepman, J. M. *Auditory discrimination test* (Manual of directions). Chicago: Language Research Associates, 1958.
Wepman, J. M., Jones, L. V., Bock, R. D., and Van Pelt, D. Studies in aphasia: background and theoretical formulations. *J. Speech Hearing Dis.,* 1960, *25,* 323-332.
Wilde, W. R. *Practical observations on aural surgery and the nature and treatment of diseases of the ear.* Philadelphia: Blanchard and Lea, 1853.
Wilson, L. F. Doehring, D. G., and Hirsh, I. J. Auditory discrimination learning by aphasic and non-aphasic children. *J. Speech Hearing Res.,* 1960, *3,* 130-137.
Worster-Drought, C., and Allen, I. M. Congenital auditory imperception (congenital word-deafness): With report of a case. *J. Neurol. Psychopath.,* 1929, *9,* 193-208.
Worster-Drought, C., and Allen, I. M. Congenital auditory imperception (congenital word-deafness): Investigation of a case by Head's method. *J. Neurol. Psychopath.,* 1929, *9,* 289-319.
Worster-Drought, C., and Allan I. M. Congenital auditory imperception (congenital word-deafness): And its relation to idioglossia and other speech defects. *J. Neurol. Psychopath.,* 1930, *10,* 193-236.

Experimental Procedures

SAMPLE-MATCHING TECHNIQUES IN THE STUDY OF CHILDREN'S LANGUAGE

PETER B. ROSENBERGER, LAWRENCE T. STODDARD, and MURRAY SIDMAN

*Massachusetts General Hospital and
Fernald State School*

PETER B. ROSENBERGER received his M.D. degree from Western Reserve University in 1960. He took his internship and residency training in pediatrics at the Children's Hospital in Boston, and in neurology at the Massachusetts General Hospital. He is currently on the staff of the Pediatric Neurology Unit at Massachusetts General Hospital, and is Assistant Professor of Neurology at Harvard Medical School. He also serves as Director of Research at the Fernald State School.

LAWRENCE T. STODDARD received his Ph.D. degree in psychology from Columbia University in 1962. Since then he has been associated with the Behavior Laboratory, Neurology Service, Massachusetts General Hospital, where he now serves as Associate Psychologist. His principal base of operations is presently at the Eunice Kennedy Shriver Center, Fernald State School.

MURRAY SIDMAN received his Ph.D. degree in psychology from Columbia University in 1952, and for the next nine years was Research Psychologist in the Division of Neuropsychiatry, Walter Reed Army Institute of Research. Since 1961 he has served as chief of the Behavior Laboratory, Joseph P. Kennedy Jr. Memorial Laboratories, Neurology Service, Massachusetts General Hospital, where he now holds the rank of Psychologist. He is currently Associate Professor of Psychology in the Department of Neurology, Harvard Medical School, and also chief of the Behavior Laboratory at the Eunice Kennedy Shriver Center, Walter E. Fernald State School.

The relationship between brain disease and disturbance in language disorder has been recognized for well over a century. The question of the extent to which specific language deficits may be correlated with specific localities of brain disease has aroused considerable controversy among neurologists and psychologists during this century. A few basic clinical-anatomical correlations appear to have survived this controversy thus far. They are illustrated in Figure 1 and are as follows:

  1. Lesions of the posterior part of the third frontal convolution of the dominant cerebral hemisphere of the normal adult appear to give rise to an interruption of the motor productivity of language, that is to say oral speech (#2 in Fig. 1). This disorder is usually accompanied by apraxia for fine motor movements of the lips and tongue, and practically always by difficulty in the graphic expression of language as well. Intact language comprehension can ususally be demonstrated.

  2. Lesions in the middle third of the superior temporal convolution (#4) produce a disturbance in language formulation and comprehension while leaving the fluency of verbal output relatively unimpaired. These are the

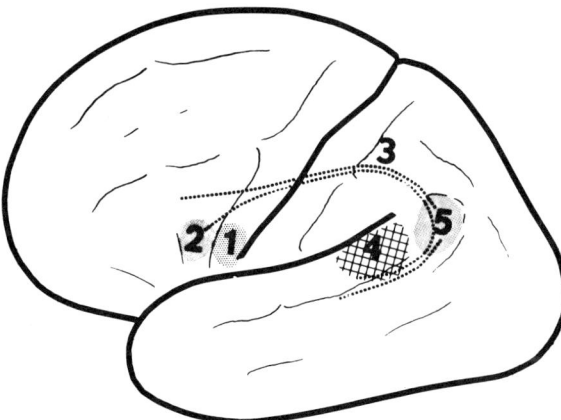

Fig. 1. Schematic diagram of language centers in the dominant hemisphere of the normal adult brain (Courtesy of Dr. Norman Geschwind).

patients whose speech includes jargon, phonemic substitutions, synonymous substitutions, circumlocutory phrases, and other similar linguistic abnormalities.

3. Lesions elsewhere in the dominant temporal lobe are frequently found in the patient whose language deficit is most prominently in the area of *word finding*. Such a patient usually has relatively intact language comprehension and relatively good verbal output, but is frequently unable to call forth from his memory precisely the right word for what he wants to say.

4. The angular gyrus of the dominant hemisphere (#5) is a much less well understood but critically important area for language. It appears that some sort of integration of visual and auditory information occurs in this region. Patients with lesions in this area are frequently dyslectic, that is, have lost their ability to read while retaining their comprehension of spoken language as well as their primary visual acuity and visual comprehension of non-verbal materials. We shall speak more of this later.

To complicate the picture even further, the child's brain violates some of the most sacred principles of classical neurology in its relation to language behavior. To begin with, a child under the age of ten years who has acquired normal language skills, and who then loses them as the result of a lesion in his dominant cerebral hemisphere, almost uniformly reacquires these language skills within a year; and there is considerable evidence that this reacquistion is accomplished by the *other hemisphere*—something which rarely if ever occurs in the adult. Second, cerebral dominance is a different phenomenon in childhood; that is, its importance to language increases with age. Thus young children more frequently show disturbances of language behavior with lesions of either cerebral hemisphere than do adults. Third, fluent aphasias are rarely seen in childhood.

What do these above considerations have to do with language of the retarded? First of all, defective language is often a retarded person's outstanding handicap. A questionnaire circulated to the ward attendants of the Fernald State School revealed that only 747 of 1,752 residents evaluated are capable of speech understandable by a stranger; and 499 of these 1,752 residents have difficulty understanding even the simple communications of the attendants (Table 1). (It must be stressed that these

TABLE 1

Survey of language skills of Fernald State School residents

I.	*Communication to Others*	
	Form left blank	27
	Unknown	12
	Makes no sounds	102
	No meaningful communication	287
	Jabbers—no words	192
	Makes sounds or signs	12
	Speech somewhat difficult to understand	373
	Speech understandable by a stranger	747
	Total residents surveyed	1,752
II.	*Receiving Communication from Others*	
	Form left blank	32
	Unknown	35
	Does not respond to gestures and/or signs	138
	Responds only to gestures and/or signs	99
	Has difficulty understanding oral communication	195
	Understands oral communication	1253
	Total residents surveyed	1,752

are questionnaire replies from untrained attendants). Second, complete neurological evaluations of nearly 1,600 of our residents show that almost 80 per cent have clinical evidence of disease of the nervous system. It is, of course, not possible to draw conclusions from these two sets of figures concerning the portion of language deficits which are caused by neurological disease. However, the mere number involved have been sufficient to stimulate our interest.

RELEVANCE OF SAMPLE MATCHING TECHNIQUES

Our use of sample matching techniques in the study of children's language was prompted by both neurological and psychological considerations. The neurological issue was raised by Geschwind (1965), who offered evidence in support of the proposition that the language capability of the human organism may be related to the ability of his brain to make direct anatomical connections between auditory and visual associations of which the animal brain is incapable. Birch and Belmont (1964) developed simple tests for auditory visual correlation and demonstrated performance deficits on these tests among poor readers.

Psychological considerations were even more persuasive. Conventional techniques of verbal communication are nearly useless in the study of language deficits, especially more severe ones. Our laboratory was already engaged in the extensive use of nonverbal techniques to study the behavior of animals and subnormal human subjects. It occurred to us that these techniques might profitably be applied to the exploration of verbal deficits as well. Specifically, the sample matching technique permits the subject to indicate his selection of choices by nonverbal responses even when the stimulus materials are verbal in nature. The technique can use verbal and nonverbal sample and choice materials interchangeably without concern about whether the subject has mastered a new response skill. In general, it allows the precise specification of stimuli presented and mode of response which, as Geschwind (1965) and others have pointed out, is so crucial in the study of language deficits.

Our technique also incorporates other features of the operant conditioning laboratory. The first is the reinforcing consequence, which immediately follows each correct response by the subject. The reinforcement not only insures stable performance and cooperation, but serves to instruct the subject in the nature of the task required. In the case of severe language deficits, this instruction often represents the only effective communication between subject and experimenter. The second is complete automation of stimulus presentation and responses recording. This minimizes equivocation in the decision as to what constitutes a response, and helps us to control for such variables as position habits.

APPARATUS AND TECHNIQUES

The subject works in a well-ventilated room approximately five feet square with sound resistant walls and door. An electric fan aides in dampening incidental noises. The subject sits facing a wall in which is mounted a display and response panel consisting of a square matrix of nine translucent windows, each two inches square and arranged in three rows of three each, separated from one another by three-quarter inch barriers. Figure 2 shows this nine-window matrix, with the outer windows illuminated and the center one dark. Figure 3 shows a child pressing one of the windows, which activates a small microswitch behind the window delivering a signal to our electronic programming and recording apparatus, more fully described by Sidman and Stoddard (1966).

Visual stimuli to be presented on the windows are photographed on 35 mm color film and projected as slides from the rear. We use a Leitz automatic slide projector. Motor driven shutters behind the windows and in front of the projector lens control the presentation and removal of stimuli. Photoelectric cells behind the windows indicate to the control and recording apparatus which window contains the "correct" choice on any given trial. One and one-half seconds elapse between the end

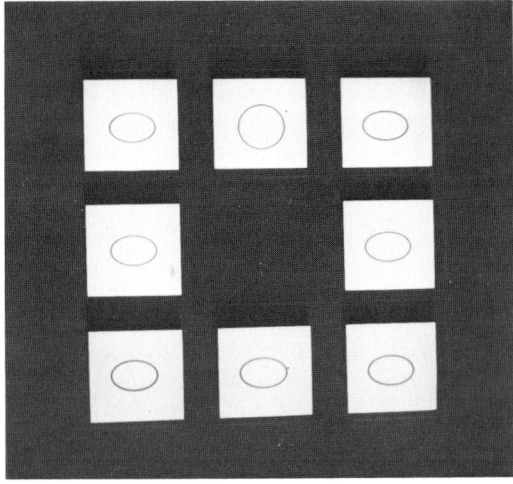

Fig. 2. Nine-window matrix of the sample matching apparatus with outer windows illuminated.

of one trial and the beginning of the next trial. The solenoid-driven shutters, the slide projector, the photoelectric cells, the rewarding devices, and the recording equipment are all controlled automatically by digital electronic circuitry.

On both the left and right sides of the matrix are plastic trays into which automatic devices deliver such rewards as candies, toys, or tokens that the child may trade later for other things. When the child presses a correct window, a chime above the matrix sounds and a reward dispenser operates. Most children receive candy-coated chocolates as their reward.

Fig. 3. Child pressing one of the windows to indicate a choice.

We tend to classify our modalities of stimulus and response somewhat over-mechanistically as "input" and "output." Of the input modalities, the visual has already been demonstrated. We are also able to provide auditory samples by means of recorded tape through a loudspeaker in the ceiling of the subject booth. The tape recorder is driven automatically and coupled with the slide projector by means of a photoelectric cell mechanism. An alternative method is to use a stereophonic tape recorder to record stimulus materials on one channel and to stop and start signals on the other. We provide tactile stimuli manually through a box which masks them from the subject's vision.

The only output modality which is automatically controlled is that of matching to visual choices. We also use vocal naming, which is recorded on tape through a ceiling microphone, and writing, which is collected on a separate piece of paper for each trial.

The various verbal and related materials available to us include single lower case

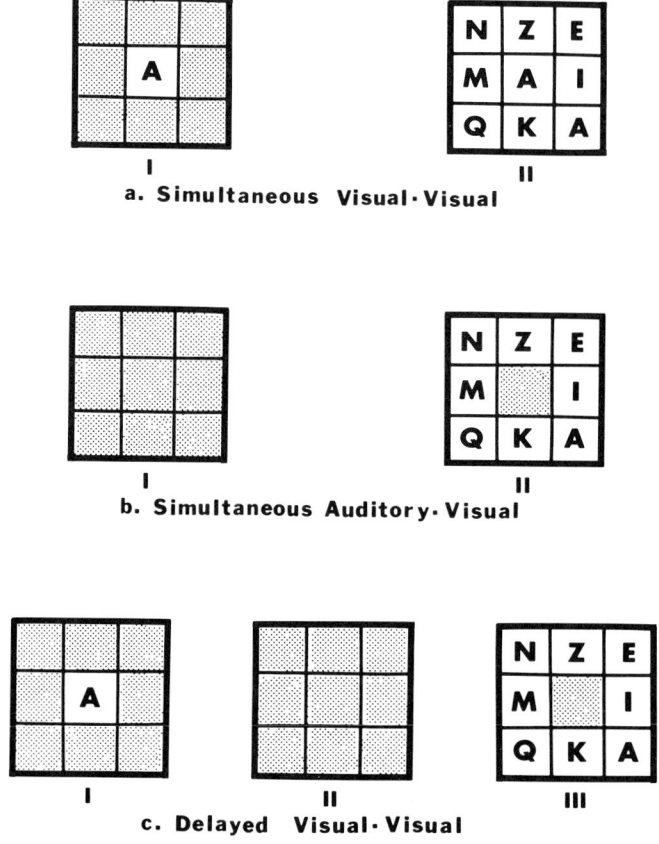

Fig. 4. Diagram of some of the sample matching paradigms available.

letters, single capital letters, simple three-letter words (which are the names of objects), pictures of the objects which those words name, three-letter nonsense syllables of consonant-vowel-consonant combinations, three-letter nonsense trigrams which cannot be pronounced, digits and names of digits, colors and names of colors, combinations of dots in various arrangements, small objects presented for tactile recognition, and photographs of those subjects.

We can also require a simultaneous or delayed sample-match, as illustrated in Figure 4. In the simultaneous match procedure, the sample appears on the center screen. The subject then touches this screen (makes an "observing response"), and the choices immediately appear on the other eight screens for simultaneous comparison with the sample. (It should be noted that in this context, "simultaneous" is a *procedural* specification. We have only indirect evidence for what the subject actually does in scanning the choices to make his selection). For the simultaneous auditory-visual match, the center screen remains blank as the auditory sample is presented repeatedly over the loudspeaker. The subject must touch the blank center screen to bring on visual choices. In the *delayed* matching procedure, the sample, either visual or auditory, *disappears* when the subject makes his observing response, and a delay of from zero to sixty seconds ensues before the choice appears. We can program either a fixed delay (same duration for every trial) or an *adjusting delay* (one which increases on subsequent trials after correct responses and decreases after errors).

APPLICATIONS TO THE STUDY OF LANGUAGE

We initially applied the above techniques to study the effects of acquired brain disease upon normally developed language in presumably normally intelligent children.

Study of Acquired Brain Disease Affecting Language

> *Case 1* (Rosenberger et al., 1969)
> A 14-year-old boy, who was in excellent health and doing generally satisfactory work in school, suffered a sudden cerebrovascular thrombosis which left him with a right hemiparesis and severe incapacitation of language skills. A carotid arteriogram showed complete occlusion of the left middle cerebral artery, suggesting extensive damage to his left or dominant cerebral hemisphere. On follow up examination two months after his acute illness he was nearly devoid of speech. Although he could write simple three-letter words to dictation, he was unable to write single letters to dictation, or to pick out on spoken command single letters which he had just written.

Over the next year we subjected this patient in a large number of separate sessions to various sample-matching tasks, usually in sets of 20 trials each. Figure 5 shows the results of these studies with single letters. Successive sessions, not equally spaced in time, are graphed along the abscissa, errors per 20 trials along the ordinate. When the samples were auditory and the choices visual, he consistently made large numbers of errors. Sessions 27 and 28, in which the error rates were low, occurred on the same day. We gave him the same series again immediately afterward with the samples removed. Error rates were still low, indicating that he had learned something about the stimuli besides what the task was calling for. New sets were constructed with samples and choices rearranged. In following sessions error rates were once again high. He also made errors in matching visual samples in auditory choices. With visual samples and visual choices, or auditory samples and auditory choices, however, error rates were consistently low.

Figure 6 shows his auditory-visual matching performance with other materials. When spoken three-letter words were matched against visually presented words, or names of simple objects against pictures of those objects, error rates were consistently low. When auditory samples were *spelled* rather than pronounced, error rates were high. When three-letter nonsense syllables or nonsense trigrams were used, error rates were even higher. The use of "nonrepresentative" nouns and non-nouns gave error rates somewhat in between.

Subsequent follow-up studies of this boy have shown nearly simultaneous occurrence of the following: drop in error rates on auditory-visual matching on single

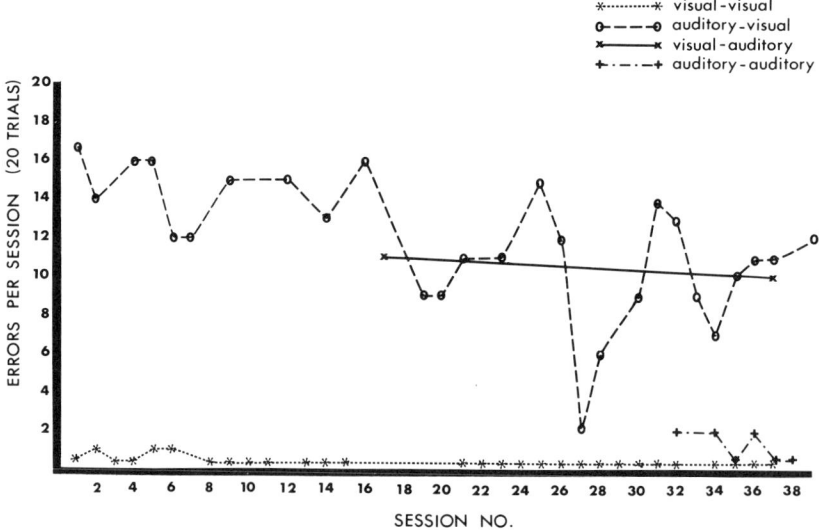

Fig. 5. Error rates in various sample matching tasks by the boy described as Case 1. The key indicates the modalities in which samples and choices respectively were presented; i.e., visual-visual indicates visual samples, visual choices.

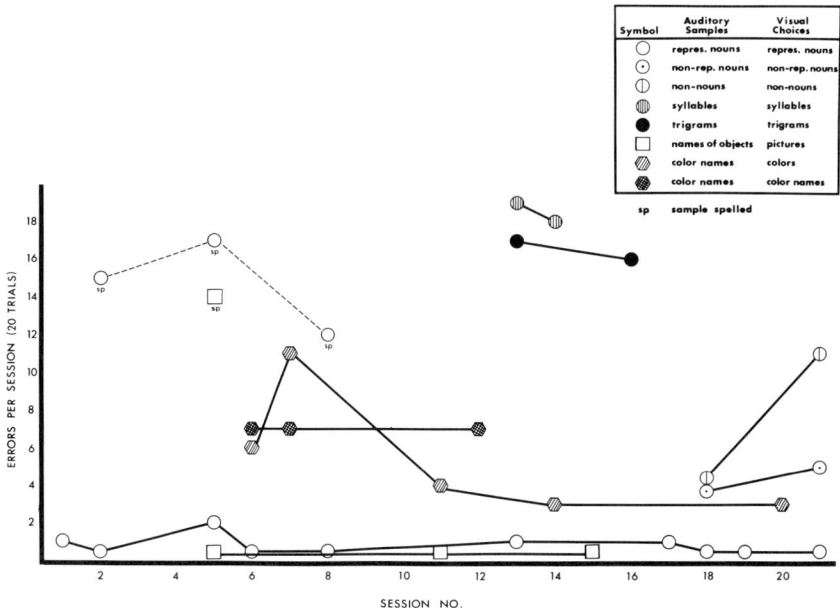

Fig. 6. Performance in auditory visual sample matching tasks with various materials by the boy in Case 1.

letters, ability to *name* single letters aloud, and increase in amount of vocal speech. These findings suggest that the ability to make auditory-visual equivalences, especially with materials with which our only experience is auditory and visual, may indeed be crucially related to the formulation of language, although the direction of the cause-effect relationship is still obscure.

Case 2

An 8-year-old boy, again with a history of normal language development and satisfactory school work, developed a rapidly progressive right hemiparesis and aphasia following a mild gastrointestinal upset. A left carotid arteriogram showed congenital malformations of both internal carotid arteries and occlusion of branches of the left middle cerebral artery. On examination a week later, he was able to repeat single words spoken to him, and even to recite several lines of familiar songs and poems. He showed deficits in both reading and comprehension of auditory information, and was able to name only a few simple objects.

Figure 7 shows the results of repeated sample-matching sessions with this boy over a four-month period, during which a predictable marked improvement in his language was noted. There are interesting differences between this and the previous case. At the beginning, this boy had difficulty with auditory-visual match not only of single letters but also of words against words and words against pictures. In addition, he made errors on the visual match of words against pictures—equivalent to a reading comprehension difficulty.

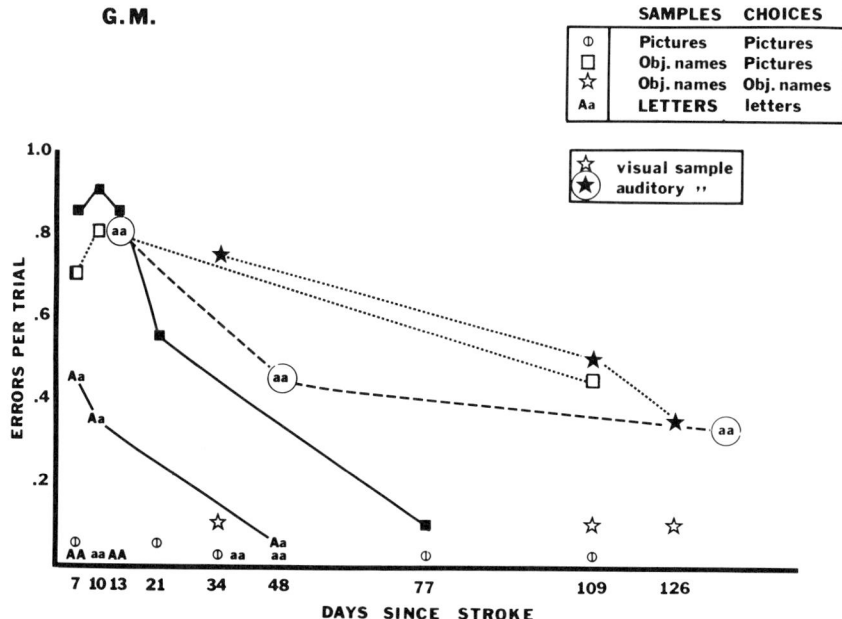

Fig. 7. Visual-visual and auditory-visual sample matching performance with various materials by subject G.M., described as Case No. 2. Shaded or encircled symbols indicate that an auditory visual sample match was required. Some of the more relevant points are connected by lines for easier comparison.

The boy also did quite well with simultaneous match or nonidentical pictures of the same object. Apparently he was either making this match purely on the basis of visual features in common, or he was able to formulate a name for the sample object to assist him in the match, although he was unable to say it aloud. We attempted to resolve this question by giving both identical and nonidentical pictures for delayed sample-matching. Table 2 shows the results. When an adjusting delay was employed, more errors were made (a shorter delay was tolerated) with nonidentical pictures in every case. Where the fixed delay was used, error rates with nonidentical pictures increased as the delay was increased; this was not the case with the identical pictures. These findings may be evidence that the boy was either not formulating a name for the sample object, or was unable to retain it as well as he retained visual images.

Case 3

A 3-year-old girl, with a normal developmental history, suffered a rapidly progressive loss of speech over a two-week period, followed by a 3-month period of decreased responsiveness to commands and conversation. The latter gradually improved, but she did not regain speech. She was seen in our clinic a year later, where the neurological examination was unrevealing. Pertinent laboratory data included electroencephalograms showing "focal

TABLE 2

Results of visual sample-matching tasks, pictures (errors/trials), Patient G. M. (MGH 159-16-68)

Adjusting delay (4 sec.)	Correct choice identical with sample	Correct choice not identical with sample
10-1-69		8/20
10-9-69	1/13	8/20
12-3-69	5/20	8/20
Fixed delay (10-22-69)		
4 sec.	6/20	8/20
20 sec.	5/20	13/20

epileptogenic activity in the left temporal and frontal regions," normal skull x-rays, normal hearing by GSR audiometry, and a normal IQ on the Leiter test.

After this girl had adapted to the experimental situation, we attempted without success to get her to match the spoken names of simple objects with pictutures of those objects. We then designed a simple ten-trial program to teach her this task. On the first trial of this program, the correct choice (the picture of the object whose spoken name was being given her as an auditory sample) was the only one visible. Over succeeding trials, the incorrect choices were gradually "faded in" by overexposure photography, until on the tenth trial all choices were of equal density. A back-up correction procedure was used; i.e., the projector reversed after each error and advanced after each correct choice.

Table 3 summarizes our experience with this procedure. Initial tests showed high error rates. She was able to get through the program well enough, but her performance broke down on subsequent test trials on which all incorrect choices were equally visible. It was important to ask at this point whether it was perhaps the skill of sample-matching which she could not manage. We know from other experiences

TABLE 3

Results of auditory-visual and visual-visual sample-matching tasks (errors/trials), Patient C. M. (MGH 131-57-24)

Date	A-V Test	A-V Program	V-V Test	V-V Program	A-V Test	A-V Program	V-V Test	A-V Test
12-11	20/20*				18/20			
12-15		0/10→3/5				0/10→ 6/10		
12-17				6/10→0/10		1/10→10/10	0/8	
7-23		0/14→7/10			7/8			
1-29				0/14→0/10		2/14→ 7/10 (letters)	2/20	18/20
						(Colors)	4/18	15/18

*Test materials are pictures of simple objects except where noted

TABLE 4

Results of auditory-visual and visual-visual sample-matching tasks (errors/trials), normal controls

Subject No.	Age	A-V Test	A-V Program	V-V Test	V-V Program
1	3-2	3/10		5/10	2/14→3/10
2	3-6	0/10		6/10	2/14→1/10
3	3-8	1/4	6/9	8/10	16/13
4	3-11	1/10		1/10	
5	4-1	0/10		8/10	12/13
6	4-2	1/10		2/10	
7	4-7	0/10		0/10	
8	4-7	3/10		5/10	
9	4-8	0/10		0/10	
10	4-8	2/10		10/10	7/14→1/10
11	4-9	1/10		7/10	0/14→1/10
12	4-10	0/10		6/10	0/14→4/10
13	4-10	0/10		0/10	
14	4-11	1/10		10/10	0/14→2/10
15	4-11	3/10		4/10	
16	5-0	0/10		9/10	3/14→3/10
17	5-7	2/10		0/10	
18	5-10	1/10		0/10	
19	5-11	0/10		0/10	

that not every normal four-year-old has mastered this skill. We gave her the simple teaching program with visual samples. She apparently caught on to the task during the program, and managed subsequent tests without difficulty. Despite this, she retained her original difficulty with the auditory-visual sample-match.

Could it be that this discrepancy between auditory-visual and visual-visual sample matching is to be expected of the normal child in our experimental context? First of all, it is the experience of a number of investigators that one cannot expect to teach the task of visual sample matching by identity to a normal child under five years old, although many younger children may be able to grasp the task. On the other hand, it is rare to see a normal child over three years of age who is not able to pick out visual objects upon hearing their spoken names. Second, we administered these tasks to a small sample of normal children between the ages of three and five years. The results are shown in Table 4. The auditory visual match task was grasped immediately by nearly every child, while the visual match task was not grasped by many of the children. A number of these children were able to learn the task by the simple fading program to which we referred above.

Summary of Cases

In summary, our experimental findings in these three cases of acquired language disorder in childhood are in many ways more interesting for their differences than for their similarities. The left and presumably dominant cerebral hemisphere was involved in each case. Beyond this, it has not been possible for us to correlate specific behavioral deficits with specific locations of disease. However, the findings of all three cases have suggested that auditory visual equivalences are indeed important to language skills. In addition, these equivalences may be studied by essentially nonverbal techniques in the proper laboratory setting.

Teaching a Retarded Boy to Read (Sidman, 1970)

Children normally understand words they hear before they learn to read with comprehension. Also, they name objects before they learn to name printed or written words corresponding to the objects. For example, the subject of this experiment, an institutionalized 17-year-old boy, microcephalic and severely retarded, was able to match pictures, colors, and printed numbers to picture names, color names, and number names that were spoken aloud to him. But he was unable to do the matching correctly when the names were presented to him visually rather than spoken. Also, he could name the pictures aloud, but not the corresponding printed words. He could not write. He showed good auditory comprehension and picture naming, but little if any reading comprehension or oral reading.

Such behavioral observations, along with theoretical conceptions of central nervous system development and structure, have led many writers to postulate that reading, a visual task, evolves from the previous learning of auditory-visual equivalences. Birch and his coworkers (1964) report positive correlations between a test of auditory-visual integration and reading achievement. Most children break through the "sound barrier" in the first or second grade, and learn to understand not just words they hear, but words they see. Yet, whether auditory-visual learning is indeed a necessary or even sufficient prerequisite for reading comprehension seems not to have been studied experimentally. The data presented here will demonstrate that certain learned auditory-visual equivalences are sufficient prerequisites, even without explicitly teaching reading comprehension.

Preliminary tests evaluated the subject's proficiency at simple comprehension and naming tasks. He was then taught to match spoken to printed words. Final tests evaluated the effects of this teaching on his reading comprehension and word naming.

The subject sat before the panel of translucent windows described above. Visual word or picture samples appeared on the center window of the matrix. Auditory samples, repeated at 2-second intervals, were dictated from tapes over a speaker (Figure 8, left column).

In matching tests, the subject pressed the center window to bring choice stimuli, always visual, onto the outer windows of the matrix. Schematic examples of the displays are in the second column of Figure 8. On each trial, one choice, the correct one, corresponded to the sample; the other seven choices did not. The subject selected and pressed one of the choice windows. His correct choices were rewarded by chimes

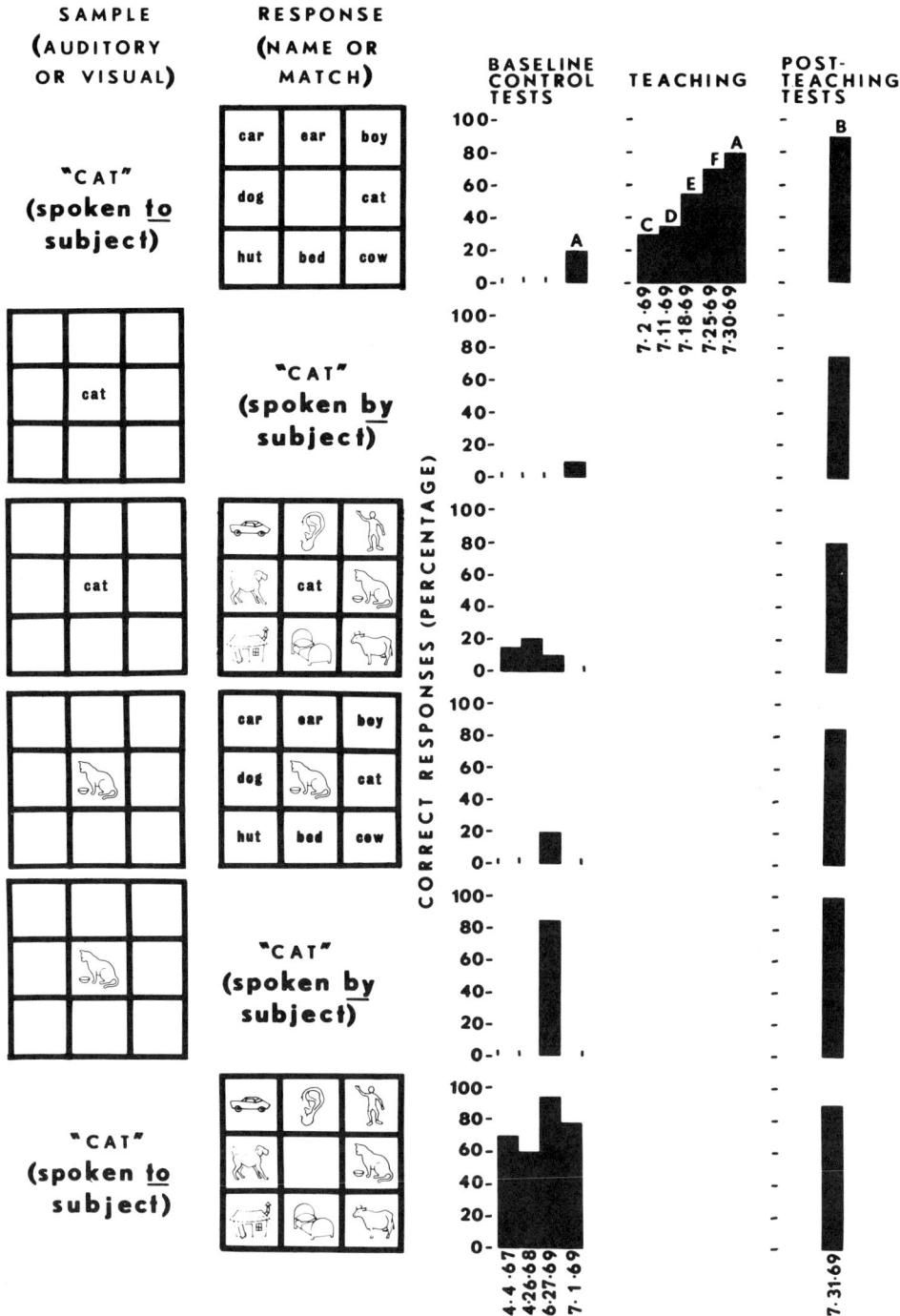

Fig. 8. Summary of results of sample matching teaching and test procedures with verbal materials in a single severely retarded boy. See text for explanation.

ringing and the delivery of a candy and a penny. No rewards followed incorrect choices. The stimuli disappeared after each choice and 1.5 seconds later a new sample began the next trial.

Each test had 20 trials. The sample and choice stimuli, taken from a list of 20 pictures, or the printed (lower case) or spoken names of the pictures, were: axe, bed, bee, box, boy, bug, car, cat, cow, dog, ear, hat, hen, hut, hoe, man, pie, pig, saw, zoo.

In oral naming tests, the subject had simply to name the sample picture or word aloud. Reward procedures were the same as in the matching tests.

The results of the preliminary tests are in the left column of bar graphs in Figure 8. Bars at the lower left show the subject's scores in tests that required him to match spoken word samples to picture choices. In four tests, administered from April, 1967, to July, 1969, he scored from 60 to 95 per cent correct, demonstrating a fair proficiency at this type of auditory comprehension. He also scored 85 per cent in naming the pictures (second row from the bottom).

In reading (all tests that involved printed words) the subject scored poorly. Continuing up the left column, these tests were: matching picture sample to printed word choices; matching printed word samples to picture choices; naming printed words; and matching spoken word samples to printed word choices. The possibility that the subject could not distinguish the printed words from each other was ruled out by his score of 95 per cent in matching printed word samples to printed word choices (not shown in Figure 8).

The subject came to the experiment knowing the equivalence of spoken words to pictures (Figure 9:I). Would teaching him the second auditory-visual equivalence, spoken words to visual words (Figure 9:II), suffice to establish reading comprehension, the purely visual equivalence of printed words to pictures (Figure 9:III, IV)? Also, would teaching him auditory-visual word matching suffice for oral reading (Figure 9:VI) to emerge?

In the teaching procedure, sample stimuli were words spoken to the subject. The

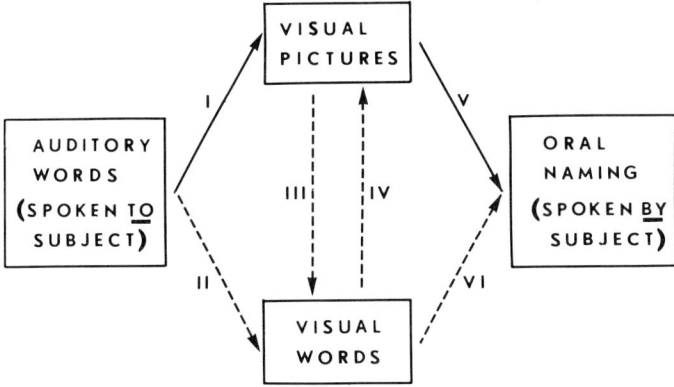

Fig. 9. Schematic diagram showing interrelationships of various specific skills involved in reading. See text for explanation.

choices were printed words. When the subject chose a wrong printed word, the display remained unchanged until he pressed the correct window. If he made one or more errors on a given trial the chimes rang when he finally pressed the correct window, but he did not receive candy or a penny. Each phase of the teaching procedure started with only two trials (sample-choice combinations), the two being repeated until the subject's first choices on both were correct. Then a third trial was added. When his first choices on all three were correct, a fourth was added. This progressive enlargement of the set continued as the subject attained each criterion of mastery, until his first choices were correct on the full set of 20 trials.

Six versions or sets of auditory-visual word-matching materials presented the same 20 sample words in different trials sequences, and each set displayed a different combination of seven wrong words along with each correct word. Set A was used for the preliminary control test. Then the subject was taught Set B until he scored 100 percent, and was tested on Set C. His low score on Set C (Figure 8, center section, first bar) suggested that his learning of Set B had been specific to the particular sequence of correct window positions and to the particular wrong words displayed along with each correct word.

The subject then learned Set C, reviewed Set B to the same 100 per cent criterion, and was tested on Set D. The process of learning, reviewing, and testing on a new set continued through Set F, and the center section of Figure 8 shows the gradual improvement on each new test. Finally, the subject was retested on Set A, which he had not seen since the preliminary test. The change from 20 to 80 percent correct on Set A demonstrated his new proficiency at the task.

After the teaching, all comprehension and oral naming tests were administered once more. Scores are in the right column of Figure 8. The subject maintained his good performance on the first auditory-visual word matching set he had learned (upper right), in matching spoken words to pictures, and in picture naming (lower right). His reading comprehension and oral reading improved greatly. Having learned to match spoken word samples to printed word choices, he was then able, without additional teaching, to match picture samples to the printed word choices, to match printed word samples to picture choices, and to name the printed words.

Given the subject's ability to match spoken words to pictures, teaching him the second auditory-visual equivalence, spoken to printed words, sufficed for the emergence of purely visual reading comprehension. A connectionistic interpretation might be that the visual words and pictures became equivalent to each other (Figure 9:III, IV) because each, independently, had become equivalent to the same spoken words (Figure 9:I, II). After the subject learned auditory-visual word matching, however, he also proved capable of visual-word naming, or oral reading (Figure 9:VI). Although the subject did not name the words or pictures aloud during the reading comprehension tests, it remains to be determined whether reading comprehension would have emerged if oral reading had not.

If naming is not necessary for visual word-picture equivalence to emerge, then words presented via the tactile modality, or even arbitrary visual nonsense syllables, would be substitutable for auditory words in this experiment. That deaf children learn to read suggests that such substitution is feasible. Furthermore, it may be possible to teach any two of the three equivalences, I, II, and III (or IV) in Figure 9, and find that the third also emerges. For example, if the subject is taught I and III (or IV), he may then be able to do II, matching auditory to visual words. If purely visual equivalences can facilitate auditory-visual equivalences, and if another modality can be substituted for the auditory, then auditory-visual learning, although sufficient for reading comprehension, will prove not to be a necessary prerequisite.

One may ask if oral reading will always emerge after a subject has learned auditory-visual word matching. Guess (1969) has shown that receptive language training need not facilitate the learning of productive speech, but the present data emphasize his conclusion that the relation expressive to receptive repertoires requires further experimental analysis. The present experiment indicates, however, that matching spoken words to pictures and to printed words (sufficient prerequisites for reading comprehension) can be taught without explicitly teaching oral reading, and therefore completely without the intervention of a teacher. It remains to be determined whether picture naming need be taught directly and whether the method can be extended to other reading material and other kinds of comprehension.

SUMMARY OF DISCUSSION

QUESTION: In the last case, where there is a failure to make auditory-visual match, what information do you have about the response to auditory signals in general?

ROSENBERGER: The best we could say was that her psychogalvanic audiometry was normal. We didn't have the materials then that we have now to test nonverbal auditory discrimination. We now have tests that can show whether a child can match a train whistle sound with a picture of a train, a police whistle with a picture of a policeman, and so forth.

QUESTION: Did she respond to verbal commands?

ROSENBERGER: We could get no response at all with verbal commands.

QUESTION: Did I undertand correctly that pretesting took place over two years, whereas the teaching took place over one month?

SIDMAN: Correct.

QUESTION: In terms of your Figure 9, would you be willing to speculate, if you were teaching these in sequence, whether you would teach the first, teach the second, teach the third, in the sequence in which they are numbered?

SIDMAN: There's a whole chain of changes to be learned here. For example, we are working with two children now who can't even do the straight visual discrimination. They can't tell the words apart as forms. We have to teach them that first before we can do any of this. So that would be a prerequisite. Other children will have to be taught literally to discriminate sounds before any of this can go on. Then they will have to be taught to produce those sounds. I don't know what the answer to that question would be. I suspect it is easier to teach them to name a picture than to name a word because children have equivalents of pictures, objects around them from the moment they can respond at all.

QUESTION: You didn't test III, but the implication is that if you teach III and not II you would generate IV.

SIDMAN: There are a number of implications like that, but there is no indication of the necessity for that sequence at all.

QUESTION: Did you have the opportunity to observe any induction of this facilitating effect outside of the set of training stimuli?

SIDMAN: No. we didn't check that. But that would really be a startling thing, wouldn't it, if we taught the child those 20 words and he not only could do those 20, but any others as well? That would really be fabulous but I just can't believe that is going to happen. It would be a miracle.

QUESTION: Would you think, however, that the bonus effect might be possible under at least extreme conditions; that is, that you would get some free ones?

SIDMAN: No, I don't think so.

QUESTION: If the child is taught phonetically, then, as it is termed in the reading field, can't he unlock the new words?

SIDMAN: Yes, having been taught phonetically and having been taught to name the picture, then I think he can do it.

QUESTION: What about any other generalizations beyond the specific pictures and the printed words you have used—that is, other representations?

SIDMAN: Our selection of pictures to start with was purely arbitrary. We didn't select a group of pictures that we had taught the child. We selected a group of pictures and then tested him on them, and he knew them. So probably he also knows the names of many other pictures as well. He also knows those same pictures in other views. We couldn't possibly have picked just the 20 views of each of those pictures that he knows and no others.

QUESTION: I'd like to ask a more general question. It doesn't relate specifically to this experiment. But you touched on the interaction of the organism, its neurological-physiological status, and certain kinds of environmental events. Now, could you speculate somewhat on the processes of language acquisition and development in the context of developmental processes? What do your data and what you have been talking about mean in terms of future directions of research with respect to problems of language acquisition and development?

SIDMAN: I'm looking forward to the very exciting prospect of being able to teach many children to read with comprehension who haven't been able to do so before, to at least get them started this way. So, even if we can't teach more complicated kinds of comprehension, at least they will now be amenable for work with a teacher. It's going to take a lot of my time in the near future, just for that one simple little bit of development of reading, of language. Giving children all of the specific prerequisites that one needs to do these tasks is a large curriculum development problem. Teaching a child to discriminate letters as forms and letter names as sounds and teaching him to produce those same patterns of sounds is a problem. I think a teacher program for retarded children must extend down to that level.

QUESTION: By extending this to more difficult material, can actual speech and more complex speech be generated by just reading?

SIDMAN: Can you do this same thing starting low with other children of single words? Could you do it with adjectives? Could you do it with prepositions? I think you can with those. Programs have been worked out using words and pictures for teaching adjectives and prepositions. I don't know about verbs. That will take more ingenuity. Probably the same general kinds of principles, but a different kind of set-up, perhaps using moving pictures rather than still pictures, will be needed to teach verbs and tenses, then phrases, sentences, paragraphs. Could the same kind of techniques be adapted? I don't know. These are all questions to be looked into. But I think they are now worth the effort.

REFERENCES

Birch, H. G., and Belmont, L. Auditory-visual integration in normal and retarded readers. *Am. J. Orthopsych.*, 1964, *34*, 852–861.

Geschwind, N. Disconnexion syndromes in animals and man. *Brain*, 1965, *88*, 237–293.

Guess, D. A functional analysis of receptive language and productive speech: Acquisition of the plural phoneme. *J. Appl. Behav. Anal.*, 1969, *2*, 55–64.

Rosenberger, P. B., Mohr, J. P., Stoddard, L. T., and Sidman, M. Inter- and intramodality matching deficits in a dysphasic youth. *Arch. Neurol.*, 1968, *18*, 549–562.

Sidman, M., and Stoddard, L. T. Programming perception and learning for retarded children. In Ellis, N. (Ed.), *International review of research in mental retardation*, Vol. II. New York: Academic Press, 1966. Pp. 151–208.

Sidman, M. Reading and auditory-visual equivalences. *J. Speech Hearing Res.*, 1971, *14*, 5–13.

THE ROLE OF VERBAL PROCESSES IN SHORT-TERM MEMORY

EARL C. BUTTERFIELD
University of Kansas

JOHN M. BELMONT
Yale University

EARL C. BUTTERFIELD is a professor of psychology at the University of Kansas and the research director at the University of Kansas Medical Center setting of the Kansas Center for Research in Mental Retardation and Human Development.

He earned his Ph.D. in 1963 at George Peabody College. He is a consulting editor for the American Journal of Mental Deficiency *and a consultant to the Joint Commission on Accreditation of Hospitals. Motivational, cognitive, and personality processes in average and retarded children are the primary areas of his research interests. He has published extensively in these fields.*

JOHN M. BELMONT is a research associate in psychology and lecturer at Yale University. He earned his Ph.D. degree at the University of Alabama in 1966. He served on the President's Committee on Mental Retardation in 1969-70 and is currently a consulting editor for the American Journal of Mental Deficiency. *His chief research interests lie in the study of learning and short-term memory processes with the retarded.*

For approximately three years we have been engaged in a research program designed to determine why short-term memory (STM) increases with age and intelligence. A major reason that has emerged is that older and more intelligent persons use more sophisticated verbal processes when they are learning or storing information they must later recall. Younger and less intelligent persons have verbal learning deficits which account in large measure for their inferior STM performance.

Learning deficits are only one of three possible process deficiencies that might account for the inferior memory performance of children and the mentally retarded. Recall deficiencies might also result from more rapid forgetting of well-learned material or from ineffective retrieval of learned material still residing in memory. When we began our research the primary hypothesis of experimenters concerned with the recall deficits of children and retardates had been that they forget more rapidly than average adults. However, a thorough review of the developmental and comparative literature on STM revealed that children and retardates do not have significantly greater forgetting rates than average adults (Belmont and Butterfield, 1969). Accordingly, we have studied the role of verbal processes in short-term memory performance with a task designed to yield direct data about learning and retrieval, rather than about retention processes.

The research reported here was supported by USPHS Grants HD-00870, HD-03008, and HD-04760.

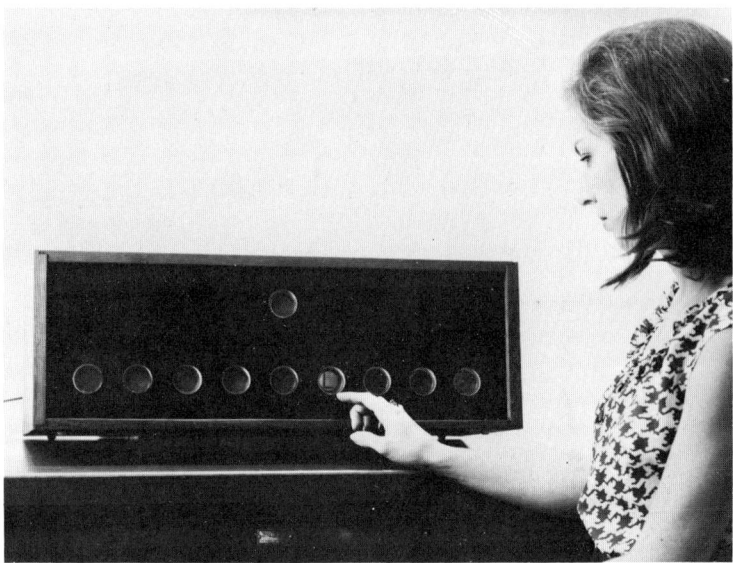

Fig. 1. Subject console illustrating the appearance of letters.

The apparatus which we have used to study the role of verbal processes in memory consists primarily of a series of projectors which present letters. The letters do not appear arbitrarily, however. The subject makes them appear by pressing a button below and in front of the console (Figure 1). The first time the subject presses the button, the first of a series of letters appears, the second time the second letter in the series appears, and so on. The order in which letters appear in the various projectors can vary. The simplest case in which the letters move one projector at a time from the subject's left to right was used to collect most of the data discussed here.

After the subject has paced himself through the entire list, he makes a probe or test item appear in the projector at the top of the apparatus. The subject's task then is to indicate the projector where the test letter appeared. For example, if an "L" appeared in the third window, and the test letter was an "L," the subject would have to press the face of the third projector to be correct.

Figure 2 is a schematic representation of the apparatus and the data resulting from a typical trial. Three-tenths of a second after the subject's first button push, an "R" comes on in the first window. It appears for 0.5 second. Then it goes away. Then, 0.3 second after the next button push, the "K" comes on in the second window, and it appears for 0.5 second, and so on. In order to study acquisition processes we collect a printed record of how long the subject hesitates between letters. The upper portion of Figure 2 portrays the amount of time that one subject hesitated after each letter of a 6-letter list. Such uneven distribution of hesitation times is typical of average adults' performance.

One of our earliest findings was that almost every adult faced with this task quickly adopts a pattern of inter-letter pauses, which may be called his acquisition strategy,

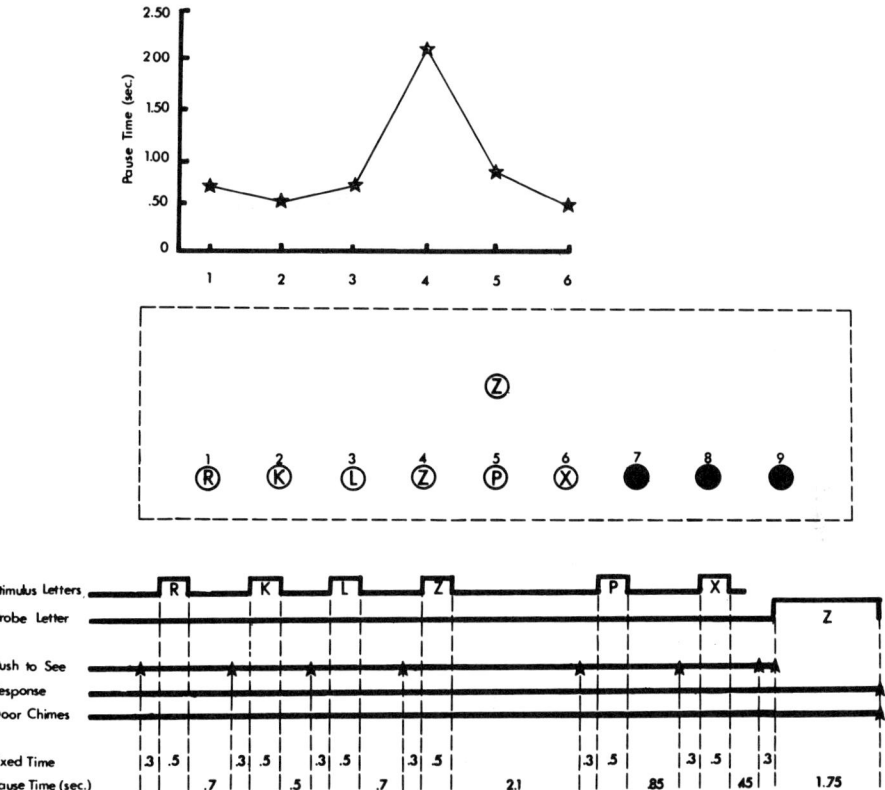

Fig. 2. Schematic diagram of subject console and illustration of a typical temporal pattern on a 6-letter list.

to which he adheres with great precision, list after list. Figure 3 shows hesitation times of two college students, one of whom worked on ten 9-letter lists, the other on ten 8-letter lists. In both cases the lists were evidently acquired in three segments, the first two (each comprising three letters) being set off by relatively long pauses. The last segment (three letters in the 9-item lists; two in the 8-item lists) received relatively little attention before S tested himself. Inferences of this kind, based on highly reliable inter-letter pause data, were confirmed by about 85 per cent of the introspective reports. That is, 85 per cent of the subjects reported verbally rehearsing letters at the points where the pause data showed long hesitations. Several additional types of evidence establish that pauses reflect rehearsal.

Subjects who are allowed to study lists at their own rate should hesitate less to rehearse lists they have previously studied than those which are novel. We have recently performed an experiment in which some lists appeared repeatedly and others appeared only once. In each block of four trials, only one list was new. The other three had each been studied once in each preceding block of four trials. The college

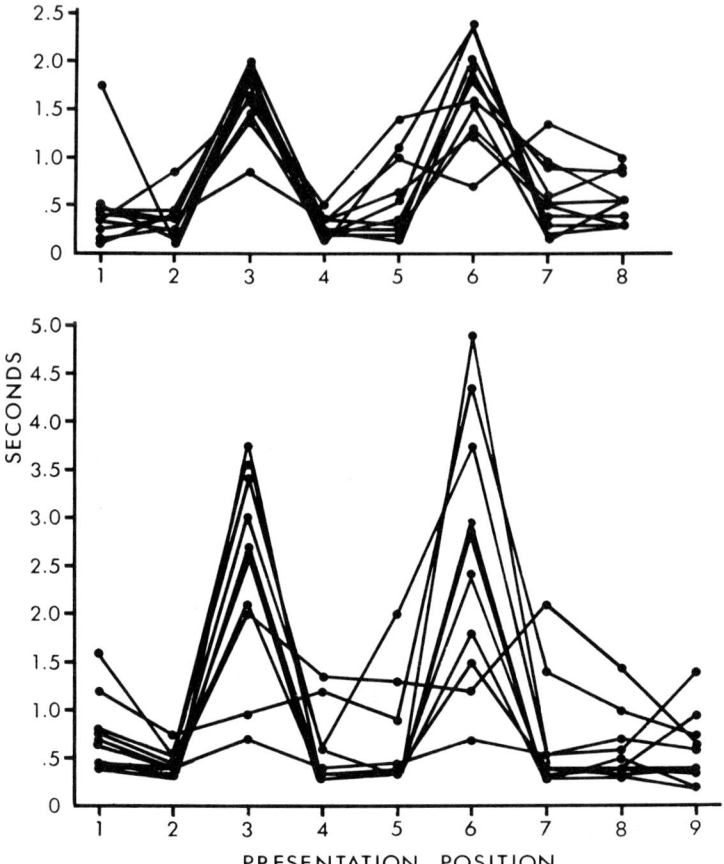

Fig. 3. Pause times of two college students on each of ten trials.

student subjects were instructed to rehearse following only the fifth and seventh letters of the 9-letter lists. Figure 4 shows the mean hesitation following each position for the repeated and unrepeated lists from the first, second, and third blocks of 12 trials. The pauses following letters five and seven decreased for the repeated lists, but not for the unrepeated ones. This is inferential evidence that pauses reflect rehearsal and is exactly consistent with the findings of a similar experiment reported by Belmont and Butterfield (1969).

If pauses reflect rehearsal, then those subjects who pause longer should recall more since they will have rehearsed more. A group of 20 college students were divided into two groups according to their total hesitation time. Those who fell above the groups' median hesitation time are compared to those who fell below the median in Figure 5. The left portion shows the average hesitation pattern of the long and short hesitation groups. The data of greatest interest are the percentage correct response curves.

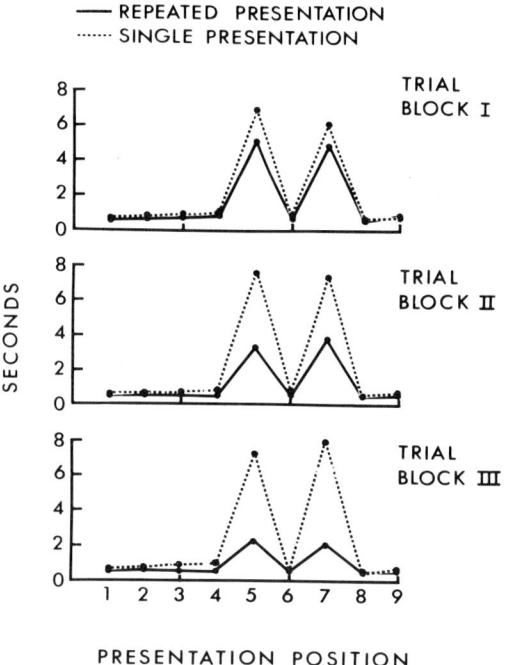

Fig. 4. Mean median pause time under repeated and single presentation conditions for each of three successive trial blocks.

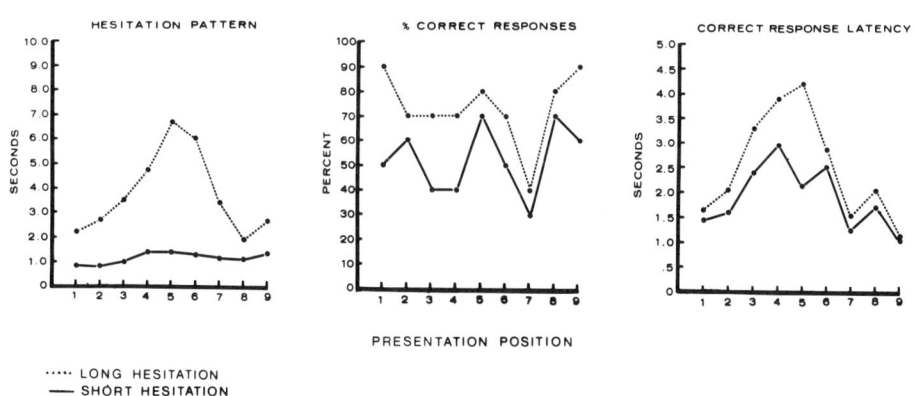

Fig. 5. Mean hesitation pattern, percentage of correct responses, and correct response latency for college students with long and short total hesitation times during acquisition.

Those who hesitated longest recalled more, as they should have if their pauses reflect rehearsal.

From the foregoing and other data (Belmont & Butterfield, 1969), it can be concluded with confidence that the pause time measure reflects the extent and distribution of verbal rehearsal used by subjects faced with our task. Our task also yields data about retrieval. Retrieval strategy is defined, independently of acquisition strategy, as the pattern which results from plotting correct response decision time over the probe letter's position in the list. Figure 5 shows this data for the long and short hesitation groups, and suggests that retrieval strategy varies with amount of rehearsal. The long hesitation group takes longer to correctly retrieve the positions of the letters from the first portion of the list.

A recently completed series of six experiments has established that there is a clear and strong relationship between type of acquisition and retrieval strategy (Butterfield and Belmont, 1971). Letters that are actively rehearsed are recalled by means of a relatively slow search of memory that begins with the first-acquired letter and proceeds serially through those actively-rehearsed letters until the correct one is found, at which point the memory search is terminated and a correct response is made. Letters that are learned by attention alone, without verbal rehearsal, are searched much more rapidly than rehearsed letters. They are retrieved from memory either by an exhaustive search which does not terminate when a correct letter is found, or by a self-terminating search that does not begin with the first attended to letter or proceeds unsystematically rather than serially. When the early letters in a list are learned by rehearsal and the later letters by mere attention, the later letters are searched before the early letters. The early letters are searched only if the probe letter is not recognized as coming from the late, unrehearsed portion of the list.

We concluded above that neither age nor intelligence relates to the slope of the forgetting curve. Differences in forgetting rate are thus apparently not the source of deficient memory in children or retardates, but two other possibilities remain. Recall may be low if the person does not completely acquire the material, or if he uses imperfect retrieval (output). The method which we have described was developed in order to examine these possibilities. The method yields three data: pauses following each letter exposure during storage, number of correct responses (R+) at each presentation postion, and latency of correct responding at each presentation position. Application of the method to college students and other nonretarded adults has shown that when storage is passive and does not involve rehearsal, (a) pause time is low, (b) R+ is high for recently-presented information but low for earlier-presented information, and (c) R+ latency is short for all correct responses. It has also shown that when intake involves verbal rehearsal, (a) pause time is high, (b) R+ is high for distantly as well as recently-presented information, and (c) R+ latency increases systematically across presentation position. These then are the basic facts which make it feasible to examine systematically the role of storage and retrieval processes in determining the memory deficits of children and retardates. The following two experiments are the beginning of such a systematic examination.

EXPERIMENT I

The first experiment was concerned with three questions: (1) Given the opportunity to pace their learning, will retarded and normal teenagers spontaneously rehearse differently? (2) If the answer to the first question is "yes," and the retardates rehearse less or distribute their rehearsal differently, can they be induced to change how they rehearse, with corresponding improvements in recall? (3) If retardates can be induced to use particular rehearsal strategies, will they maintain the induced strategies when released from the induction condition? To answer these questions, all subjects were first permitted to pace their own acquisition of material to be recalled. This allowed appraisal of their spontaneous strategies through measurements of pause time. Experimental subjects were then instructed to use a combination of active rehearsal and passive attention, while the controls continued uninstructed. This allowed assessment of whether instructions in acquisition improves retardates' recall (R+). Finally, the experimental or instructed subjects returned to the free-strategy condition, on which the controls remained. This allowed determination of the short-term durability of the instructed strategies.

Method

Subjects. The subjects were 20 institutionalized mildly retarded teen-agers (IQs from 55 to 70) and 20 normal high school juniors and seniors, ages 16–18 years (here to be called adults). The adult and retarded groups were randomly divided in two halves each, leaving two groups of ten retarded and two groups of ten normal teenagers.

Procedure. The experiment was run in three parts, each of the first two having 18 lists, and the third having 12. Each list was a different meaningless combination of six letters from the 12-letter pool: A, C, E, H, K, L, N, P, S, U, X, and Z. The sequence for each list was: the subject (S) pushed-to-see, lag (0.3 second), letter#1 (0.5 second), pause; S pushed-to-see, lag, letter #2, pause; . . .; S pushed-to-see, lag, letter #6, pause; S pushed-to-see, lag, probe-letter onset. At this point S pushed the key covering the projector in which he recalled having seen the probe letter. If correct, a door-chimes rang. In either case, the probe letter went off with the response. The next trial began after ten seconds, during which the experimenter changed the program control card. Each of the pauses in this sequence was determined by S; the pattern of pauses is the measure of his acquisition strategy.

The position of the probe letter in the list varied haphazardly across trials, but each of the six positions was correct once in each six-trial block. The projectors were always activated from S's left to right, beginning with the far-left projector. Unused projectors were covered with black paper plugs.

Instructions for Part I were the same for all subjects. The letter exposure and test procedures were described without alluding to possible strategies of pausing while learning the lists. For Part 2, ten normals and ten retardates were instructed to use a 4–2 strategy. This is a strategy of going rapidly through the first four letters saying each one aloud, pausing long enough after the fourth letter to rehearse the four as a group several times aloud, then going through the last two letters with no pause before pushing to see the probe. The remaining ten (control) subjects in each group received no special instructions for Parts 2 or 3. Part 3 instructions for the 4–2 groups emphasized that the subject was free to do the task as he liked, thus presumably liberating him to return, if he wished, to his Part 1 strategy. The two three-part conditions of this experiment may be symbolized as N/N/N (no special instructions given in any part) and N/4-2/N(4-2 acquisition strategy enforced in Part 2; no enforced strategy in Parts 1 or 3). Both the N/N/N and N/4-2/N sequences were given to ten retarded and ten normal children.

Results and Discussion

Pause Time. The median pause time following each letter during each of the experiment's three blocks was calculated for each subject. The means of these median times are plotted separately for retardates and normals in the upper panels of Figure 6.

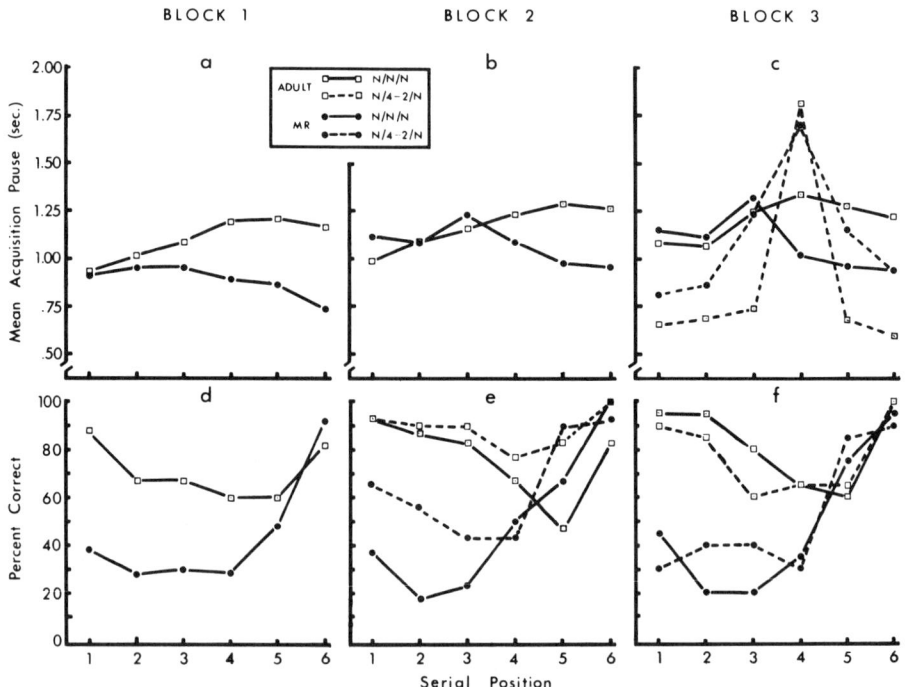

Fig. 6. Mean acquistion pause and percentage of correct responding for normal and retarded subjects in each block and condition of Experiment I.

During Block 1, when all subjects received the N condition, the 20 retardates decreased their pauses as they proceeded through the six letters, whereas the 20 normals increased and then decreased slightly. A 2 × 6 Intelligence × Position analysis of variance showed that these differences are reliable. The Intelligence × Position interaction was significant ($F_{5/190} = 7.55, p < .001$). Positions × Subjects analyses within groups showed that for the retardates, position 2 > position 5 > positon 6, while for normals, position 1 < positions 3 − 6 and position 2 < positions 4 − 6. The two groups were significantly different only at position 6. Although they spent nearly equal amounts of time overall, the normals reliably increased their pauses as the information load increased, but the retardates reliably decreased their pauses.

Mean pause times for the normal and retarded N/N/N groups for Blocks 2 and 3 are shown as solid lines in Figure 6b and 6c. The pause pattern demonstrated in Block 1 by all 20 retarded and all 20 normal teen-agers was shown throughout the experiment by the N/N/N groups. A 2 × 6 × 2 Intelligence × Position × Block (2 & 3) analysis was performed on the data from the N/N/N conditions only. As in Block 1, the Intelligence × Position interaction was the only reliable effect ($F_{5/90} = 3.09, p < .005$).

The 4-2 instructions had a clear and marked effect during Block 2. Both normals and retardates paused only after the fourth letter, verifying their use of rehearsal or secondary memory (SM) for the first four letters and no rehearsal or primary memory (PM) for the last two. In Block 3 (Figure 6c, dashed lines) both the normal and retarded subjects seem to have maintained something of their Block 2 strategy, but the hesitation at position 4 during Block 2 was much longer ($\overline{M} = 6.25$ seconds) than during Block 3 ($\overline{M} = 1.75$ seconds). Even this brief average pause during Block 3 was not general. Rather, the majority of subjects returned to the inactive strategy they had employed in Block 1, and did not pause at all. A few of both the normal and retarded subjects carried their Block 2 strategy into Block 3, though even these hesitated less at letter 4 than they had in Block 2. The accuracy data indicate that whether the subject carries the instructed Block 2 strategy into Block 3 is an important individual difference.

Accuracy. The percentages of correct responses (%R+) plotted over positions for Block 1 are shown in Figure 6d, and they closely resemble curves reported by Ellis (1970). The notable features are the normals' high primacy performance contrasted with the retardates' low primacy, and the high recency performance of both groups. The recurrence of identical patterns in the N/N/N subjects' Block 2 and 3 performance demonstrates the reliability of these data, which invite a straightforward interpretation: PM is used well by both groups, but is effective only for the most recent items, positions 5 and 6. Only the normals effectively use SM, which is responsible for the relatively long retention required for recall of early items. The inference that poor SM is responsible for the retardate's ouput deficiency for the early letters is strengthened by the acquisition pause data, which indicate that the normals increased their pauses as memory load increased while the retardates did not. These pause data provide direct evidence for an SM deficiency at the input stage among retardates. The retardates failed to commit the letters to a durable SM system, so they could not later retrieve them.

The purpose of the 4-2 condition in Block 2 was to determine whether, if forced to use an SM strategy, the retardates would improve in their primacy performance. Their Block 2 recall accuracy did improve, having just doubled in the first three serial positions. In contrast to this marked gain, the %R+ curve for the 4-2 retardates in Block 3 fell to control levels, suggesting that whereas they did adopt a partially successful SM strategy in Block 2, they reverted to PM in Block 3. However, like the Block 3 pause data, these averages are not general. Figure 7 shows the %R+ and pause times for the four retardates who used a clearly active pausing strategy during Block 3 compared to the six who did not. It is important to note that this division of subjects was based solely upon whether they showed increases in pause time during Block 3.

In Figures 7a and 7d it may be seen that under the initial free-strategy condition the groups did not differ in either pause time or %R+. In Block 2 the subjects who were destined to retain an active strategy in Block 3 spent insignificantly less time rehearsing following the fourth letter ($t = 1.7, p < 0.20$), but the groups were dramat-

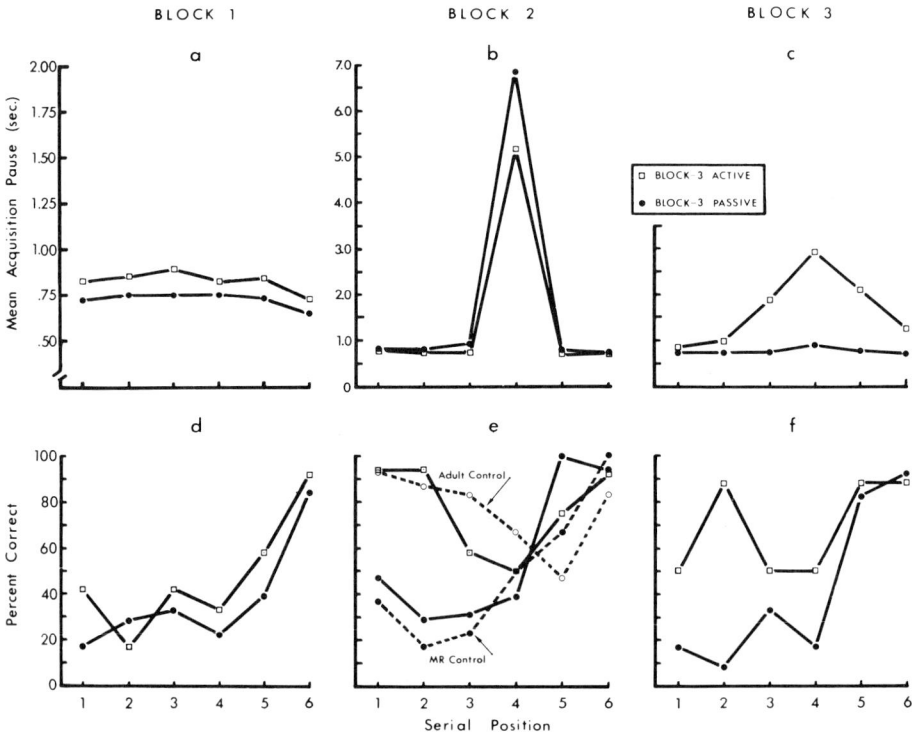

Fig. 7. Mean hesitation times and percentage of correct responses for retardates who did and did not hesitate during Block 3 of Experiment I.

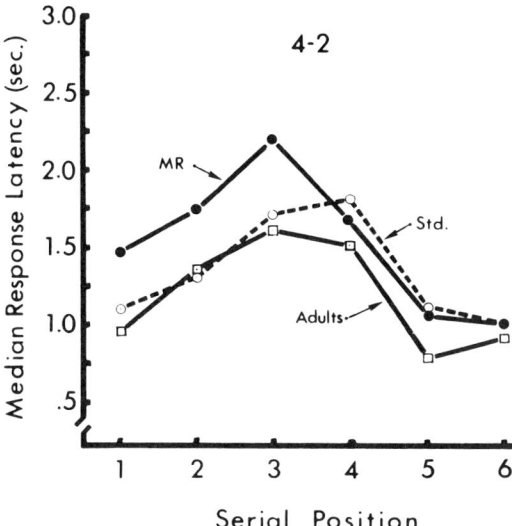

Fig. 8. Mean median correct response latency during Block 2 of Experiment I for retardates and adults who maintained an active pause pattern in Block 3.

ically separated on Block 2 %R+. As seen in Figure 7e, those who would later retain an active strategy were close to the normal control level (shown as dotted curve), while those who became passive in Block 3 were close to the retardate control level, and this separation continued in Block 3. What looked in Figure 6 like a moderate Block 2 gain in %R+ and a Block 3 retention of active strategies is thus seen as a total failure by six of the subjects to improve, despite their apparent use of the 4-2 strategy in Block 2, combined with a leap to practically normal accuracy by the remaining four subjects. The average mental ages of these groups are 10.38 and 10.31 years, respectively; evidently neither the traditional measure of intellectual level nor performance in an initial uninstructed condition predicts this remarkable individual difference among institutionalized retardates in their ability or willingness to profit from instructions to use a clearly beneficial memory strategy.

In Experiment I, four retardates and five adults carried the 4-2 strategy into Block 3. Figure 8 shows the median R+ Lat computed from all of the scores given by each of these groups at each serial position in Block 2. It also shows mean values calculated by averaging the median R+ Lat of ten adults instructed to use a 4-2 active-passive strategy (Belmont and Butterfield, 1969). Considering that the five adults in Experiment I could yield a maximum of only 15 scores at each position, the function very satisfactorily duplicates this standard. They show an increase in R+ Lat across the first three positions, a sharp decrease between the last of the four actively-learned and the first of the two passively-learned letters, and rapid responding to the passive letters. The retardate's SM segment also shows the expected rise, but it is much higher than the standard, showing that they retrieved more slowly from SM than adults. Thus, even those retardates who benefited from the 4-2 strategy seem to have had more difficulty retrieving information from SM than adults.

The data of Experiment I speak clearly to most of the issues which they addressed. The Block 1 performance shows that retardates have a definite SM deficit as indexed both by pause time and R+ in the primacy portion of the lists. The Block 3 pause times and Blocks 2 and 3 R+ show that about half of the retardates benefit from instructions to employ an adult-like acquisition strategy. Although the half of those retardates who thus benefit recall as accurately as adults, their correct response latencies are considerably longer than the adults in the SM portion of the lists. This suggests that these retardates have something of a retrieval deficit, and makes it reasonable to suggest that those retardates who do not benefit may have even more serious retrieval problems.

EXPERIMENT II

The purpose of Experiment II was to clarify and extend the results of Experiment I. First, it was designed to determine whether intellectually average children differ from adults with respect to pause time in ways similar to how retardates and adults differ. Second, it was designed to see whether the form of the retrieval strategy used by children is the same as that used by adults when they are instructed to employ the same acquisition strategy. Third, the experiment was intended to provide evidence concerning whether speed of retrieval from SM develops with age.

Method

Subjects. The subjects were ten normal 9-year olds (IQs 95–115, $\overline{M}$ = 107.7) and ten normal 13-year olds (IQs 96–110, $\overline{M}$ = 102.5).

Procedure. The apparatus was the same as in previous experiments. The procedure, which was the same for all subjects, was a 3-Block N/4-3/N sequence, with 21 free-strategy trials in Block 1, 21 enforced, overt 4-3 rehearsal trials in Block 2, and seven free-strategy trials in Block 3. All lists had seven letters, and each serial position was tested once in each seven-trial series. Blocks 1 and 2 were each preceded by seven practice trials.

Results and Discussion

The mean median Block 1 pause times of the 9- and 13-year olds were compared with a 2 × 7 Age × Position analysis of variance. This analysis revealed a reliable Age × Position interaction reflecting the greater increase across positions by the 13-year olds. This evidence that active acquisition strategies do develop with age is consistent with our earlier findings (Belmont and Butterfield, 1969).

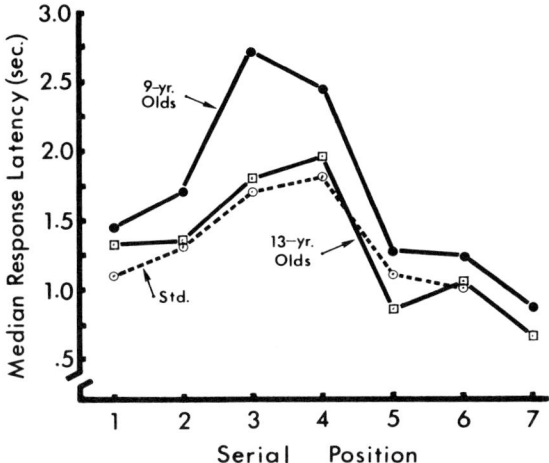

Fig. 9. Mean median correct response latency for nine- and 13-year olds who employed an active pause pattern in Block 3 of Experiment II.

As in Experiment I, it was clear from the Block 3 pause times that some subjects had not been sufficiently influenced by practice on the Block 2 active-passive strategy to maintain an active strategy in Block 3. The analysis of Block 2 R+ Lat was therefore made on data from the four nine-year olds and seven 13-year olds who carried the 4-3 acquisition strategy into Block 3. Figure 9 shows the median median R+ Lat curves for the two age groups. As in the previous experiments, the R+ Lat curves reflect the active-passive acquisition strategy at both age levels. Moreover, the lower-age longer-search relation again obtains in the active segment of the list, with the 13-year olds' retrieval appearing to be at the standard-adult level.

CONCLUSIONS

The purpose of these experiments was to study two suspected sources of STM deficiencies in retardates and children: Acquisition and retrieval strategies. Bearing in mind that only one of several possible STM tests was used to study a narrow range of subject characteristics, several firm conclusions can be made. Almost all educable teenage retardates and many of their normal mental age peers use passive intake strategies which restrict their recall to only the most recently acquired information. About half of these subjects respond with dramatically improved recall accuracy when they are forced to adopt acquisition strategies which embody a combination of active rehearsal and passive attention, but as yet there is no index to predict which subjects will enjoy this improvement. Those who do improve not only show marked gains in recall of distant information, they also reveal an information retrieval strategy which is essentially normal except for the overall speed with which it is employed. In view of these findings it is fair to conclude that retardates and young children have a severe STM input deficiency which, however, can sometimes be ameliorated. In addition to the deficit in input strategy there is a sluggishness of retrieval processing which obtains in retardates and young children even when these subjects are showing adult input processes.

We suspect that the deficient intake process in the active memory system observed in children and retardates cannot help but be reflected in many tasks which require durable memory. Moreover, it is likely that as in the present study, relatively simple procedures for ameliorating the deficiency for at least some subjects can be found for other memory-dependent tasks. Thus, Gerjuoy and Spitz (1966) found that precategorized lists facilitated clustering in retardates' free recall. Perhaps instructions to cluster would do an even better job, just as instructions to label and rehearse the pictures might have improved recall in the young subjects studied by Flavell, Beach, and Chinsky (1966). The present study concurs with the results of these others in showing a verbal mediation production deficiency in children, but it also provides evidence that, in many cases, the deficiency is not the result of an inability to use verbal mediators, but rather a simple failure to realize the mediational potential of those verbalizations.

The role of retrieval strategies in the recall deficits of children and retardates is less clear than the role of acquisition strategies. Those subjects who failed to benefit from intake instructions may have done so because their primary deficit was one of retrieval. Alternatively, the intake instruction may not have been delivered appropriately. Perhaps a shaping process or reinforcement for acquisition behavior would result in improved recall for all children and retardates. Since retrieval cannot be studied well unless the subjects are recalling accurately, the R+ Lat data of the subjects who did not benefit provide no clues to whether further attacks on intake or ouput will be more fruitful. Raising the recall accuracy of all children and retardates to adult levels remains a challenge, as does speeding up the retrieval of those children and retardates whose accuracy deficit is eliminated by simple intake instructions.

SUMMARY OF DISCUSSION

QUESTION: You mentioned at one point that subjects recalled more accurately if they were allowed to recall the final items in a list before the initial items than if they had to recall the initial items first.

BUTTERFIELD: That's right.

QUESTION: Is that surprising to you?

BUTTERFIELD: No, it wasn't. You see, it allows the subjects to take advantage of two very different kinds of memory. The distinction here is between primary and secondary memory, or perhaps active and passive memory are more descriptive terms. People can remember a little bit very well for a short period of time by acquiring it passively, but they remember more for a longer period of time by acquiring it actively. If you have a fixed list length—in our case nine items—you can either work very hard and acquire all of them actively by rehearsing all the way through the list —that is, you can use active memory for a lot of material—or you can work a lot less hard and rely on passive memory for the last few items, thereby reducing the amount of information you have to commit to secondary or active memory. But in order to do that, and recall accurately, you have to recall the passively learned items first. So by having our subjects recall the last items in the lists first we gave them the opportunity to immediately spit out the last few items, the ones they passively learned, before recalling the actively learned ones, thereby reducing the total rehearsal time and increasing the accuracy of both.

QUESTION: This reminds me of a study on remembering telephone numbers, in which the experimenter had the subjects learn the numbers in the forward direction, but then dial the last four numbers before the first three.

BUTTERFIELD: That will never get you the right number.

QUESTION: Not unless you change the whole telephone system. But this was a laboratory experiment, not real life.

QUESTION: Was recalling the last letters first the most accurate condition with the least errors?

BUTTERFIELD: Yes, and subjects spontaneously adopt that strategy. If you allow subjects freedom to recall in any order they wish, from one-third to one-half of them spontaneously recall the last ones first. It's really easier.

QUESTION: That's the same thing that is happening in the telephone experiment. And, as a matter of fact, it would take several billion dollars to change the telephone system so that that would work. But that would reduce the number of errors.

BUTTERFIELD: Yes. There is a simpler, cheaper way which won't go quite as far, and that is to make the prefix, the first group of numbers longer than the suffix. We now have three numbers followed by four: 123-4567. If you just reverse that, make it four followed by three, 1234-567, the telephone numbers would be a lot easier to remember, too.

QUESTION: These studies were all visual memory studies?

BUTTERFIELD: The stimuli were presented visually, but the rehearsal is auditory. The subjects are required to rehearse out loud in most of the experiments. A verbally controlled strategy.

QUESTION: But never combined in presentation with auditory?

BUTTERFIELD: No, we have never presented stimuli in the auditory fashion, but others have. Not the same kind of research. I know of no one who has done it with retardates, for example.

QUESTION: It seems that people react differently to different kinds of material— that is, sentence-like materials versus items that are relatively unrelated?

BUTTERFIELD: They do.

QUESTION: Would you speculate that your results would hold with different kinds of material?

BUTTERFIELD: Fortunately, there are some data. I don't really have to speculate very much on that. I haven't collected it, but Wilkes and Kennedy in England have. The procedures are not identical to the ones that we have used, but they are similar. They have used different types of sentences. That is, they varied the grammatical structure of the sentence and had subjects learn them by first showing them a card and then taking it away and having them say them out loud so that they can measure where they hesitated during the sentence. And then, after the subjects had learned them extremely well, they would systematicaly ask them what word follows each word in the whole sentence.

They found that the kind of strategy, pausing, that the subjects used varied with the type of sentence. Their subjects' pauses are in the same ballpark as far as time is concerned as ours are. And there was a close relationship between recall time and both structure of sentence and hesitation time. It looks very much as if the same sorts of regularities exist for sentence material as for individual letters. What I should go on and say, though, is that these are rote strategies. There is no doubt of that. There are some subjects, a small group, considerably less than 10 per cent, who really confuse the data. They go flat out through the list, not hesitating at all, so they look very much like mentally retarded people. If you ask these people what they are doing, they report using coding strategies. For example, people will do things like think of the names of friends whose initials are the same as pairs of letters in the list, so as they go through the list all they have to do is say, "Jack Katz," or what have you. At the end of the list they have only to recall four names. They apparently do it very quickly. One reason we haven't done anything with such strategies is that our measure is simply lost in the face of that kind of behavior. You don't get any pauses, and that is our primary acquisition measure. Fortunately, we don't run into subjects like that too often, but there were two in twelve in that first experiment I showed you. That is high. We don't generally get that many.

QUESTION: You can always ask them.

BUTTERFIELD: Ask them what?

QUESTION: What strategy they are using.

BUTTERFIELD: Oh, yes, you could. Part of the trouble though is that if you want to study that sort of thing you just have to run through huge numbers of people to get enough who do it spontaneously. We could try manipulating it, try to get people who don't normally use some kind of fancy strategy to use one. We just haven't gotten that far yet.

QUESTION: Have you considered using retarded people with very low verbal skills as opposed to retarded people with relatively high verbal skills? It's all verbal rehearsal?

BUTTERFIELD: I have considered it, but have not done it systematically. It is very difficult in this task to study the kinds of things we study if a person doesn't already know the alphabet, for example. So the answer is, generally, no, I haven't. I think if we were to use different kinds of stimuli, stars, squares, or circles or that kind of thing, then we could, and I am becoming more interested in doing that. Because we do have to screen our retarded sample now fairly severely. We are restricted to the upper levels.

QUESTION: There were retarded people who didn't continue to use the strategy you taught them in phase two—there were people who did use it in phase two apparently, but were not being very correct. You feel the reason for that is they didn't have an adequate retrieval strategy?

BUTTERFIELD: That's a possibility.

QUESTION: It also could be they really weren't doing the same thing even though they were saying the letters out loud.

BUTTERFIELD: That's possible too.

QUESTION: They didn't know how to commit them to memory, so to speak. And if you did a different kind of training . . .

BUTTERFIELD: That's quite possible, and people have raised that point every time I have talked about this. All I can say for sure is that we need to try some other kinds of training techniques. This is obviously a very simple one and it doesn't take advantage of the kinds of things that we know we can use. We gave subjects in these experiments no extrinsic reason to do well. We just assumed they wanted to be right. We didn't give them any incentives whatsoever, or what we did give them were not contingent on correct responding. That could be tried.

REFERENCES

Belmont, J. M., and Butterfield, E. C. The relations of short-term memory to development and intelligence. In L. P. Lipsitt and H. W. Reese (Eds.)., *Advances in child development and behavior,* Vol. 4. New York: Academic Press, 1969. Pp. 29–82.

Butterfield, E. C. and Belmont, J. M. Relations of storage and retrieval strategies as short-term memory processes. *J. Exp. Psychol.,* 1971, 89, 319–328.

Ellis, N. R. Memory processes in retardates and normals. In N. R. Ellis (Ed.), *International review of research in mental retardation,* Vol. 4. New York: Academic Press, 1970. Pp. 1–32.

Flavell, J. H., Beach, D. R., and Chinsky, J. M. Spontaneous verbal rehearsal in a memory task as a function of age. *Child Devel.,* 1966, 37, 283–299.

Gerjuoy, I. R. and Spitz, H. H. Associative clustering in free recall: Intellectual and developmental variables. *Am. J. Ment. Deficiency,* 1966, 70, 918–927.

INDEX

Acquisition of language
  ambiguities resolved in, 4–5, 60
  competence in, 6, 7, 9
  and discrimination of consonants, 137, 138, 177, 179, 185
  and emerging grammars, 20–23
  imitation in, 9–10, 11, 12–13, 14–15, 84–85
  innate capacity for, 6–7, 13
  interpersonal factors in, 32, 44–45, 133–135, 138–140
  labeling in, 24, 43–44, 96
  learning theory of, 128–133
  memory in, short-term, 7
  neurologic aspects of, 16, 76
  in normal and retarded children, 45–46, 47–48
  perceptual mechanisms in, 7
  performance features of, 6, 7, 9
  pivot words in, 10, 15, 19, 22, 27, 29
  primary linguistic data in, 7, 15
  psycholinguistic model of, 5–17, 135–136
  and reacquisition, 122
  and referential processes, 26, 37, 44, 45, 49, 60–64
  semantic features in, 3–5, 11, 19–33
  single-word utterances in, 23–25, 32
  and syntax. *See* Syntactic component of grammar
  training programs for. *See* Training programs
  and underlying intent of speech, 21, 27–28, 30, 33, 134
  unique utterances in, 29, 30
  universals in, 6–7
Age factors, in assessment of language development, 147, 166
Ambiguity in language, 4–5, 60
Animal communication, 54, 70
Arousal thresholds, in childhood, 132
Articulation skills, measurement of, 145, 165
Assessment of language development, 77, 143–168
  and audiology, 169–187
  in dysphasia, 195–201
  expressive language in, 144–145, 156–163
  longitudinal studies in, 165, 168
  receptive language in, 144, 148–155
Audiology, 169–187
  Bekesy procedure in, 181, 184
  central tests in, 181, 186
  for deaf subjects, 181, 184–185
  discrimination studies in, 177–181, 185
  in dysphasia, 197, 201–202
  evaluation of procedures in, 183
  for nonverbal children, 177
  for preschoolers, 183, 185–186
  reinforcement in, 172, 183
  stimulus control in, 174–175
  and stimulus-interference training, 175
Auditory-visual sample-matching studies, 211–229
Auditory-vocal functioning, in dysphasia, 196, 199, 200
Awareness, and language development, 144

Behavioral systems
  and assessment of language development, 143–168
  and audiologic research, 170–184
  See also Reinforcement; Training programs
Bekesy audiometry, 181, 184
Brain disease, and language disorders, 211–213, 217–223

Choice processes, by listeners, 58–59
Cognitive structure in grammar, 21, 36
Comparison stage, in communication, 58, 67–68
  in children, 60, 61, 63
Competence in language acquisition
  development of, 6, 7
  in prelinguistic stage, 9
Comprehension
  in dysphasia, 193–194, 199
  and imitation, 12–13
Consonants, discrimination of, 137, 138, 177, 179, 185

Deafness
  Bekesy audiometry in, 181, 184
  and speech development, 6, 7, 131, 137
Development of language. *See* Acquisition of language
Dialects, and language training, 121
Disadvantaged children, modification of speech in, 114–118
Discrimination
  in audiometry, 177–181, 185
  development of, 144
  in dysphasia, 197, 201–202
Drills, grammar, 44
Dysphasia
  auditory-vocal deficit in, 196, 199, 200
  case studies of, 190–191
  comprehension in, 193–194, 199
  current research in, 195–201
  description of language in, 193
  and dyspraxia, 194
  group studies of, 191–192
  historical studies of, 189–193
  imitation in, 199, 202, 204

and intelligence, 194–195
    language-related behavior in, 189–205
    memory function in, 198–199
    mild, 192, 194, 195
    neurologic factors in, 201, 203
    oral-motor function in, 196, 197
    types of children studied, 192

Efficiency of training programs, evaluation of, 84–85, 87
Emerging grammars
    cognitive notions in, 21, 36
    relational notions in, 21–23, 24–25, 31
    study of, 20–23
    syntactic patterns in, 20, 26–27
Environmental factors, in training programs, 88, 118
Evaluation of language development, 143–168
Expressive language, 144–145
    assessment of, 156–163

Facility in training procedures, evaluation of, 85

Generality of training procedures, evaluation of, 84
Generalizations in language, 86, 87, 90, 105, 113, 228
Generative grammars, 5, 20–23, 41, 99
Gestures, and referential behavior, 56–57
Grammar
    acquisition of. *See* Acquisition of language
    components in, 3–5
    emerging. *See* Emerging grammars
Grammatical organization, training program for, 96–100

Head Start program, language studies in, 118
Hearing loss
    Bekesy audiometry in, 181, 184
    and speech development, 6, 7, 131, 137
Hesitation time, in memory studies, 232–236, 238–239, 242–243

Imitation
    and acquisition of language, 9–10, 11, 12–13, 14–15, 84–85
    in dysphasia, 199, 202, 204
    elaborate, production of, 110–111
    as expressive behavior, 145
    in language training, 82–83, 89–90, 100–104, 108–113
    of motor behaviors, 108–109
    nonreinforced, 102, 109
    and reinforcement, 95, 102, 108
    teaching of, 95
Initiating behaviors, 145
Innate capacity, for acquisition of language, 6–7, 13
Integration, and language development, 37

Intelligence, and dysphasia, 194–195
Intent, underlying speech, 21, 27–28, 30, 33, 134
Interpersonal nature of speech, 133–135, 138–140
    See also Social interaction
Intervention model of language acquisition, 11

Labeling behavior, 24, 43–44, 96
Learning theory, and speech retardation, 128–133
Listener process
    in children, 63–64
    and communication disorders, 134, 139–140
    referential, 58–59
    and suspended judgments, 59
Longitudinal studies of language development, 165, 168

Maturation, and speech development, 128
Memory, short-term
    in communication, 58, 68–69
    in dysphasia, 198–199
    and language acquisition, 7
    verbal processes in, 231–247
Metareferential acts, in conversation, 54, 66
"Monster" model, of Osgood, 36–38
Motor behavior, imitation of, 108–109
Mute psychotic subjects, language training in, 108, 110

Neurologic factors
    in acquisition of language, 16, 76
    in dysphasia, 201, 203
    in language disorders, 211–213, 217–223
Nonlinguistic clues, use of, 28, 48
Nonsense materials, studies with, 61–63, 68–70
    in dysphasia, 197, 198
Normal development, compared to retardates, 45–46, 47–48

Operant procedures. *See* Behavioral systems
Organic factors
    in dysphasia, 201, 203
    in language disorders, 211–213, 217–223
    in speech development, 128, 131
Osgood's "monster" model, 36–38

Perceptual mechanisms, in language acquisition, 7
Performance characteristics of language acquisition, 6, 7
    in prelinguistic stage, 9
Phonologic component of grammar, 3–5
    development of, 11
Physical clues, use of, 48
Physical factors
    in dysphasia, 201, 203
    in language disorders, 211–213, 217–223
    in speech development, 128, 131
Pivot words
    in acquisition of language, 10, 15, 19, 22, 27, 29
    in language training, 77, 80–82, 87, 90

INDEX

Plurals, training program for use of, 97–99
Pointing responses
  in audiometry, 177
  in training programs, 86–87
Prelinguistic stage of language development, 9
Prepositions, comprehension of, 164–165
Primary linguistic data, and language acquisition, 7, 15
Probabilistic vocabulary, in referential processes, 61–63, 68–70
Psychoacoustic discrimination program, 179–180
Psycholinguistic acquisition model, 5–17, 135–136
Psychotic mute subjects, language training for, 108, 110

Reacquisition of language skills, 122
Reading, teaching of, 119, 223–227, 229
Receptive language, 144
  assessment of, 148–155
  in language training, 86, 87
Recordings of conversations among retardates, 48
Referential processes of language, 26, 37, 44, 45, 49
  in children, 60–64
  choice processes in, 58–59
  comparison stage in, 58, 60, 61, 63, 67–68
  development of, 53–70
  gestures in, 56–57
  in listeners, 58–59
  probabilistic function in, 61–63, 68–70
  research in, 54–57
  sampling in, 58, 67–68
  in speakers, 57–58
  surrogate referents in, 54, 64–66, 70
  theory of, 57–59
Rehearsals, verbal, in memory studies, 233–236, 237–242
Reinforcement
  in audiologic research, 172, 183
  for grammatical organization, 97
  and imitation, 95, 102, 108
  inappropriate quality of, 131–132
  in language training, 76, 83, 84
  and social interaction, 118, 129
Relational notions, in emerging grammars, 21–23, 24–25, 31
Representational levels, in language development, 36, 37, 49
Responsive behaviors, 145
Rule-bound organization of language, development of, 93–100

Sample-matching studies, 211–229
  applications of, 217–227
  simultaneous or delayed, 217
  techniques of, 214–217
Sampling process, in communication, 58, 67–68
Semantic features in language development, 3–5, 11, 19–33
  and emerging grammars, 20–23
  and single-word utterances, 23–25, 32
  and syntax, 36, 37, 49
  and treatment of language disorders, 25–27
  and underlying intent of speech, 21, 27–28, 30, 33, 134
Short Increment Sensitivity Index (SISI), 175–177
Simplistic grammar, development of, 93–105
Single-word utterances, in childhood, 23–25, 32
Social interaction
  and language development, 32, 44–45, 133–135, 138–140
  as reinforcer, 118, 129
Sound, imitated, in language training, 82–83
  See also Imitation
Speaker-listener relationships, 5, 7, 45, 53–70, 133–135, 139–140
Speaker process, referential, 57–58
  in childhood, 63–64
Stimulation, inappropriate, 132
Stimulus control, auditory, 174–175
Stimulus-interference training, in audiometry, 175
Surface structure of grammar, 36, 45, 100
Surrogate referents, use of, 54, 64–66, 70
Syntactic component of grammar, 3–5
  development of, 10–11
  in emerging grammars, 20, 26–27
  and language development in retardates, 35–49
  methods for improvement of, 42–45
  semantic aspects of, 36, 37
  surface structure in, 36, 45, 100
  and transformations, 36, 38–41

Tacting behavior, 24, 43–44, 96
Tests
  audiologic, 169–187
  of dysphasic children, 195–201
  of language development, 77, 143–168
Training programs, 42–45, 75–122
  assessment procedures in, 77
  and basis for speech therapy, 132–133
  for disadvantaged children, 114–118
  in dysphasia, 201
  efficiency of procedures in, 84–85, 87
  environment affecting, 88, 118
  facility of, 85
  generality of, 84
  grammar drills in, 44
  for grammatical organization, 96–100
  imitation in, 82–83, 89–90, 100–104, 108–113
  interactions in, 44–45
  labeling in, 43–44
  loss of skills after, 122
  for memory deficits, 244
  operant language modification in, 107–122
  pivot-open phrases in, 77, 80–82, 87, 90
  pointing responses in, 86–87
  procedural lattices in, 76–79, 83–85
  for reading skills, 119, 223–227, 229

receptive vocabulary in, 86, 87
reinforcement in, 76, 83, 84
for rudimentary speech development, 110–114
semantic factors in, 25–27
for speaker and listener skills in children, 61, 64, 70
for spontaneous language improvement, 114–118
systematic approach to, 75–91
validity of, 83–84, 87, 89, 90
verbal bombardment in, 43

Transformations, 5, 17, 36, 38–41, 47, 48–49
  development of, 42–45

Understanding, as receptive behavior, 144
Unique utterances, in language development, 29, 30
Universals, linguistic, 6–7

Validity of training procedures, evaluation of, 83–84, 87, 89, 90
Vowel-consonant distinctions, 137, 138